D0983855

The Color of Sex

New Americanists  *A Series Edited by Donald E. Pease*

# The Color of Sex

*Whiteness, Heterosexuality, and*

*the Fictions of White Supremacy*

Mason Stokes

Duke University Press   *Durham & London, 2001*

© 2001 Duke University Press
All rights reserved
Printed in the United States of
America on acid-free paper ∞
Designed by Rebecca M. Giménez
Typeset in Carter & Cone Galliard
by Tseng Information Systems
Library of Congress Cataloging-
in-Publication Data appear on the
last printed page of this book.

# Contents

# Acknowledgments

I sometimes think I finished this book solely to have this opportunity to thank the following people.

Debbie McDowell guided this project with enthusiasm and rigor in its earlier life as a dissertation. The best teacher I've ever had, and my favorite kind of scholar, Debbie has shaped my thinking in ways that defy traditional notions of acknowledgment. Her presence is felt in each of these pages, and the example she sets is one I intend to hang onto.

Eric Lott took enormous care with early versions of these chapters. Festooned with Eric's inscrutable marginalia, drafts long feared dead came back to life, suddenly shiny with potential.

Dana Nelson, both in her scholarship and in her unflinching commitment to academic community, has been the best kind of inspiration. She's fabulous.

Ken Wissoker and the folks at Duke University Press have demonstrated an utterly invigorating faith in this project. I owe a huge debt to the anonymous readers at Duke, whose comments made the revision process interesting in ways I hadn't thought possible.

A version of chapter 3 has appeared previously in *American Quarterly*. I thank Lucy Maddox and the readers at *American Quarterly* for their extremely useful guidance.

I am blessed with a geographically scattered cohort of scholars whose work and friendship continue to sustain me, despite the distance between us. Daylanne English, dear friend and comrade, excites me in both mind and heart. Karen Shimakawa was an early hero of mine; she's who I want to be when I grow up. Amy Ghaemmaghami couldn't have come into my life at a better time, offering her friendship and her intellect when I desperately needed both. Lisa Samuels has seen me through a variety of relocations and reorientations; I continue to benefit enormously from knowing her.

In ways big and small, Derek Nystrom, Tim Wager, and Rod Waterman have made both my work and my life better places.

Since 1997 I have been privileged to work with a host of truly inspiring teachers and scholars in the Skidmore English department; I thank them all for the community they have offered me. My chairs during this time, Sarah Goodwin and Susan Kress, have created a space for the kind of teaching and scholarship that I've always wanted to do. Linda Simon, coconspirator from day one, is to me that rarest and most valuable of combinations: friend and mentor.

My community at Skidmore extends beyond the halls of the English department, and I thank my friends and colleagues across the college for helping me understand the real value of our collective endeavor. In particular, I thank Jennifer Delton for disagreeing with me in the most interesting, provocative, and useful ways imaginable; this work is better for it. Susan Walzer is one of the smartest and most generous people I know; being her friend is a wonderful thing.

These next are more difficult to categorize:

I thank Anne-Elizabeth Murdy, for understanding the roots of this work as only she can.

Kim Langford and Adam Daniel, for their wide-eyed faith in the importance of good times.

Mike Furlough, for almost fifteen years now.

Bill Verner, for his love and support when I needed them most.

Michael Miller, for giving me the reason to do the most difficult and important thing I've ever done, and for everything since then.

Mike Bennett and Juan Battle, not only for providing a fabulous downstate retreat but for caring enough about family to create an extended one—and for making me a part of it.

My uncle and name-giver, for his creative spirit.

Finally, my parents. In her life and in her death, my mother set an example of strength and sureness of character that I will always draw on. I also thank my father, whose willingness to embrace challenge and adventure comes as a welcome reminder of new possibilities, of new hope.

This book was written in the spirit of such hope, and I thank all of these people for the things that made it possible.

# White Fictions

Were I to state here, frankly and categorically, that the primary object of this work is to write the negro out of America, and that the secondary object is to write him, (and manifold millions of other black and bicolored caitiffs, little better than himself,) out of existence, God's simple truth would be told. —Hinton Rowan Helper

Writing and racism. White supremacy and the text. What this passage from Helper's *Nojoque; A Question for a Continent* (1867) makes clear is the interdependence of the two—the construction of white supremacy as a textual practice, whereby ink on a page and the circulation of books work to fix racial identity and its supposedly attendant qualities. Once fixed in print, Helper's "negro" can be written away like so many dinosaurs, the victim of the textual weight of mid-nineteenth-century anthropology. Or of Thomas Jefferson's *Notes on the State of Virginia* (1784), where Jefferson infamously writes, "Never yet could I find a Black that had uttered a thought above the level of plain narration; never seen even an elementary trait of painting or sculpture. Religion indeed has produced a Phillis Whately [*sic*] but it could not produce a poet. The compositions published under her name are below the dignity of criticism" (140). In Jefferson's view, blacks are incapable of saying or thinking anything worth writing down, worth making into text.

And yet so much of African American literary history, especially in the nineteenth century, attaches a supreme importance to the power of the text as a path to freedom and its attendant grace, humanity. Think of Frederick Douglass's 1845 *Narrative*, both a textual badge of his humanity, according to the dehumanizing racial logic of the Enlightenment, and a record of literacy as a road to freedom. Douglass's first literary production is actually the fictionalized pass he forges to effect his escape. That his fellow slaves are forced to eat these fictions when their plan is discovered testifies simultaneously to the subversive power of black writing and to the oppressive bodily economy of the black text—that piece of writing that *is* black body, that gets subsumed under the sign of black flesh.

Or think about Linda Brent's textual manipulations of white authority in Harriet Jacobs's *Incidents in the Life of a Slave Girl* (1861), where Linda uses literacy to invert the power relations of slavery, of black and white. Through the power of the pen, Linda convinces her master that she has escaped to the free North, though her body still resides in the cramped spaces of her grandmother's attic, firmly embedded in slave country. Although literacy can render black freedom as a convincing fiction, the double location that Linda occupies—slave and "free"—metonymizes the dilemma of African American writing in the mid–nineteenth century. The textual power Linda acquires never arrives without a dangerous ambiguity, particularly for those whose access to it is always contested. For Jacobs herself, textual power becomes a route to freedom and bodily autonomy as well as another type of slavery. Bound by the conventions of literary expression, Jacobs struggles to preserve her newly acquired "humanity" amid the dehumanizing ethos of sentimental fiction and the white middle-class values that sustain it.[1]

Or more recently, think of Sethe's dilemma in Toni Morrison's *Beloved* (1987), her discovery that Schoolteacher's nephews have been keeping a written record of how she doesn't quite measure up to their notion of humanity. Listing her "human characteristics" on one side of the page and her "animal characteristics" on the other, these boys typify much of the nineteenth-century white-supremacist discourse that Helper represents and that Douglass, Jacobs, and others struggled so mightily against. Sethe's reaction to this tabulating of humanity is painful and instructive, as she realizes her own complicity in the process: "I made the ink," she tells Paul D. "He couldn't have done it if I hadn't made the ink" (271). The "it" in Sethe's sentence moves outward in various directions, referencing the specific (Schoolteacher's tabulating and hierarchizing of humanity) as well as the general (slavery itself). The ink is at the root of both. Implicated in the same bodily/textual economy as Douglass, Sethe's blackness both produces the possibility of the nephew's text and becomes it, as she disappears under the more powerful sign of the written word—the sign of humanity that erases the humanity of others.

All by way of saying that writing, particularly in the nineteenth century, was a site where race got manufactured, deployed, disseminated, contested, and claimed. Where bodily hierarchies acquired legible form. Where the debate over slavery achieved its prominence, and perhaps its greatest effect. Where people like Helper tried to write people like Jacobs out of the country, and out of existence. At the very site of textual possibility—where dark letters hover on a white page—the differences between black and white became even more pronounced, and even more troubling.[2]

Helper knew something about the power of the written word. George Fredrickson has called Helper's first work, *The Impending Crisis of the South* (1857), "the most important single book, in terms of its political impact, that has ever been published in the United States" ("Introduction" ix). Best described as a racist, antislavery polemic, *The Impending Crisis* became the subject of bitter debate in Congress and largely shaped much of the prewar discussion of slavery, free soil, and states' rights. In a complicated series of political moves, Helper's book became a key component in the 1858 fight over the Speakership of the House of Representatives, a fight that eventually strengthened prosecessionist sentiment among southern representatives (Fredrickson, "Introduction" xii–xix).

Given Helper's radical antiblack, antislavery stance, it's worth reconsidering the method proposed in the passage that heads this introduction. Helper intends not to burn, lynch, vote, chase, terrorize, or otherwise harass "the Negro" out of America; rather, he intends to *write* "him" out of America.[3] How does he imagine that such textual fiat is possible? A glance at the table of contents for *Nojoque* provides a surreal yet instructive preview: "The Negro, Anthropologically Considered, An Inferior Fellow Done For; Black, A Thing of Ugliness, Disease, and Death; White, A Thing of Life, Health, and Beauty; The Servile Baseness and Beggary of the Blacks; Removals, Banishments, Expulsions, Exterminations; A Score of Bible Lessons in the Arts of Annihilating Effete Races; White Celebrities, and Black Nobodies" (ix–x). Against the textual weight and authority of anthropology, Helper suggests, the Negro doesn't stand a chance. "Blackness" and "Whiteness," rendered textually, become things, canvasses for the collection of moral and physical properties. The Bible becomes a how-to manual for would-be colonizers and exterminators.[4]

And as Helper suggests elsewhere in the preface, yet another textual authority looms over the scene of his writing—namely, what would come to be called Social Darwinism, whose chief proponent was English sociologist and philosopher Herbert Spencer. Putting his faith in the "present economy of Nature" (vii), Helper weighs the following "consoling and cheerful consideration" against the plague of "coal-black and copper-colored caitiffs": "The appointed period of their tenancy upon the earth will soon be up; and then, like the short-lived ephemera of a summer afternoon, they shall all speedily pass away, and thenceforth and forever be known only, if known at all, in fossil form!" (vii). Although Helper doesn't directly invoke Spencer here, his presence is most surely felt. His *Principles of Biology,* published in 1864, provided a textual authority for this kind of exterminationist thinking, introducing a phrase that would (mistakenly) get associated with Darwin, "the survival of the fittest."[5]

There is, however, an interesting irony in Helper's version of Spencer's "survival of the fittest," one that returns us, once again, to the familial connection between writing and racism. According to Helper, once the Negro has gone the way of the "toxodons, the glyptodons, the mastodons, and thousands of other extinct species of animals" (vii–viii), he will only exist "in fossil form" (vii). Although I doubt that Helper was actually referring to his book as one of those forms, I want to suggest that it was—and is—a fossil-like reminder of one man's representation of "the Negro." Helper surely thought, optimist that he was, that his own words would outlast their subject and that in the absence of actual Negroes, those words would create the final and lasting "truth" of a race that no longer existed.

That textual representation could, in fact, manufacture "the Negro" had been proven in a long line of literary antecedents to Helper, the most famous of which was surely Harriet Beecher Stowe's *Uncle Tom's Cabin* (1852), published a scant fifteen years before *Nojoque,* and only five years before *The Impending Crisis.* Stowe's work demonstrated the incredible power of the written word both to alter and become part of the American racial landscape. Stowe's goal was to make her Negro America's Negro, to make the docile and Christlike Tom the universal face of the American slave. Although Helper's lingering presence certainly indicates at least a partial failure on her part, the attempt had an enormous transformative power, one lasting well into the next century. The power of Stowe's representation shaped the literary conjunction of race and writing in countless ways, from the many anti–Uncle Tom novels of the 1850s and 1860s to Thomas Dixon Jr.'s determination, on seeing a stage version of Stowe's story in 1901, to set the record straight and tell the "true story" of the South, the Negro, and slavery (Cook 105). The result would be *The Leopard's Spots* (1902), a novel of racial hatred that sold almost as well as Stowe's.

And yet, while Stowe's novel has lasted into the late twentieth century, becoming, in fact, part of "the canon," Dixon's and Helper's works have virtually disappeared from our critical awareness. Although part of me sees this as a perfectly happy occurrence ("Good riddance, racist scum!"), a larger part believes that the disappearance of these white-supremacist texts from our vision of the American literary landscape renders that landscape false and incomplete, a testament to a literary history that didn't really happen. Although scholars have cataloged the incredibly prolific and offensive output of antiblack writing between 1852 and 1915, few have read these works seriously as revealing and ambiguous textual productions. This book offers these texts—from plantation romances to theological tracts to popular film—as a shifting, complicated, yet continuous record of how white Americans lived and commodified racist ideologies in the latter half of the nineteenth century.

At the same time, I contextualize this white-supremacist writing vis-à-vis the interventionist efforts of African American writers and activists. Although my primary object here is to pressure the dissonances within white-supremacist literary representation, I have no desire to do so in a vacuum. As Ida B. Wells notes in *Crusade for Justice,* too much has been lost because "only the southern white man's misrepresentations are in the public libraries and college textbooks of the land" (5). To focus on the discourses of white supremacy without paying attention to those black writers who wrote actively against those discourses would be to reify the structural power that white supremacy has worked to claim. It would be to allow whiteness the very tautology and exclusivity that it needs to survive.[6] Instead, I strive throughout to keep one eye trained on the ways in which black writers and activists both responded to and shaped the debate over racial difference in this country—how writers such as Harper, Jacobs, Douglass, Du Bois, and countless others refused to grant whiteness the intellectual space it sought and required. These black interventions ranged from the book-length (Sutton Griggs's *The Hindered Hand,* for example) to the devastatingly precise (Anna Julia Cooper's brisk dismissal of William Dean Howells's *An Imperative Duty:* "Mr. Howells does not know what he is talking about" [201]).

The most extended treatment of such intervention occurs in chapter 4, which I devote to Charles W. Chesnutt's *The Marrow of Tradition* (1901). Chesnutt's novel strategically refigures turn-of-the-century white-supremacist narratives, turning white anxiety against itself in a brilliant recasting of dominant sexual ideologies. Chesnutt's literary intervention also reveals the difficulties of writing "against" such ideologies, exposing how the omnivorous energies of whiteness fracture any strictly binary model of racist domination, on the one hand, and antiracist resistance, on the other. To imagine that Chesnutt could write entirely outside the structures of whiteness would be to underestimate the protean potentials of white supremacy, its uncanny ability to throw its voice. Although Chesnutt's novel is clearly distinguishable from the white-supremacist fictions I treat here, it bears a relation to them that isn't purely oppositional. It belongs among these white-supremacist fictions not because it is itself white supremacist but because its encounter with white supremacy reveals the seemingly impervious nature of whiteness, its knack for making friends of enemies.

Even as I acknowledge, however, the importance of African American responses to American racism, I still want to claim whiteness and textual white supremacy as my primary foci, my main objects of inquiry. Although I recognize the dialectical give-and-take of competing "racial" voices, I have no intention of re-creating a debate here, of sketching in full the shape this conversation took during its time. I've resisted any inclinations to refute, point by point, the racist arguments put forth by the writers I examine. Although such a refutation may be worth doing, this is not the space for it. My primary goal is to chart the workings of whiteness through sustained attention to these seldom studied white-supremacist texts. Consequently, the texts themselves—with all of their hatred and venom—will demand my primary attention, as well as the majority of the following pages. Only by taking them seriously as richly ambivalent textual productions and by devoting to them the kind of attention too often reserved for "serious" works of literature will these hateful works pay off in the kinds of broadly instructive ways that I think are both possible and desirable.

## Justifications

My focus throughout is on white racism as a popular discourse, one aimed at and received by a significant number of people. Charles Jacobs Peterson, for example, wrote his proslavery novel *The Cabin and Parlor* (1852) directly on the heels of Stowe's *Uncle Tom's Cabin*, hoping, like so many other proslavery novelists, to cash in on the enormous popularity of Stowe's novel. These anti–Uncle Tom novels were quickly written and designed to sell by the thousands so as to influence the ongoing debate over slavery. Metta V. Victor's *Maum Guinea and Her Plantation "Children"* (1861), the dime novel I examine in chapter 2, sold well over one hundred thousand copies, enormous sales for this genre and time. Its audience, like that of the dime novel in general, consisted of a wide array of people, from shop-floor workers to merchants, from seamstresses to the president.[7] Dixon's *The Leopard's Spots,* like several of his race novels, sold so well that it is credited with establishing Doubleday, Page and Co. as a major publishing house. It also helped make Dixon extremely wealthy and famous. Even the ethnologists and theologians whose work I examine in chapter 3 can be seen as popularizers of a more elite discourse, dedicated to making their scientific and religious racism palatable and palpable to "the masses."

The texts I've chosen, with certain exceptions, move quietly beneath our contemporary critical radar. They aren't studied, and too often aren't taken seriously. They announce themselves, from the beginning, as avowedly white supremacist in their orientation. Like Helper, they foreground the propagation of white supremacy as their primary goal and disdain what might be called the merely literary exercise of symbol and myth. As a result of their conscious identification with whiteness as a structural ideology, these works better demarcate its shape, its constitutive parts, than more canonical nineteenth-century meditations on whiteness.[8] Though Melville's and Poe's works offer a rich field for reading race in the nineteenth century, *Maum Guinea* provides a more fertile space for this kind of analysis, precisely because Victor's status as a successful writer of dime novels demonstrated time and time again her ability to shape narrative to the pressures of popular desire.[9] When the desire for a large audience in midcentury America meets a "romance of slavery" told with supposedly antislavery leanings, the product is, to say the least, richly instructive and heavy with ambivalence. The writers I examine were dedicated to establishing and buttressing a specifically popular racism, one they hoped would seep into every thread of the American fabric so as to become a pervasive determinant of that fabric. I'm concerned throughout with white supremacy and whiteness as live cultural forms, lived and inhabited by the man and the woman on the street.

Of course, my attention to "the popular" as a literary category has an institutional history, one that can be traced back to various moments and to various critics (Helen Papashvily, Judith Fetterly, Nina Baym, Ann Douglas, Janice Radway, Nancy Armstrong, and Michael Denning, to name just a few). For my purposes, however, it is useful to see the most recent phase of that history as being inaugurated by the publication in 1985 of Jane Tompkins's *Sensational Designs: The Cultural Work of American Fiction, 1790–1860*. Tompkins's book has had an enormous impact on literary studies in the years since its publication, and its shadow certainly hangs over my own work. It marks something of a paradigm shift in literary studies, establishing at least two tenets that we now tend to take for granted and that lie at the root of the analyses that follow. First, Tompkins argues that a text's popularity, in and of itself, justifies our critical attention to it. As Tompkins writes about the works of Stowe, Brown, Cooper, and Warner, "the enormous popularity of these novels, which has been cause for suspicion bordering on disgust, is a reason for paying close attention to them" (124). Second, Tompkins argues that aesthetic judgment has a history, and she makes visible the modernist criteria that have shaped that history. As she writes, "In modernist thinking, literature is by definition a form of discourse that has no designs on the world. It does not attempt to change things, but merely to represent them, and it does so in a specifically literary language whose claim to value lies in its uniqueness. Consequently, works whose stated purpose is to influence the course of history, and which therefore employ a language that is not only not unique but common and accessible to everyone, do not qualify as works of art" (125). With these two claims, Tompkins helped open up a new space for literary analysis, legitimating a kind of highbrow attention to the lowbrow, the application of New Critical skills to texts that the New Critics would most likely have found beneath their contempt.[10]

Although my readings here owe a particular debt to Tompkins, the differences in our approaches ultimately outweigh the similarities. An obvious difference is contextual. You can hear in Tompkins's work an explicit defensiveness about her project, a defensiveness absolutely reasonable in 1985, but perhaps no longer necessary. The study of popular fiction has become something of an industry in the late nineties, owing in part to Tompkins, but to others as well. This isn't to say that the prevailing modernist criteria that Tompkins was writing against no longer hold sway, but that she and others have pried open some critical space around those criteria, making room for other evaluative standards.

If it's no longer necessary to be defensive about one's attention to popular texts, what's left for one to be defensive about? Well, an attention to white-supremacist popular texts, for starters. This concern marks a shift from a defensiveness about form to a defensiveness about content, and it's worth pointing out that Tompkins tends to deemphasize the content of the popular forms she examined. As she writes, "Because I want to understand what gave these novels force for their initial readers, it seemed important to recreate, as sympathetically as possible, the context from which they sprang and the specific problems to which they were addressed. I have therefore not criticized the social and political attitudes that motivated these writers, but have tried instead to inhabit and make available to a modern audience the viewpoint from which their politics made sense" (xiii). Tompkins's neutrality on "the social and political attitudes that motivated these writers" may have been necessary given her historical moment, but it was only possible because she did in fact assign a content to these texts, one that was always already subversive. For Tompkins, the sentimental novel is "a political enterprise, halfway between sermon and social theory, that both codifies and attempts to mold the values of its time" (126). And I would add, since Tompkins doesn't, "for the better." For isn't this phrase implicit in Tompkins's claim that "the sentimental novelists elaborated a myth that gave women the central position of power and authority in the culture" (125)? Tompkins is ultimately interested and invested in these texts to the extent that they constitute subversive interventions in a patriarchal culture. I go to the trouble to make explicit Tompkins's claim here not because I disagree with her—the myth she elaborates is an attractive one—but to ask what happens if instead of adding "for the better" we are compelled to add "for the worse." For this is surely the case with the white-supremacist texts I examine here, none of which can be heroically defended as a neglected but subversive intervention in normative cultural politics.

I'm following, then, Ann Cvetkovich's argument that mass cultural forms don't have to resist oppression to be worth studying and interpreting. As she writes in *Mixed Feelings,* "Critics who argue for the political and aesthetic reevaluation of mass culture or women's culture can confuse the critically interesting with the subversive, forgetting that a work does not have to be resistant to be worth interpreting, and that an intervention within the institution of literary criticism is not always a synecdoche for other forms of resistance" (38).[11] My attention to these enormously popular but critically neglected works constitutes, I think, just such "an intervention within the institution of literary criticism." Whether this intervention pays what we might call oppositional dividends, it is meant to shift the way literary critics think about race and literature in the nineteenth century. It is meant, in short, to make visible a strain of American writing that critics have preferred to neglect. Although this neglect is certainly understandable, given the sometimes awkward good intentions of American literary studies, it has been neither accidental nor incidental to the shaping of what we mean when we talk about American literature.

In fact, the novels I read here occupy something of a switchpoint in the relation between institutional literary studies and popular fiction. Before critics like Tompkins began making a different argument, it was easy to dismiss novels like *The Clansman* not because they were racist but because they were "bad," offering critics a way to keep the American canon (allegedly) free of racism without really addressing the problem of racism. Not surprisingly, the formal judgment has proven easier and less messy than the ideological judgment, since the ideological judgment may raise other, equally messy questions: for example, "What if American literature, as well as our study of it, actually bears something of a structural relation to American racism?"

But given the shift that Tompkins's argument helped inaugurate, it is no longer possible to take the easy way out. We can no longer say that overtly racist novels are beneath our critical attention because they are melodramatic or because they are conventionally plotted. If this is the case, and given their tremendous sales, what excuse do we have to ignore them? That they are racist? Even a sympathetic glance at the heart of the American canon would prove that this hasn't previously been a criterion for exclusion. That they are explicitly racist? This would surely involve us in a labyrinthine hypocrisy, forcing us to admit that we prefer our racism to be implicit. That we prefer "literary" racism to "trashy" racism. That racism is tolerable if it's embedded in a New Critical subtlety.

The fact that these novels are explicitly and proudly racist does not justify our lack of attention to them. Rather, their racial hatred actually requires our attention. Those of us engaged in antiracist work within the academy can't afford to turn away from the overtly racist work that precedes us. Rather than ignore the textual racism of the literary past precisely because it's in the past, we should let it tell us as much as it can about that past, as well as the present. Although there's a risk that the spotlight I'm calling for may simply revivify some of the ugliest currents of American literary history, I believe that the current moment requires us to take that risk. With racial violence and white-supremacist organizing once again on the increase, we neglect at our peril these surreal visions into the workings of white racial anxiety and hatred. Although it's become something of a cliché to argue that you have to understand racism in order to deflate it, it's no less true.

In addition to this overtly political justification, there are other reasons for our attention to the fictions of white supremacy, reasons having to do with the construction of American literary history. To ignore these often repugnant texts would be to participate in that most long-lasting of American critical fictions: that American literature is always a heroic literature, that it has always been a literature of subversion (even revisionists like Tompkins fall into this pattern). We like to imagine American writers as lone voices speaking truth to power, as heroic individuals resisting the contaminating taints of modernity. The reality has been, as we should surely know by now, too often the reverse, and time spent with the novels I examine here may go a long way toward revising a vision of American literary history that is, perhaps, too comfortable for its own good—and for ours.

Another benefit to be derived from a serious attention to the literature of racial hatred relates, somewhat ironically, to African American literary history. The texts I examine made up the difficult context for much African American literary production in the mid– to late nineteenth century, and a detailed understanding of their inner workings will give us a much clearer sense of the task facing African American writers during this period. Although others have described the vexed space of nineteenth-century black writing—the difficulty of writing under the simultaneous burdens of entertaining a mass audience and proving one's humanity—the texts I examine here offer a more detailed vision of the literary landscape facing writers like Douglass, Jacobs, Harper, Chesnutt, and others.[12] For example, an awareness of Victor's *Maum Guinea and Her Plantation "Children,"* a dime novel published in the same year as Harriet Jacobs's *Incidents in the Life of a Slave Girl,* enlarges our appreciation of Jacobs's ability to create a new genre out of the inadequacies of those available to her. An understanding of the racist theology I take up in chapter 3 provides a necessary context for novels like Pauline Hopkins's *Of One Blood,* a novel that dramatizes the difficulties of negotiating and appropriating a racist science for antiracist purposes. Familiarity with this antiblack theology also deepens our appreciation for the ways in which black writers continued to claim and reinvent the Christian tradition as a space of hope and liberation, despite the steady and often surreal drumbeat of biblically sanctioned racism. An understanding of Thomas Dixon's almost monolithic dominance of race fiction at the turn of the century gives us new insight into the challenges facing Charles Chesnutt, Sutton Griggs, and Pauline Hopkins, all of whom wanted not only to sell books but to wrest away from Dixon the terms of racial discourse. In other words, although white-supremacist fiction bears an obviously antithetical relationship to African American literary history, a true appreciation of that history is only possible when we know what it was up against.

### Whiteness/Heterosexuality

This attempt to shift the geography of American and African American literary history comprises a significant part of what I hope to accomplish here. In addition, however, and on a more theoretical level, this book intervenes in a body of work that is coming to be known, for good or for ill, as whiteness studies. In short, this book extends the growing critical emphasis on whiteness as a form of textual, political, and sexual anxiety. The virulent racism of the texts I read here brings whiteness forcibly into view as both normative disciplinary presence and anxious response. Although "whiteness" and "white supremacy" don't name the same thing, white supremacy turns out to be a particularly good lens on whiteness. White supremacy is a form of whiteness, one of its particular manifestations. It usually describes a specific and historical eruption of white political energies, as in the Dixon novel I examine in chapter 5. In part, white supremacy makes whiteness possible because it allows whiteness the space of moderation and normality that it needs to survive. White supremacy, so often imagined as extreme, allows whiteness once again its status as the nonthreatening, as the good. White supremacy, then, becomes something of a scapegoat for whiteness, the convenient location of white violence and lawlessness, distracting our attention from the violence and lawlessness of whiteness itself. Although whiteness and white supremacy are certainly related, they do bear important differences, and I attempt to hang onto those differences in the pages that follow. However, since I'm interested in disrupting the false binary between "good" and "bad" forms of whiteness, there will be times when whiteness and white supremacy do in fact take on the same meaning in my analysis, when whiteness becomes white supremacy, and vice versa.[13]

Although I want to defer until my epilogue a fuller treatment of the possibilities and perils of whiteness studies, I do want to highlight here my primary angle of vision on whiteness: its ambivalent proximity to, and interaction with, heterosexuality. A central contention of the readings that follow is that whiteness works best—in fact, that it works only—when it attaches itself to other abstractions, becoming yet another invisible strand in a larger web of unseen yet powerful cultural forces. My focus on avowedly white-supremacist texts forces into relief the alliances on which white supremacy depends. Dixon's concern with racial purity, for example, makes his novel a better place to understand how gender and sexuality make whiteness a literary and cultural possibility. His single-mindedness on race exposes things about sexuality—specifically heterosexuality as simultaneously a normative standard and a deeply ambivalent structure of desire—that might be left unseen in another work lacking Dixon's polemical drive. I'm interested in whiteness at what could be called its most transparent moments, precisely because in these moments we're able to see its location within a larger system of oppressive and normalizing structures.

For my purposes, the chief ally in whiteness's normalizing mission is heterosexuality, which Monique Wittig defines, with admitted difficulty, as "a nonexistent object, a fetish, an ideological form which cannot be grasped in reality, except through its effects, whose existence lies in the mind of people, but in a way that affects their whole life, the way they act, the way they move, the way they think. So we are dealing with an object both imaginary and real" (40–41). In Wittig's thinking, heterosexuality's power to promote its own invisibility is so complete that "the straight mind cannot conceive of a culture, a society where heterosexuality would not order not only all human relationships but also its very production of concepts and all the processes which escape consciousness, as well" (28). Those "processes which escape consciousness" are the primary breeding ground for heterosexuality's normalizing and self-generating power. And the same holds true for whiteness. As an example, reread the first passage from Wittig quoted above, but imagine that she's defining whiteness, not heterosexuality. What she's talking about is the very air we breathe, the stuff that creates us with no reminder that it is doing so.

What's alluring about Wittig's definition of heterosexuality, however, is also what makes it problematic. In Wittig's hands, heterosexuality becomes a universal force, always already the invisible stuff of the universe. As a mystical presence, it lacks material particularity. However, as scholars are now demonstrating, heterosexuality has a discrete history, one that allows us to avoid too much dependence on the provocative vagaries deployed by Wittig. Jonathan Ned Katz traces this history in medical literature of the late nineteenth century, charting the ways in which heterosexuality made its gradual journey from perversion to its modern incarnation as an immensely powerful normalizing force. According to Katz, *heterosexuality* first appeared in the American medical lexicon in 1892 in an article by Dr. James G. Kiernan (19).[14] For Kiernan, *heterosexuality* signified the perverse, since it referred, in part, to male/female sexual behavior divorced from reproductive imperatives. Since reproduction normalized different-sex eroticism, sexual pleasure occurring outside a reproductive context was seen by Kiernan and others as unhealthy, as pathological. At the time of Kiernan's article, Richard von Krafft-Ebing was also using the word *heterosexual* in his landmark study, *Psychopathia Sexualis.* Krafft-Ebing shares Kiernan's sense that "heterosexual" signifies a nonreproductive, pleasure-centered pathology, but, contrary to Kiernan, Krafft-Ebing begins to position heterosexuality as a normalized, healthy, different-sex erotic standard. Because Krafft-Ebing discusses heterosexuality alongside case studies of men troubled by homosexual desire, heterosexuality begins to assume its shape as a cure for deviance, as a thing to strive for. The process of normalizing heterosexuality was continued by Freud in his "Three Essays on the Theory of Sexuality," where "heterosexuality" comes to mean the healthy, natural endpoint of one's sexual maturation. As Katz writes, Freud "helped to constitute our belief in the existence of a unitary, monolithic thing with a life and determining power of its own: 'heterosexuality'" (66). Katz continues, "Freud's explicit uses of the word *heterosexual* helped to constitute a different-sex eroticism as modern society's influential, dominant norm" (66).

Although I've taken the space to sketch this brief history, a history that coincides with the period under consideration in this book, we must keep in mind an important qualification. What I'm talking about here is, to some extent, a history of language. Although it's possible, à la Katz, to construct an etymological history of heterosexuality's birth, it's important not to overestimate the extent to which this history tells us something about the lived experience of the time. To imagine that the appearance of words like *heterosexuality* in medical journals exists in a causal relationship with people's sexual behaviors is to overestimate the popular currency of medical discourse and to underestimate the unchartable complexity of sexual behavior. George Chauncey Jr. makes this point in his pioneering work on early medical uses of the term *homosexual:*

> It would be wrong to assume, I think, that doctors created and defined the identities of "inverts" and "homosexuals" at the turn of the century, that people uncritically internalized the new medical models, or even that homosexuality emerged as a fully defined category in the medical discourse itself in the 1870s. Such assumptions attribute inordinate power to ideology as an autonomous social force; they oversimplify the complex dialectic between social conditions, ideology, and consciousness which produced gay identities, and they belie the evidence of preexisting subcultures and identities contained in the literature itself. Although the literature is one of the sources most easily accessible to historians, we must

guard against attributing to it a more central role in the formation of sexual identities than it actually may have played. (115)

We ignore such a warning at great cost.

This does not mean, however, that words don't matter. Rather, the shifting medical terminology of this period marks the public face of liminality. It suggests that sexual behaviors, as well as the names for those behaviors, are in a period of flux and transition, that categories are being made and unmade in response to the anxieties that attend any period of upheaval. We shouldn't imagine that etymology tells us anything precise about "heterosexuality," but we shouldn't underestimate how language comes to signal and mirror a period of uncertainty, a period of movement. Katz recognizes as much when he writes that "in the last decades of the nineteenth century, the new term *heterosexual* moved into the world, sometimes linked with nonprocreative 'perversion,' sometimes with 'normal,' procreative, different-sex eroticism" (55).

Although it is impossible to pinpoint a precise moment when *heterosexuality* came to mean what we now take it to mean, it is possible to use this changing language as the visible sign of a broad shift from a reproduction-based sexuality to a pleasure-driven heterosexuality, and it is this broad shift that I want to hang onto. For whiteness bears a necessarily anxious relation to reproduction, a relation mediated through the not-always-dependable structure of heterosexuality. As Richard Dyer writes, "All concepts of race are always concepts of the body and also of heterosexuality. Race is a means of categorising different types of human body which reproduce themselves. It seeks to systematise differences and to relate them to differences of character and worth. Heterosexuality is the means of ensuring, but also the site of endangering, the reproduction of these differences" (*White* 20). The Women's Christian Temperance Union understood as much when, in 1885, its Social Purity Division adopted the slogan "The White Life for Two," a phrase that economically figures one aspect of the relation between whiteness and heterosexuality (D'Emilio and Freedman 153). Through its use of this slogan, the WCTU signaled the centrality of heterosexuality to the maintenance of both the white race and a "white" morality.

As Dyer points out, although heterosexuality is absolutely necessary to the reproduction of whiteness, it is also the means through which whiteness can lose itself. At the heart of both outcomes lies the tricky matter of desire, an inherently unstable quantity—part longing, part repulsion, part fascination, part horror. The texts I examine here reveal what happens when race and sexuality meet, when the desire for whiteness meets its own ambivalence. The result, not surprisingly, is an obsessive attention to amalgamation, that site where heterosexuality endangers rather than ensures white reproduction. Robert J. C. Young suggests that racial theory is itself invested in—if not defined by—the compulsive imagining of interracial sex. As he puts it in this wonderfully over-the-top passage, racial theory has historically depended on a

> voyeuristic tableau of frenzied, interminable copulation, of couplings, fusing, coalescence, *between races*. At its core, such racial theory projected a phantasmagoria of the desiring machine as a people factory: a Malthusian fantasy of uncontrollable, frenetic fornication producing the countless motley varieties of interbreeding, with the miscegenated offspring themselves then generating an ever-increasing *mélange,* "mongrelity," of self-propagating endlessly diversifying hybrid progeny. . . . Nineteenth-century theories of race did not just consist of essentializing differentiations between self and other: they were also about a fascination with people having sex—interminable, adulterating, aleatory, illicit, inter-racial sex. (181)

With such amalgamationist terror at its root, it would be surprising if the relationship between whiteness and heterosexuality were neat and tidy. The truth of desire is messy.

Partly responsible for this messiness, in addition to the amalgamationist fervor described by Young, is a homosocial desire that I take to be a constitutive component of both whiteness and heterosexuality. In the readings that follow, I'm interested in how white women become silent markers in the systems of exchange that make both whiteness and heterosexuality cultural givens. Simultaneously imagined as the key to whiteness's future and its weakest defense, white women enable whiteness at the same time that they are denied its fruits. They make it possible, yet are kept from the fullness of its franchise, given their status as women in the always patriarchal shape that whiteness assumes. At the same time, I emphasize a similar role played by black men, who, through the hysterical imaginings of white men, become the sexual threat and object of sexual desire that simultaneously threaten and buttress the heterosexual expectations of whiteness. White supremacy, then, can be usefully understood as a homosocial network that commodifies and appropriates the bodies of white women and black men in order to consolidate both whiteness and heterosexuality as governing ideologies, ever present abstractions, condensed forms of panic, and political structures.

By invoking the category of the homosocial, I mean to borrow from and extend the work of Eve Sedgwick, whose model of the homosocial triangle (itself borrowed from Claude Lévi-Strauss and Gayle Rubin, among others) continues to have enormous critical currency. By homosocial, Sedgwick means the structural logic of male/male relations that requires a woman in a mediating position, in a position of exchange. Like Sedgwick, my goal is to "draw the 'homosocial' back into the orbit of 'desire,'" positing "the potential unbrokenness of a continuum between homosocial and homosexual" (*Between* 1). As others have pointed out, however, Sedgwick's homosociality becomes something of a different creature—more complicated, less universally applicable—if we consider how race, as well as gender, determines the workings of desire.[15] Although I explore this in more detail in chapter 5, for now let me simply point out that the homosocial may be a necessary component of any attempt to keep whiteness white, to keep whiteness pure. If, as Dyer points out, "race is a means of categorising different types of human body which reproduce themselves" (*White* 20), white reproduction becomes a necessarily unstable process. To reproduce whiteness sexually is to risk contamination, and so heterosexuality becomes a threat to whiteness, one that can only be avoided if that heterosexuality is ultimately less important and less central than the homosociality that it facilitates. Homoeroticism becomes, paradoxically, the only structure of desire that can keep whiteness white. Thus the homosocial becomes not merely a constitutive element of patriarchy, or of the sex/gender system, or of heterosexuality, à la Sedgwick, but of whiteness.

*White Weddings*

Our critical attention should be focused on race and sexuality as equally important and interdependent categories, since whiteness and heterosexuality come most clearly into view in proximity to one another. Their invisibility depends on the invisibility of the connective threads that link them together. It's my goal here to make this connective tissue visible. Whereas whiteness appears more often than not as an ideological abstraction, heterosexuality is made visible primarily through its forms, the chief of which is marriage. Of course, marriage and heterosexuality don't name the same thing; rather, marriage is a structure of heterosexuality, a visible form of heterosexual desire. Katz emphasizes the materiality of marriage by defining it as "a social organization of kinship relations, of economic alliances, of property transfer, and of pleasure" (175).[16] Although this definition might seem to take the romance out of its subject, it's useful to us for precisely that reason. The relations of money and property, of pleasure and kinship—and I would add politics—reveal the social infrastructure that marriage is at least partially designed to create.

Time after time in the readings that follow, marriage becomes the mannequin on which whiteness and white supremacy are draped. Marriage consolidates white-supremacist desire, often providing the political motivation for that desire. The link between marriage and whiteness can be seen most clearly as a generic property. Most of the works I read here depend on that most dependable of plots: the complicated yet ultimately satisfying journey toward marriage. The presence of this plot itself is far from remarkable. But what happens, we might ask, when the marriage plot becomes the narrative superstructure on which an avowedly white-supremacist polemic is hung? What happens at the intersection of the white-supremacist plot and the marriage plot that makes each a central component of the upcoming narrative closure? If both white supremacy and marriage must be established facts by novel's end, what is their real relation to one another, both within and without the pressures of narrative? The symbiotic relationship between these racial and sexual compulsions is so tightly woven that it's worth prying them apart in order to witness their separate shapes and the congruity that these shapes allow, and even demand.

As a way to untangle and clarify the symbiotic relationship I'm describing, we might ask what structural similarities plots of besieged heterosexuality and besieged whiteness share, and why these plots tend to demand wedding bells as a salvational trope. Richard von Krafft-Ebing's famous case studies of heterosexually challenged Victorians offer a useful parallel to the white stories I read here, since they also depend on marriage for both political and narrative closure.[17] After hypnotism, a Mr. von X, who had complained of "unnatural" thoughts and acts concerning other men, "still had sympathetic feeling for some men, but never anything like love. He occasionally had pleasurable coitus with women, and now thought of marriage" (Krafft-Ebing 342). A Mr. von Z., having undergone Krafft-Ebing's treatment, is described as "lastingly cured," and "occupied with thoughts of marriage" (347). And after forty-five treatments, a Mr. R. "became engaged to a young lady some weeks later, and presented himself again, after six months, as a happy bridegroom" (354). In all these cases marriage comes to the rescue of besieged masculinity, making that masculinity whole again by redirecting its supposedly pathological sexual desires.

Although I don't mean to suggest that the white-supremacist texts I examine enact the same type of conversion narrative, where homosexuality is the disease and marriage the cure, I do think the structural similarity between the plots of beleaguered heterosexuality and beleaguered whiteness is enormously instructive. In the case of the white-supremacist texts, marriage often carries with it the same magical, curative properties described by these nineteenth-century sexologists, though the pathology differs. In the works I read, the disease isn't homosexuality, but a weakening and sickened form of whiteness. Marriage becomes the restorative, the social form that buttresses whiteness in its cultural decline.

Or at least that tries to. In this formulation—with marriage successfully coming to the rescue of whiteness—whiteness and heterosexuality become normative copartners, both invested in buttressing and feeding off of the cultural normativity of the other. This is, in fact, often the case, as chapters 1 and 2 demonstrate. I should add, however, that this only tells part of the story. As I argue in chapters 4 and 5, as "heterosexually" becomes, around the turn of the century, a more visible and scientifically demarcated category, its infrastructure actually becomes less, rather than more, stable, particularly in relation to the structures of whiteness. Although the forms of heterosexuality—marriage, for example—pretend to create racial order out of mongrel chaos, the pretense is never entirely persuasive. In some cases, heterosexuality's "coming to the rescue" not only doesn't "save" whiteness; it in fact reveals things about heterosexuality—and about whiteness—that their adherents would be shocked to discover. There's an important sense in which whiteness and heterosexuality actually threaten one another, a way in which the system of desire unleashed by a newly emergent heterosexual pleasure principle threatens the racial purity on which whiteness depends. Given this ambivalence, it's worth charting the movements of these two structures of feeling, hoping, in the process, to get a more accurate picture of the early days of white heterosexuality.

In short, I'm interested in determining when whiteness and heterosexuality are playing for the same team, and when they are not. Or, to borrow a much richer metaphor from Richard Dyer, I want to examine heterosexuality as "the cradle of whiteness" (*White* 140). In this formulation Dyer implies not only that heterosexuality gives birth to whiteness but that it nurtures whiteness, attending to its needs and soothing away its anxieties. Heterosexuality becomes the loving parent. This is certainly true, but only up to a point. For as we all know, parent/child relationships aren't always healthy. Envy, jealousy, anxiety, selfishness, overinvestment, underinvestment, abuse—this is also the stuff of the cradle, a cradle that heterosexuality can rock with a vengeance. Only by allowing whiteness and heterosexuality the freedom to be themselves—multiple, fractured, incoherent—will we get a sufficiently nuanced picture of the true relation they bear to one another as they struggle to define, once and for all, the color of sex.

# Chapter One

# "De White Man in Season"

There is one thing I would like to say to my white fellow countrymen, and especially to those who dabble in ink and affect to discuss the Negro; and yet I hesitate because I feel it is a fact which persons of the finer sensibilities and more delicate perceptions must know instinctively: namely, that it is an insult to humanity and a sin against God to publish any such sweeping generalizations of a race on such meager and superficial information. We meet it at every turn—this obtrusive and offensive vulgarity, this gratuitous sizing up of the Negro and conclusively writing down his equation, sometimes even among his ardent friends and bravest defenders. Were I not afraid of falling myself into the same error that I am condemning, I would say it seems an *Anglo Saxon characteristic* to have such overweening confidence in his own power of induction that there is no equation which he would acknowledge to be indeterminate, however many unknown quantities it may possess.—Anna Julia Cooper

Just a few months after the publication of *Uncle Tom's Cabin* in book form, an article in the proslavery *Pennsylvanian* issued a call to literary arms. Commenting on the book's early and significant sales, the article backhandedly praised "the enthusiastic abolition fanatics" for recognizing that "cunningly written fictions" provide the best forum for the propagation of antislavery sentiment, since "the great mass of the people cannot be induced to listen to their mad ravings, or read their essays." The article then calls for literary rebuttal: "In order to meet the fallacies of this abolition tale, it would be well if the friends of the Union would array fiction against fiction. Meet the disunionists with their own chosen weapon, and they are foiled. The friends of the Union have no fiction enforcing and defending the guaranties of the Constitution, or advocating the rights of our Southern brethren; but the sooner we have, the better; the people love light attractive reading, and it is in disseminating works of this kind that the fancy is pleased and the mind influenced."[1] One of the first to heed this call to arms was Charles Jacobs Peterson, a Pennsylvania writer and magazine publisher who published *The Cabin and Parlor; or, Slaves and Masters* late in 1852 as a rebuttal and revision of Stowe's incendiary novel.[2] Put simply, *The Cabin and Parlor* takes the main ingredients of Stowe's novel and turns them on their head. A crisis at the "big house" causes the separation of a white family rather than a slave family. Fugitive slaves find despair and poverty in the North as opposed to freedom and Quakers. The young white son finds himself dying of poverty in the wage labor of the North rather than presiding at the salvational death of a heroic slave in the South. In short, this novel of slavery somehow finds a way to show how tough it is to be white in the 1850s—especially if your whiteness is of the aristocratic mold. Which, of course, was the only real whiteness going.

I want to use Peterson's novel—a much richer text than it is ever given credit for being—to work through the interlocking relations of class, gender, and whiteness. More specifically, I want to explore how crises of class and gender actually produce whiteness as a "racial" category—how the tensions surrounding labor and gender at midcentury fuel whiteness as a looming abstraction that both covers up and answers to the pressures of white labor and black slavery. As David Roediger has argued, the ideological construction of labor in the early part of the nineteenth century occurred within a context where race was always an issue. As Roediger writes, "Antebellum white workers could not begin to describe themselves without reference to the fact of slavery and, increasingly, to the ideology of race" (*Wages* 20). In Peterson's novel, this fact gets played out in intriguing fashion, as the remnants of a southern planter family are forced to earn their own bread, no longer aided by their legions of slaves. By putting his white characters through this crisis of labor—which is at the same time a crisis of whiteness—Peterson highlights the extent to which whiteness exists simultaneously as anxiety and uncertainty *and* as a normative and disciplinary social structure. Its success in the second of these seemingly antithetical modes is absolutely dependent on its invisibility in the former. By rescuing his white characters at novel's end and restoring them to their former caste, Peterson inadvertently demonstrates whiteness's absolute dependence not only on the black slave but on the white worker, who is crucial to the novel's happy resolution but necessarily absent from it. And he does so in a way that grants to whiteness a hypervisibility, making clear its multiple potentials for success as well as failure.

Peterson is an intriguing figure for many reasons, despite his virtual disappearance from various mappings of nineteenth-century American letters. If he is remembered at all, it is for his fleeting association with Poe, whom he worked with for a time and who later described him as one of many journalistic "ninnies." Ninny or not, Peterson founded and edited the most popular woman's periodical in mid-nineteenth-century America, *Peterson's Magazine*, which was designed to fill a niche being gradually vacated by his friend and mentor George Graham. Peterson recognized that *Graham's Lady's and Gentleman's Magazine* was "verging into solid literature slowly, cutting the fashion plates . . . and indulging in more heavy prose" (Nipps 238). Peterson intended to make his own magazine "light, spicy, romantic, and lady-like" (Nipps 238), and to offer it at a cheaper cost than his competition. The eventual sales figures chart Peterson's success in offering the magazine-buying American public—particularly women—exactly what it wanted. By 1866 *Peterson's* had the largest circulation of any ladies' periodical in the world (Stearns 211).

As Barrie Hayne has argued, Peterson's success can be largely attributed to his absolute faith in moderation. In a letter to James Russell Lowell, Peterson described himself this way: "I am *no* teetotaller, *no* abolitionist, *no* transcendentalist, *no* peace-man, or any of that sort. . . . Heaven intended me for a conservative in everything except politics. I hang on to the old religion & and the old doctrines, until the evidence in form of a novelty becomes not only equally strong but preponderating. . . . It takes strong testimony to persuade me I am wiser than my fathers" (qtd. in Hayne 512–13). Although this heartfelt adherence to the status quo is partly responsible for the popularity of Peterson's magazine, the extent to which he intentionally kept politics out of its pages is also significant. The Civil War years offer one example. As Hayne writes, "One can read *Peterson's* in the years 1861–1865 without being at all aware of the war raging beyond" (514–15). Though a Union man himself, Peterson obviously recognized that his audience wanted the opposite of what the war provided: calm rather than stress, normalcy as opposed to chaos. At least within the pages of *Peterson's Magazine,* everything could remain the same.

I'm interested in Peterson precisely because he adhered so firmly to the middle ground. "His mind was distinctly average," writes Hayne (512). In reading his magazine and his novels, "one may properly feel in touch with what the average man—and, especially, the average woman—was thinking in those years" (512). "If it is the plain we seek," Hayne concludes, Peterson may be our best guide (512). Although I want to avoid fully endorsing these appraisals of Peterson's character ("the normal" is notoriously hard to quantify, and harder still to prove), I agree with Hayne to the extent that Peterson's cultivated and self-conscious moderation makes him an intriguing lens through which to view the immoderate issues of his day—namely, race, caste, and gender.

Although Peterson's tendency to hug the middle of the road makes his views on slavery worth exploring, he is an equally interesting figure because he represents the tip of the anti–Uncle Tom literary iceberg.[3] While it's become a cultural commonplace that the publication of *Uncle Tom's Cabin* drastically altered the course of nineteenth-century American politics, few people talk about the impact Stowe's novel had on the publishing industry and on popular American letters in general. Put simply, Stowe's book offered itself as a new model of literary success. If one wanted to sell thousands upon thousands of copies, it seemed to suggest, one merely had to pen a novel about slavery—be it pro or con.[4] Writers hoping desperately to capture the attention, and the money, of the American middle class had finally found their subject.[5]

A survey of the "New Publications" column in the *New York Tribune* during the last three months of 1852 offers a narrative history of the emergence and reception of Peterson's novel. First announced as "In Press" on October 2 (an announcement repeated five more times), *The Cabin and Parlor* was finally published on October 29, by which point eighteen thousand copies had been presold in ten days and a fourth edition of eight thousand more was in printing.[6] The ad announcing its publication called Peterson's novel "the greatest book of the century, far surpassing Mrs. Stowe's far-famed work of 'Uncle Tom's Cabin,'" and contained a long excerpt from a review in the *Philadelphia Evening Bulletin* that hailed the novel's powers of narrative, description, and most of all, argument. An advertisement a week later proclaimed sales of twenty-two thousand copies and excerpted positive reviews from the *Boston Post*, the *Christian Observer*, the *Philadelphia Dollar Newspaper*, the *Saturday Courier*, and the *Baltimore Clipper*. On November 18, another ad announced that twenty-five thousand copies had been published of *The Cabin and Parlor*, "the ONLY REAL ANSWER TO UNCLE TOM'S CABIN yet published."[7]

Peterson's novel also received a good deal of attention in the national magazines, including Peterson's own. A humble blurb from the December issue focused almost exclusively on the book's physical qualities, calling it "as handsome a volume as has been issued this year." The notice, presumably written by Peterson himself, referred readers to the advertisement on the magazine's front cover for "the character and merits of the work" and noted that twenty thousand copies had been sold in the space of a month. *Godey's* called *Cabin* a "most thrilling narrative which will . . . forcibly appeal to the good sense and judgment of [Peterson's] readers" and noted that the book has been "generally and favorably noticed by the press."

*Cabin* attracted the most ink in a widely read editorial by George Graham in the February 1853 issue of *Graham's Magazine*. Titled "Black Letters; Or Uncle Tom-Foolery in Literature," Graham's article decried the wave of "literary nigritudes" (214) then flooding the market and focused primarily on the great evil perpetrated by Stowe in *Uncle Tom's Cabin*, an evil that has made "the shelves of booksellers groan under the weight of Sambo's woes, done up in covers" (209). Graham sees Stowe as merely the most famous instance of a larger perniciousness: "Our female agitators have abandoned Bloomers in despair, and are just now bestride a new hobby—an intense love of black folks, *in fashionable novels!*" (209).[8] Although the majority of Graham's review deals with *Uncle Tom's Cabin*, a significant section reviews Peterson's novel, yoking it together with Stowe's work as "the bane and antidote" (212).[9] Though Graham faults *The Cabin and Parlor* for its occasional instances of "outrageously bad" dialogue, he firmly believes that Peterson bests Stowe in terms of plot and story. That he chose to review these two novels side by side lends significant credence to Peterson's status as chief rival to Stowe, at least in the early part of 1853.[10]

Charles K. Whipple, in the November 5, 1852, issue of the *Liberator*, also grants Peterson this status, though he does so by way of attacking his argument point by point. Calling *Cabin* better than other anti–Uncle Tom novels (*Uncle Tom's Cabin as It Is,* by William L. G. Smith, and *Aunt Phillis's Cabin,* by Mary Henderson Eastman), Whipple devotes most of his energy to summarizing Peterson's main points and then attacking the seven false suppositions on which his novel depends.[11] Whipple recognized *The Cabin and Parlor* as a better novel than other anti–Uncle Tom novels precisely because it treats a complex social problem without entirely dismissing the complexity. Peterson's portrayal of free blacks living in northern ghettos carries a good deal of ugly truth, which Whipple acknowledged. Likewise, Peterson's analysis of northern wage labor, with its attendant and desperate poverty, holds up even today as a thorough critique of one phase of capitalism. Peterson at least attempts to acknowledge and maintain the complexity of labor relations in order to counter the sometimes simplistic notions that Stowe finds herself dependent on in *Uncle Tom's Cabin.* For this reason, if for no other, Peterson's novel should be of interest to us, not because it is staunchly proslavery but because in its proslavery stance it stumbles on some rather trenchant analyses of slavery's subsidiary structures—a rigid class system, for example, or the bindings and stresses of gender.

*The Cabin and Parlor* achieves its complexity and ambiguity through the radical reorientations that occur within it. An aristocratic Virginia family loses everything through the death of the patriarch and is thus forced into a kind of "white slavery." With the death of the father, and the incompetence of the mother, responsibility for the family's continued existence falls to the beautiful daughter, who is forced into school teaching. In order not to be a burden, the young son goes to Philadelphia to make his way in the business world, hoping through fame and fortune to reinstate his family in their former graces. In all of these situations, the terms of slavery are reversed, as whites find themselves slaving in an economy pitted against them, since they no longer have the magical protections of the planter class. In *Cabin,* the work normally heaped on the backs of slaves is, through a weird transference, returned to the backs of whites, who feel the heaviness of labor, the difficulty of subsistence, the tenuousness of the economy and their place within it. What's worse, the unmarried but beautiful daughter must now bear the brunt of labor, ruining her chances at a future match because her purity and whiteness are now soiled—not through a sexual contamination but through the dirt of work, a dirt that implies a sexual sullying without fully enacting it.[12]

These primary reorientations—the loss of caste and the forced movement outside gender roles—manifest themselves in the novel through an increasing occupation with whiteness as a once beautiful abstraction, now fallen to the real world of dirt and labor. Although whiteness hovers over the novel as a poignant reminder of the lost city, in actuality it exists only as anxious response to the changing conditions brought about by the tenuous and always conflicted nature of American slavery. It appears most clearly when that slavery is threatened. With the temporary suspension of black slavery in the novel, brought about by the death of Mr. Courtenay and the loss of the plantation, whiteness takes on increasing importance at its weakest moment.

Before turning to the specifics of Peterson's novel, however, I want to look briefly at one aspect of the response generated by Stowe's novel, particularly as it relates to the fact of a woman working. The young daughter's labor in *The Cabin and Parlor* has its real-world analog in Stowe's labor with her pen. The hostility that greeted Stowe's work—and here I use "work" to mean labor—will be instructive when we turn our attention to Peterson's horrified and conflicted representation of female labor and its implications for whiteness as a cultural and political franchise.

*Disciplining Stowe*

Let the woman learn in silence with all subjection.

But I suffer not a woman to teach, nor to usurp authority over the man, but to be in silence.—1 Timothy 2.11–12

In his review of *Uncle Tom's Cabin* for the *Southern Literary Messenger*, John Thompson reaches back to this piece of biblical authority as divine sanction for his utter condemnation of Stowe and her book. Stowe, associated in Thompson's mind with those "diaper diplomatists and wet-nurse-politicians" who make up the "school of Woman's Rights," defies the "letter of scripture" when she attempts to tell men how to live their lives (631). And lest the southern reader think Thompson too harsh in his treatment of this "lady novelist," he begins by drawing an important distinction. Echoing Macaulay, who had asked whether the work of lady authors should be examined with the same critical lens used for their male counterparts, Thompson argues for a bit of critical gallantry. As long as ladies refrain from such male subjects as history and philosophy, he argues, their fictional works should be given the benefit of the doubt, recognizing the "immunities of the sex" (630). But having sketched out the duties of the chivalrous reviewer, Thompson goes on to make a crucial distinction between "*lady* writers and *female* writers" (630). "We could not find it in our hearts," he writes, "to visit the dulness or ignorance of a well-meaning lady with the rigorous discipline which it is necessary to inflict upon male dunces and blockheads" (630). He continues: "But where a writer of the softer sex manifests, in her productions, a shameless disregard of truth and of those amenities which so peculiarly belong to her sphere of life, we hold that she has forfeited the claim to be considered a lady, and with that claim all exemption from the utmost stringency of critical punishment" (630). Enter Mrs. Stowe, a decidedly female writer who, according to Thompson, has looked "beyond the office for which she was created—the high and holy office of maternity" (631).

Thompson was not alone in his focus on Stowe's unladylike behavior. George F. Holmes, reviewing *A Key to "Uncle Tom's Cabin"* for the *Southern Literary Messenger,* lumps Stowe together with Fanny Wright and George Sand, authors whose work, he argues, has "unsexed in great measure the female mind" (323). It's important to remember, however, that when Holmes speaks of "unsexing," he doesn't imagine that Stowe somehow loses a gendered subjectivity. Rather, she trades one sex for another; she is not unsexed but "sexed," though sexed male. As the following passage from Holmes's review suggests, Stowe becomes the phallic writer, wielding the pen as an instrument of sexual violence. No less is at stake than "female purity" itself: "It is a horrible thought that a woman should write or a lady read such productions as those by which [Stowe's] celebrity has been acquired. Are scenes of license and impurity, and ideas of loathsome depravity and habitual prostitution to be made the cherished topics of the female pen . . . ? Is the mind of woman to be tainted, seduced, contaminated, and her heart disenchanted of its native purity of sentiment, by the unblushing perusal, the free discussion, and the frequent meditation of such thinly veiled pictures of corruption? Can a . . . man think of their being habitually read by ladies without shame and repugnance?" (322).[13] Though sex isn't explicitly named in this passage, it is surely the subject. "Tainted," "contaminated," "seduced"— Holmes relies on notions that equate the acts of reading and writing with the loss of female virginity. He echoes the language of sex as robber of virtue—as something that draws one in only to despoil. But there's an interesting reversal at work here. Holmes would not have ladies (and he means southern white women) read such works because they will be seduced and tainted, their purity lost. He neglects, of course, the specifics of the "scenes of license and impurity" that Stowe relates. *Uncle Tom's Cabin* contains hints of sexual behavior only to the extent that Stowe writes about a slave economy in which black women are property first, always subject to the advances of their masters. Holmes, reading the rape of slaves as "habitual prostitution," transfers agency from white men to black women, disentangling white masculinity from its role in this debasement. His ultimate move, though, is to project the phallic power that white men exercised within slavery onto Stowe herself, who in his account becomes the despoiler of white southern womanhood. Holmes's fear of an imagined feminine power creates its figurative reality. Stowe is the rapist, who, by putting pen to paper, becomes the instrument that robs the plantation mistress of her southern purity, her female delicacy. White men have been completely removed from their role in this alleged corruption of white purity. Because Stowe writes about the rape of black women, she is responsible, according to Holmes, for the rape of white women, invoking the contempt for white women barely hidden in the cult of southern womanhood.

William Gilmore Simms, a leading southern champion of slavery, offers a more vivid example of the white male anxiety I'm tracing. According to Simms, "Mrs. Stowe betrays a malignity so remarkable that the petticoat lifts of itself, and we see the hoof of the beast under the table" ("Review" 226). One can only wonder what causes the petticoat to lift "of itself," though Holmes's fear of Stowe as despoiler of women certainly gives us a clue. At any event, whether the lifted petticoat reveals demonic hooves or a dangling pen, Simms's metaphor casts Stowe as a hypermasculinized and sexual figure of pure evil— Satan with an erection.

In *Novels, Readers, and Reviewers* Nina Baym ably disentangles the conflicting energies at work in this type of feminine labor, and she does so in a way that highlights the importance of discernible demarcations between certain types of literary work—the maintenance of certain "spheres" and "arenas" wherein women may safely labor. Baym quotes an 1855 review of a reissue of Austen's *Pride and Prejudice* that explicitly maps the terrain appropriate for female pens: "We entertain the profoundest respect for female genius," the reviewer writes, "and are well assured that, when confined to its proper sphere, its productions are not only ornamental, but requisite to the completeness of any national literature" (qtd. in Baym 255). The reviewer continues by making a distinction that explains in large measure the male uproar generated by Stowe's novel: "We would not see our wives or sisters plunge into the arena of politics or meddle with pursuits unsuited to them; but in the walks of fiction or romance, in song, and in all those branches of intellectual culture where tenderness and sensibility are required, the finer and more delicate mind of woman might greatly aid the full development of human nature" (qtd. in Baym 255). Stowe's sin was that she collapsed the categories this reviewer insists on establishing. *Uncle Tom's Cabin*—a political romance, a fictional polemic—refused neat boundaries separating masculine from feminine. This erasure of cultural markers constituted a supreme threat to those who needed those markers for the maintenance of their cultural power.

The spatial metaphors used against feminine authorial power have clear racial resonances as well, particularly in the case of Stowe. In an attack on Stowe's physical appearance, Simms lamented that Stowe had not lived her life in the "ample" and "sufficiently comfortable" Negro cabins in Carolina, for "had you always dwelt in such a habitation," he tells her, "how greatly would it have improved your aspect under the hands of the daguerreotypist" (238). Aside from merely suggesting that Stowe would have been happier in the sunnier climate of the South, Simms specifically locates Stowe's happiness within a Negro cabin—at home with, presumably, black men. Simms's hysterical response to Stowe, coupled with Baym's comments about boundaries and arenas, partially explains why metaphors of spatial segregation are often used when women act in an "unladylike" manner. Like Thompson's notion of a woman's "sphere of life" and "the office for which she was created" (630), Simms's language speaks to the perceived necessity for a distance between southern women and forces of possible (black) contamination. The most popular image of the southern plantation mistress being kept on a pedestal similarly encodes a white male fear of amalgamationist contact.

As writer, and thus as sexual threat, Stowe possesses a power that clearly worries Holmes and other male critics of her novel. Holmes's claim that Stowe is "unsexed" masks his fear of the opposite—that she is "sexed" in such a way as to threaten his own masculinity, his own right to phallic power. Consequently, Stowe's labor produces a coalescence of male anxieties involving the status of whiteness as a normative and disciplinary abstraction. Since whiteness in its normative mode is based in part on white female purity, immobility, and leisure, Stowe becomes both symbol and indicator of whiteness's decline. As worker, writer of fiction, and dabbler in sex and politics, she makes whiteness visible because she threatens the men who benefit most from it.

But perhaps Thompson, Holmes, and Simms, worried as they are about Stowe's "defilement" of southern womanhood, are exaggerating the extent of the problem. A letter originally published in the *New Orleans Picayune,* and reprinted in the *Liberator* of March 4, 1853, would have served to assuage these men's fears. In the letter, an anonymous southern woman writes to her sister in the North about how Stowe's book has affected her. The southern woman does "not like this said Harriet, for she has proved herself false to her womanly mission—a stirrer up of strife, rather than a 'peace maker'; deficient in the delicacy and purity of a woman, inasmuch as she has painted from her own, libidinous imagination, scenes which no modest woman could conceive of." Like Holmes, this correspondent feels Stowe "has unsexed herself." Reading Stowe's book has changed this southern woman's life, and here is where those men fearful of Stowe's impact will be relieved:

> The reading of her work has had one good effect on my mind—it has given me a horror for what we call clear, strong-minded women. Before I was somewhat inclined to sympathize with some of the supposed wrongs of women . . . , but I would rather be a bondswoman on one of the southern estates than be Harriet Beecher Stowe.
>
> I tell my "lordly half," I would promise to "obey" now more loudly, were we to be married over again . . . , and I thank the man Harriet for opening my eyes to the perils surrounding a woman

who believes herself sufficient unto herself; I thank the man Harriet for making more of a true woman of me.

This last phrase is truly suggestive and absolutely congruent with the fear of the female phallus betrayed by the male reviewers of Stowe's novel. Made a "true woman" by "the man Harriet," this letter writer, although disgusted by the "sexual" content of Stowe's novel, resorts to a sexualized language to describe this disgust. Reading *Uncle Tom's Cabin* is figured as an act of sex itself, though the southern woman would not want to repeat the encounter. The lesson learned, after this one-time dalliance with the forbidden, is that women must be protected from sexual threat, and that a woman writing constitutes just such a threat. Simms could not have wished for a happier scenario, a better prescription for domestic bliss.

As the above reviews suggest, the southern response to *Uncle Tom's Cabin* was far from favorable.[14] This should come as no surprise, since this book sought to undermine the fundamental institutions and ideals of the South, a book that, if its thesis were taken to heart, could begin the process of dismantling American slavery and thus change forever the shape of American social and political life. Southern reviewers and politicians were quick to recognize the very real threat that Stowe's novel posed, both to their cherished notions of "southern womanhood" and to the institutions they represented.[15]

On one level, of course, *Uncle Tom's Cabin* is a novel about the great American "race question." Its thesis is simple: if blacks are indeed human, if they feel the same emotions and are capable of the same intellect as whites, slavery cannot be justified. But as the above reviews demonstrate, there is a great deal more going on here. The fact that *Uncle Tom's Cabin* was written by a woman and that it dramatizes female characters who occasionally defy the rule of their husbands made it inevitable that "race" would not be the only battleground demarcated by this novel. The vehemently misogynist attacks of reviewers like Thompson, Holmes, and Simms bespeak a sense of patriarchy under siege, of male power seriously threatened. And when we consider how notions of southern womanhood were constructed, it becomes clearer why a novel about race would raise such fears about gender. Womanly purity and racial purity are both part of the same idea, an idea rooted in patriarchal institutions and systems of control. Societal taboos against miscegenation (or, to use the nineteenth-century vernacular, "amalgamation") placed the primary burden for maintaining racial purity not on the master who may be abusing his female slaves sexually but on the plantation mistress, whose job it was to guard her own purity so as to ensure the purity of whiteness's future.[16]

But there's a cyclical dynamic at work here. Although it's true that white women were made to bear the burden of racial purity, any threat to that purity got transmuted, through the energies of patriarchy, into a threat against white men, who then found it even more necessary to shore up the franchise of whiteness. This franchise depends on a dialectical movement between the anxious response to racial threat and the normative force that results from that response. Whiteness insists on female purity, but it only really appears in the absence of that purity. Similarly, whiteness depends on female docility and leisure, but it only appears when women break a sweat. If Stowe has the gall to work for her living, to enter the male realms of politics and letters, then the southern sense of life is already beginning to crack, the fissures in the master's house beginning to widen. It is as if white men in the 1850s were beginning to glimpse a reality that Frances Harper would make pithily explicit some years later when she said, "I do not believe that white women are dewdrops just exhaled from the skies" (218).

Peterson's *The Cabin and Parlor* offers a provocative and illuminating pathway into the issues I've raised thus far. Peterson's plot focuses on the fragility of whiteness and the relation of this fragility to a shifting economy. At its center are fears and questions about the role of independent white women within the unstable pre–Civil War South. *Cabin* is motivated, in various ways, by Peterson's sense that whiteness is under attack and that women are somehow to blame. His narrative staging of this siege will, I think, help us better understand the difficult logic that makes Stowe, for example, the biggest threat to southern womanhood.

### Reorientations

"The lord knows, a black skin, in these nineteenth century days, is quite a blessing." (152)

The wind moaning through the creaking trees, and sighing over the white, desolate expanse of fields, made her heart beat quick with vague terrors. Every instant the landscape in sight narrowed its circuit, the dark horizon shutting in, closer and closer, on all sides, till the round wall of blackness seemed to her straining eyes actually to be in motion, and advancing upon her. The village, but now in full sight, was no longer visible. Farm-house after farm-house was devoured in succession, by the greedy night. A universal chaos of darkness seemed overtaking the world. (161)

These passages from *The Cabin and Parlor* emphasize the dialectic of envy and fear so often on display in white representations of blackness. Although black skins may be enviable commodities (more on the tortuous logic of this mid-nineteenth-century desire in a moment), blackness itself is a great stalking beast, gradually closing in on the "white, desolate expanse of fields," as well as the desolate young white woman hoping to traverse them. In the second passage Isabel Courtenay, the novel's heroine, is lost in a snowstorm and struggles toward home. The snowstorm, oddly figured as a "round wall of blackness," demonstrates the intensity of Peterson's need to keep whiteness reserved for all that is good and calming. The snow possesses Isabel of "vague terrors." She is afraid, but is unsure exactly of what. The storm hits as she returns home from a hard day of work: "The suddenness of the storm appalled Isabel. Already the beaten foot-path had disappeared" (162). The advancing wall of blackness obscures the much traveled path. Having gone to work, Isabel can't find her way home again. Quite simply, Isabel, remnant of one of Virginia's long-standing aristocratic families, has lost her way.

*The Cabin and Parlor* is about just that—formerly wealthy whites who have lost their way in a radically changed economic and social landscape. Whereas *Uncle Tom's Cabin* portrays the chaos that descends on black lives once the finances at the "big house" are threatened, Peterson is more interested in the financial destruction visited on the whites themselves. When the Courtenays are thrown into insolvency at the sudden death of Mr. Courtenay, they are left to fend for themselves in a world turned upside down. The house, the property, and the slaves must all be sold. They have nothing but the help of Dr. Worthington, a family friend of moderate means who can only do so much.

Peterson makes perfectly clear how far the mighty have fallen. "Few were as well descended as they," he tells us, going on to list the triumphs of previous Courtenays: the one who "entered England with the Conqueror," the "several Courtenays [who] followed Richard of the Lion Heart to Palestine," those who "had fought in the wars of the Roses" (12). But as Dr. Worthington sadly remarks when settling the estate for his now destitute friends, "How these old families do die out" (50). The Courtenays' prospects are bleak indeed. Mrs. Courtenay, long accustomed to life's luxuries, is rendered completely helpless by the sudden turn of events: "Of the world she knew little. She was, indeed, as simple, in this respect, as a child" (13). Isabel, a beautiful young woman rumored to be engaged to a Mr. Noble, is deprived of this happy prospect by Mr. Noble's sudden departure once the family's financial state is made known. More concerned with her family's future than her own, however, Isabel decides to get a job teaching school, a decision that Dr. Worthington greets with abject horror. "The worst thing a young lady can do," he tells her, "especially in the South here, is to undertake to earn her own living; for it practically prevents her from ever making a desirable match" (38). Dr. Worthington is so horrified by Isabel's plan that it "deprived him of his self-command" (38), signaling that his own autonomy is somehow at stake here. The fear of female independence (we hear the emphasis in the phrase "her own living"), disguised as southern male chivalry, is not at all surprising in a novel devoted to the plight of a family without a patriarch. Despite Worthington's fears, however, Isabel doesn't have much of a choice. And so the family settles into a modest dwelling, and Isabel sets up a school for the neighborhood's lower-middle-class whites, "tall, awkward girls, with bare feet, unwashed faces and 'unkempt hair'" (61).

The rest of the novel traces the grueling hardships experienced by this once aristocratic family now that they have been denied the primary source of their former power: money and property. Mr. Noble's hasty departure foreshadows future difficulties, as the Courtenays seek their way in the world, their stock in the value of whiteness declining rapidly. Or to borrow a formulation from George Lipsitz, who sees whiteness as a self-perpetuating force fueled largely by self-interest, their "possessive investment" in whiteness is no longer paying the dividends it used to.[17] Isabel, who had once "exhorted admiration even from rival belles" (14), is no longer so attractive—at least not in the eyes of Mr. Noble. And although Peterson's ironic naming of this anything-but-noble character is meant to suggest the pettiness of a system in which money equals beauty, this irony does nothing to refute the fact of such a system. Isabel, deprived of her family fortune, is a belle no more, and can no longer be seen "in a robe of simple white . . . , her rounded arms bare to the shoulder, and the delicate fabric of her dress hanging, like a cloud-wreath, about her graceful figure" (14). The "white," so simple before the fall, is more complicated now—woven of "delicate fabric" indeed. And everyone knows that a complicated white is no white at all.

Written nine years before the onset of the Civil War, this novel already feels the coming upheaval. If such a family as the Courtenays can be so quickly transfigured, even given their connections to William the Conqueror, where does their power really lie? What is left for a white skin to signify? The image of the "black" snowstorm with which I began is particularly telling. Snow—normally associated with the purest of whites—becomes in Peterson's mind a "round wall of blackness." And in the context of the novel this odd metaphor makes complete sense. It's not just the "blackness" that stalks Isabel, but the terrifying possibility that "white" can no longer be so easily distinguished from "black." The black snowstorm metaphorically signifies a disturbing slippage, and it's this slippage that closes in on Isabel after she returns from a hard day of teaching those dirty, unkempt girls.

The novel's central premise is that whites, accustomed to the finer things in life, suffer far greater than blacks when those finer things are denied. The demise of the Courtenay estate will also mean the auction of its slaves, but since they're used to such uncertainty, where's the harm? Besides, the neighbors won't let slave families be separated. In a jab at Stowe, Dr. Worthington denies that such separations even occur. "We read of such things in novels sometimes," he says (39). In this novel, though, nothing of the sort takes place; the neighbors do indeed buy the slaves as families. But they care nothing for the plight of the Courtenays, since they're too busy buying their former assets at auction. Mrs. Courtenay "thought it strange that none of those people, who were so eager to possess themselves of her former home, exhibited the slightest desire to call upon her" (50). It's as if association with the fallen Courtenays could hasten the inevitability of their own fall.

And so, in a reversal of Stowe, it is the Courtenays, not the slaves, who must be separated. We learn of the certainty of the separation from Uncle Peter, one of the Courtenays' most loyal servants, who works to convince his fellow slaves that they will be in paradise compared to their beloved masters: "Dey [the Courtenays] cannot stay togedder, when dey are poor folks, don't you know dat, 'specially as dey all women or children? No; de one will go to de right, an' de oder to de left, dat each may make a libin. Eh! de life of de slave is hard, I 'fess. But harder is dat of de white man in season, 'specially when de Lord sends poverty on de widders an' orphans" (44). Peter's prophesy comes true almost immediately, as Horace Courtenay, "a bright intelligent lad of thirteen" (13), insists on going north to earn his wages so as not to be a burden on his sister's now limited means. His departure sets in motion a perversion of the plot Horatio Alger would make famous some fifteen years later, as Horace's bright hopes for success in the industrial North end in his death from overwork and lack of care. The Horace plot is actually closer in kin to many proslavery fugitive slave plots, where the fugitives inevitably find misery and hardship in the North and eventually beg to return to their masters. Horace plays this role in whiteface.

Peterson makes Horace's "fugitive slave" status clear by including a "real" fugitive slave plot meant to parallel his journey north. Charles and Cora, slaves on the former Courtenay plantation, take the opportunity of the change in ownership to make their escape, much against the sage advice of Uncle Peter. Solidly within the proslavery literary tradition, they find nothing but hardship and despair in the industrial North, which was foreshadowed the moment Cora left the Courtenay plantation: "As the mansion disappeared behind them, in the shadows of night, she felt like Eve when our first mother left Paradise for ever" (49).[18] Forced to live in "the black suburb," a ghetto portrayed in horrendous detail, Charles's job keeps him away from his wife six and a half days out of the week. When Cora gives birth to a son, the situation becomes even more dire.

The fugitives' position in the black suburb parallels Horace's new abode, located in the worst part of what is apparently an Irish neighborhood. That Horace finds his new home in an Irish neighborhood is particularly fitting, since, as Roediger has argued, "Irishness" came to signify a kind of whiteness that somehow was and wasn't white, a liminal space between clearly demarcated racial categories.[19] Horace's first vision of his new home reminds the reader not only of Horace's former surroundings but of the status of whiteness in the northern ghettos: "The main door-way was open, and disclosed what had once been a handsome hall, wainscoted to the height of three feet, but the once white paint was now of a dirty lead-color, while the paper on the wall was grimed with smoke and age. . . . Altogether, nothing had ever given Horace such an impression of filth and misery" (93). Essentially, this new home is the old Courtenay mansion projected into the amalgamated future. The best that whiteness can now muster is a "dirty lead-color." Horace, described by Peterson as "The Northern Slave," finds himself in the same condition as those ex-southern slaves, Charles and Cora. All three live in miserable conditions, unable to find work that will fully support them. And although Horace is unaware of his physical proximity to Charles and Cora, he does use Uncle Peter as a barometer of his new position in the world: " 'What would Uncle Peter,' he said, 'think, if he could see me now? Sunk to a level with his own children, perhaps to a lower one, for, on fifty dollars a year, I can't live, I fear, as well as they do' " (90). Whiteness is measured by blackness, and the distinctions are becoming superfluous. Peterson's implicit comparison here is between wage labor in the North and slave labor in the South, echoing the popular proslavery argument that depended on northern capitalism as a barometer to prove slavery's relative humanity.[20] If the white slave is no better off than the black slave, then not only is slavery justified, but racial distinctions are getting lost in the shuffle.

This racial blurring threatens not only Horace but his sister as well, hundreds of miles to the south. For Horace's descent into poverty and the "dirty lead-color" of his new living quarters signify a corruption that, when applied to Isabel, becomes uniquely sexual. In a conversation with his fellow errand boys—working-class urchins knowledgeable beyond their years—Horace realizes that his beloved sister's purity is somehow at stake. When the young boys discover that Horace has a sister, they take an immediate interest, especially when Horace admits that he "never saw any one so handsome" (99). The errand boys' intentions toward the lovely Isabel become clear:

> "And where do you keep this choice bit? She's a milliner of course," and he winked at the other boys, who, adepts already in the cant phrases of vice, laughed at the coarse jest.
>
> Horace looked from one to the other, tears of rage and mortification in his eyes. At last he said, speaking with spirit.

"I don't know what you mean. But sister Isabel's a lady, and wouldn't speak to such a fellow as you, that she wouldn't."

"Oh! she is a lady, that's too good," retorted the lad, laughing immoderately. (99)

Isabel's position follows her brother's, the only male left in the family to defend her honor. Though Horace is right that she certainly would not speak to the likes of these boys, the boys would most definitely speak to her. No protocol could keep them from speaking to a woman in Isabel's position. Though Isabel remains comfortably distant from the boys at the moment, the distance closes with every new day. Financially dependent on poor whites as a teacher of their children, Isabel's hold on whiteness may be even more precarious than that of the errand boys who plague her brother.

If the North provides the novel with examples of Isabel's future suitors, it also introduces the white male hope of salvation in the figure of Mr. Walworth, a young, wealthy Virginian visiting the city. Walworth is kept quite busy, in fact, coming to the rescue of various characters in the novel. At the earnest request of the Irish landlady he provides a doctor for Horace, though the medicine comes too late. He rescues Charles from jail after he is falsely arrested for complicity in a riot in the black suburb. And he rescues Cora and her baby from the same riot, spiriting them to safety just before their apartment is sacked.

The riot, and Walworth's proximity to it, provides an opportunity for Peterson to foreground the connection between racial mixture and the disappearance and violent reassertion of whiteness. Interestingly, the extended riot scene creates quite a bit of sympathy for the black inhabitants of the suburb, as Peterson graphically portrays the brutishness of the white mob. The riot begins when, according to one white participant, the blacks "had the impudence to have a procession, . . . and one of the butchers, downtown, threw a sheep's pluck at a big buck nigger strutting in front. The black rascal had the insolence to throw it back" (199). Thus begins a long night of fire and terror, as a white mob, aided by the inaction of the police, proceeds to burn down the entire black suburb. Peterson pulls no punches in his portrayal of these white rioters: "The savageness of the mob, which had appalled Walworth at first, grew more awful every minute. A hapless black, laid up with rheumatism, and unable to fly, with the rest, at the first assault, was dragged from the cupboard into which he had crawled, beaten with stones, trampled under foot, kicked in the face, and left, at last, apparently dead in the street. . . . The brutality of the rioters increasing with what it fed on, they soon ceased to spare any one, even females, against whom no accusations were made" (212). The scene draws to a close as one of the rioters yells "burn the black scoundrels alive in their dens" (213), a suggestion quickly acted on.

Peterson's depiction of the riot certainly creates sympathy for the burned-out and beaten blacks. This is not, however, his point. His incessant focus on the brutality and savagery of the white mob is meant not to show the reader how cruel whites are but rather to dramatize the ultimate degradation of whites once they are deprived of their racial power. Despite segregation in the industrial North, whites and blacks find themselves inhabiting similar spaces. Their interactions are frequent and not always determined by the white-supremacist power base of slavery, as in the South. They must compete for the same jobs. Consequently, much like the entrance hall of Horace's tenement building, whiteness has become a "dirty lead-color," and white people have become capable of savage brutality. Aware of these new circumstances, the mob chooses brutality to reestablish those rapidly fading racial distinctions. Denied the privileges of their possessive investment in whiteness, these rioters use violence to clarify once again the difference between white and black—between the mob and its victims. The seeping away of whiteness leads to violence as a means of restoring its power.

And although much of the mob is made up of working-class whites, Peterson makes it a point to show the participation of the white upper-middle class, showing how the loss of white privilege extends to those who actually benefited most from it. As one character remarks to Walworth, "You will see, to-night, that while the active work will be done by the coarsest ruffians, there will be looking on, and passively, at least, engaged in the riot, thousands of comparatively well-dressed men" (201). If this is the case, then what separates the genteel Dr. Worthington, for example, from these dirty white savages? In Peterson's vision, the sickness of northern capitalism is contagious and can too easily infect those who consider themselves far removed from it. Northern wage labor, as a replacement for southern slave labor, will eventually lead to the complete erosion of whiteness as a signal of gentility. If such is the case, whiteness will have nothing left to signify—least of all purity. All barriers will be down.

Of course, the notion of purity existing anywhere rapidly becomes obsolete in this novel, as the plot's return to the South indicates. Returning to the fallen aristocracy, Peterson's apocalyptic vision shows whites dependent on blacks for their very existence. Why should such dependence be worthy of remark? After all, what was American slavery if not a system in which whites were dependent on the bodies and labor of others for their prosperity? What's remarkable about Peterson's depiction of this dependence is its transparency. In a relatively minor series of scenes, Peterson unwittingly shows us not only the machinery of slavery but the difficulties involved in keeping that machinery well-hidden. Peter's wife Violet overhears Isabel's mother and little brother scold their sister for providing nothing but bad bacon for their evening meals—the only meat she can afford on her teacher's salary. As her brother says, "Yes, Alfred thinks sister Isabel naughty, because she won't give him chicken like she used to" (154). Aunt Violet reports this scene to Peter, crying "oh! Lord, dat ebber it should a come ter dis" (157). Since Peter and Violet have chickens to spare, they hatch a plan to provide two for the Courtenays' next meal. They must give the gift anonymously though, for as Peter tells Violet, "It'll nebber do to let ole missis know whar dey came from. Dat would be worse trouble of all" (157). Peter continues his goodwill mission throughout the winter, saving his former owners from hunger and misery.

This episode is important because it follows by some fifty pages one of the novel's many authorial intrusions in which Peterson explains the differing characteristics of the white and black races. Peterson writes: "Self-reliance is the peculiar characteristic of the Anglo-Saxon. In him the feeling is developed to such an extent, that any restraint on it is intolerable. He explores unknown seas, and dares unheard of perils, merely from the love of adventure or the hope of fame. In a lesser degree the other white races imitate this, decreasing in energy, however, as they recede from the former stock, and approach the dark races. When the native African is reached, we find him content with his hut and his palm shade, never venturing beyond his own continent of his own accord" (110–11). And only three chapters later we see the Courtenays, self-reliant no more, dependent on those "dark races" for their next meal. I point out this textual contradiction not for its own sake but in order to get to a more important one. Peterson's use of Emerson's noted phrase of a decade earlier raises serious questions about self-reliance as a trademark of white races. What can self-reliance possibly mean in this context, where slavery makes whites literally dependent on blacks for their livelihood? Where is the "self-reliance" of whiteness as an abstraction even, if its power is dependent on that other abstraction, blackness? Peterson's plot highlights the utter and complete dependence of his white characters: their dependence on wealth and property; their dependence on blacks for their next meal; their dependence on "independence" and "self-reliance" as ideals that create the illusion of their freedom. The novel shows both the fragility of that illusion and the slaves' awareness of the fragility. What else can explain Peter's suggestion that it would be worse than the hunger itself if the Courtenays discovered the black skin of their benefactors?

Peter and Violet work hard to hide the economics of slavery. Everyone knows that under American slavery black labor leads to white comfort. But in this specific case, where the white family needs a chicken, the underlying economy must remain hidden. The scene speaks, it seems, to the slaveowners' larger need to hide the circumstances of their prosperity and to preserve the "naturalness" of their whiteness with its attendant privileges. Peterson's faithful slaves conceal from the owners the one piece of information that would lead to white guilt and unease. Thus the responsibility for this guilt is conveniently transferred from whites to blacks. The transaction is so cleanly polished that Isabel can only stare in "amazement" at those first two chickens: "Had they dropped visibly from heaven, she could not have felt more intensely that the hand of Providence was in all this. As yet she had no suspicions of the source from whence the timely succor came" (157). The notion that the birds come from God rather than slaves simultaneously renders slavery invisible and naturalizes it as part of divine providence.[21]

Much of *The Cabin and Parlor* derives its energy from a refusal to acknowledge the systems of exchange that make it possible for white landowners to benefit from slavery without witnessing the actual sweat of their slaves. The novel shares this refusal with its characters. The "hand of Providence" works in the fields, not black men and women. Frank dependence on this Godlike intervention merely makes one a Christian, whereas an admission of white dependence on black labor would make whites lazy, helpless, and utterly undeserving of their material comfort.

What Peterson doesn't seem to realize is that through his plotting of white difficulties he makes it absolutely clear that whites are incapable of making it on their own. For no matter how valiantly Isabel may struggle, we've already seen how she needs help from other quarters. This dependence makes itself felt yet again as the novel approaches its happy ending. Whereas the episode of the chickens dramatizes white dependence on blackness, the novel's resolution enacts women's dependence on men. Peterson, troubled by the significance of Isabel's efforts to "earn her own living," ends the novel by reinscribing his heroine within the family's former home, with the good Mr. Walworth as its new patriarch. After performing his humanitarian efforts in the North, Walworth travels to Virginia to tell Isabel and her mother of Horace's death. The romance is quick and expected, since Horace's deathbed descriptions of his beautiful sister have already captivated Walworth. He travels south to claim his prize. And through a complicated series of financial and legal reversals, with Walworth and Dr. Worthington as principal agents, the Courtenay fortune and property is suddenly returned to its "rightful" owner.

### Restorations—Black No More

With the money and property restored, the wedding that was deferred from the novel's opening pages finally takes place, becoming a significant agent in the narrative reconstruction of whiteness. Whereas Mr. Noble had beaten a hasty retreat when the Courtenay estate collapsed, Mr. Walworth not only engineers the family's restored status but marries into it. And although Peterson takes pains to tell the reader that Walworth's only motive is his pure love for Isabel, the novel's structure demands that we see Walworth and Noble as bookends—the one fleeing when the money is gone, the other loving as the money returns. In both cases, Isabel's marriage is only narratively possible when she is just what her name suggests.

The novel's final pages have the aura of a coronation. The bridal party, making their triumphant return to the Courtenay plantation, see all their former servants arrayed in formation before the house's portico. The slaves, it seems, are as happy at their new prospects as the newly married couple:

> As the bridal company approached, Isabel on one arm of Walworth, and Mrs. Courtenay on another, the emotion of the servants, which had been restrained with difficulty, broke forth into loud sobs of joyous weeping and exclamations of delight and benediction. Uncle Peter, with tears rolling down his cheeks, was the first to speak.
>
> "God bless yer, ole missis. God bless yer, chile. God bless yer master!" These were his words as, almost choked with happy feelings, he welcomed Mrs. Courtenay, Isabel, and Walworth. (321)

With the marriage of Walworth and Isabel, the interrelated structures of whiteness and slavery are once again secure. The final benediction is Peter's to give, as he confers his blessings on the marriage and the slavery that it reconstitutes. The scene concludes with Tony, the plantation's principal violinist, playing "The king shall have his own again," that "famous old Jacobite tune" (322).

Though Walworth is presumably "the king" to which the song refers, the plantation was never his to begin with, thus making the modifier "again" inappropriate. But if we see this event not as the arrival of Walworth but as the far more important return of white male power, then the song's title makes complete sense. Whiteness is king once again, and the world is restored to its former order. And if Peterson has his say in the matter, this is how it shall stay. He devotes his final two paragraphs to the reader, asking us to "be the good master" and mind our own business. He writes, "If ever you are tempted to speak harshly of social institutions other than your own, recall the words of Christ, 'He that is without sin, let him cast the first stone'" (324). If no stones are cast, Peterson reasons, the Courtenays and others like them can wallow in the security of their ill-gotten booty, black no more.

The restoration of whiteness at novel's end makes it clear that although women may be responsible for maintaining the purity of whiteness, whiteness itself is predominantly a male franchise, a constitutive element of the patriarchy that Walworth reestablishes. The novel couldn't have ended on such "happy" terms had not male power come to the rescue. It's the reappearance of white masculinity—killed off with the death of Mr. Courtenay in the novel's first pages—that makes it possible for the novel to conclude. Only with Walworth's appearance can Isabel be safely reigned in again.

But if Walworth represents the reappearance of white masculinity, he also represents its redefinition, a point that will become increasingly important as we witness, in the following chapters, the coming-into-being of heterosexuality as a definitional category. In Peterson's hands, Walworth stands as an oddly hybrid figure, made up equally, it seems, of masculine and feminine characteristics. Three times Peterson calls our attention to this gender hybridity: "As he spoke, his eyes filled, for Walworth, like every true heroic soul, had a heart tender as a woman's" (242); "He spoke gently, as a woman would; kindly, as a brother might" (285); and finally, "But now a hand was laid on [Isabel's] shoulder, and a manly voice, yet one made, by sympathy, almost feminine in tone, said . . ." (306). Although Peterson's novel precedes by at least forty years the naming of "normal" male/female erotic relations as "heterosexual," it's useful for my purposes to see Walworth as a figure for heterosexuality itself, a self-contained, naturalized, and perfect system that, already containing both male and female, no longer needs Isabel for its perfection. She has become redundant, and thus oddly superfluous. And although my claim that Isabel is no longer necessary to Walworth's heterosexuality may strike the reader as odd, particularly since they have just been married, that redundancy is, as the coming pages will show, precisely the point. Although Isabel does indeed secure her place within what we would call a heterosexual structure of family, it's worth remembering that Walworth is, at least figuratively, that structure in its entirety. He is already, by himself, an organic, natural, and thus perfect fusion of male and female, those two forces allegedly striving for balance and union throughout the universe. This only reinforces our earlier sense that the return of whiteness here has very little to do with actual women and much more to do with white masculinity's omnivorous ability to ventriloquize everything that it is not: Peter, as he pronounces his blessing on slavery; Isabel, as she once again accepts her place away from worldly contaminations.

The reorientations that occur in Peterson's novel signal the displacement of white men as economic providers. Mr. Courtenay dies before the novel has fairly begun. Horace dies in his attempt to take his father's place. If Isabel can indeed provide for her family, then white men lose both racial and masculine authority. Of course, the possibility of Isabel's autonomy is only suggested so that it can be denied. The novel closes with a reconstruction of the southern aristocracy, of whiteness as a flamboyantly masculine franchise. Isabel, we assume, will never again have to work amid barefoot and unkempt school children. She was forced by the changing economy (but really by Peterson) to reach outside her prescribed boundaries. In so doing she threatened the fall of whiteness. Her relocation within those boundaries makes the world safe once again.

There's an important way, however, in which Peterson's treatment of Isabel as a laborer is at odds with much of what we know about Peterson himself, particularly his editorship of his magazine. This tension can be productively isolated in our attempt finally to understand this strange novel. According to Stearns, Peterson "often boasted . . . that his magazine was largely edited and written by women" (212). The following notice from the March 1845 issue of *Peterson's* is intriguing, particularly given the argument I've been making here: "The plan we have chalked out for the conduct of this magazine will make it a complete treasure house for the production of female writers, so that its volumes will hereafter be referred to as containing the best refutation of the mistaken opinion that the intellect of woman is inferior to that of man. . . . It cannot but be a source of gratitude to every lover of light literature to note the rank held by the female writers of the country" (qtd. in Stearns 212). And yet, although Peterson seemingly accepted women working in this public sphere of letters, it's important to recognize how this acceptance was always contingent on womanly subordination to male power and control. Ann S. Stephens, a popular writer of fiction, was listed as the coeditor of *Peterson's Magazine* until 1847, but Peterson was always the acting editor (Stearns 211–12). In an article titled "Literary Ladies" published in the April 1843 issue, Stephens herself constructs the walls demarcating acceptable feminine spaces. Citing the positive examples of Catharine Sedgwick, Lydia Digourney, and Lydia Maria Child, Stephens praises these authors for exerting their "mental wealth to render domestic life lovely, and to persuade their sisters into content with the blessings of their natural condition" (Stephens 98). "Their fiction was full of truthfulness," Stephens continues, "and the sweet lessons which it gave were calculated to exalt woman in *her own sphere, but never to entice her beyond it*" (98, emphasis added). As Nina Baym observes, this kind of literary moralizing, in which women editors participated, was intended to "neutralize the threat of the woman author by setting her to work on behalf of true womanhood" (255).[22]

The tension in Peterson's representation of feminine autonomy — women must be strong, but only in the context of a subordinate relation to male power — finds an analogous tension in his representation of class as a social determinant. For all its faults, portions of *The Cabin and Parlor* constitute a sustained and persuasive critique of capitalism. Horace's journey north and various set-piece arguments about the forms of labor available in the modern world allow Peterson to portray northern wage labor as a more vicious form of slavery than the southern variety. As Roediger and others have pointed out, northern antislavery activists often linked wage labor and slave labor in hopes of enlisting the working class in their campaign against southern slavery.[23] Peterson, however, wants it both ways. He attacks, yet depends on, the relations of labor in the North as a way to buttress the humanity and feasibility of southern slavery. For Peterson, an attention to the vicissitudes of class — particularly among whites — provides further ammunition for his proslavery narrative.

These narrative tensions involving class and gender can be better understood when we recognize the overwhelming effect color has on the story Peterson is telling. If we remove Peterson's argument concerning the cruelties of northern wage labor from its context within slavery, it's persuasive and, for its time, surprisingly radical. However, its location within a novel about whiteness as a tenuous social force drains its progressive energy in order to shore up the racial bulwark. The Courtenays' decline makes the representation of poverty necessary so that the novel's restoration of the southern aristocracy will be all the more satisfying. Once the Courtenays have reassumed the power of whiteness, however, those whites who lack such power are dismissed from the novel's pages. Their plight continues, but it no longer concerns Peterson, since slavery is once again intact. In Peterson's hands, Horace's time in the North isn't so much a biting critique of northern capital as it is a misdirected glorification of the southern agrarian lifestyle — of which slavery is a defining component. Although Peterson's critique of northern wage labor isn't entirely hollowed out by this shift of priorities, the need to restore the Courtenays to their former grandeur changes the context of that critique so radically that its logic finally fails.

A similar argument can be made about the novel's temporary re-laxation of gender roles, which was always dependent on a shift in the Courtenays' class status. The formerly aristocratic Isabel can and must work for her family's living, but only because black slavery has been temporarily suspended, at least so far as it touches the Courtenays. With this suspension, whiteness appears only as imperiled cultural property, since the absence of black slavery necessitates the presence of "white slavery." With the return of the Courtenays to their rightful place as slave owners, Isabel can and must return to her role as mis-tress of the plantation, a role requiring the supervision of labor, but not the labor itself. Isabel's labor is so much of a threat that it must be rebuked in two ways. She must fail at it and be saved from it.

In *The Cabin and Parlor* the complexities of social relations dis-appear once the narrative aim is the restoration of the white fran-chise. In fact, it's absolutely necessary that they do so. As long as the errand boys who were Horace's colleagues remain narratively rele-vant, whiteness exists as peril. They are what Horace had become. As long as the Irish mother who takes Horace in remains a part of Peterson's story, whiteness exists as peril, because she is what Mrs. Courtenay and Isabel could become. The continued representation of working-class whites—men and women alike—would make the novel's conclusion impossible, since that conclusion restores a white-ness that can only exist comfortably in the absence of its loss. But it can exist comfortably in the presence of Uncle Peter and Aunt Vio-let, and the legions of slaves restored to Courtenay ownership. In fact, if what Peterson shows us about white workers in the North is true, the newly constituted Courtenay aristocracy—a purely discursive aris-tocracy necessary to the requirements of literary genre—may be the only place where whiteness can exist comfortably. The question left at novel's end is for how long.

# Chapter Two

# Sympathy and Symmetry: The Romance of Slavery in Metta V. Victor's *Maum Guinea and Her Plantation "Children"*

It would seem as if this people anew had builded a tower of Babel, and that a confusion of tongues had begun the work of separation and iso-lation,—their first step in the downward path of barbarism.—Ethiop (William J. Wilson)

That which you behold is but the shadow of a reflected form and has no substance of its own.—Ovid

Imagine the story Chaucer would tell if commissioned to write an antebellum romance of the southern plantation. The result might be something like the narrative technique Metta V. Victor adopted for her novel *Maum Guinea and Her Plantation "Children," or, Holiday-Week on a Louisiana Estate: A Slave Romance* (1861)—a cross between John Pendleton Kennedy and Chaucer, *The Canterbury Tales* meets *Swallow Barn*.[1] As we began to see in *The Cabin and Parlor*, the empha-sis here is on courtship, the public face of what will come to be called heterosexuality. As John D'Emilio and Estelle B. Freedman have ar-gued, courtship developed differently in the planter South than it did in the North, remaining largely within the realm of the patriarchal family unit. Absent the separate spheres that characterized northern middle-class families, courtship in the South remained "public rather than private," and "economic considerations continued to be signifi-cant" (D'Emilio and Freedman 94). This public, economic face of male/female relations becomes, for Victor, an appropriate structure through which to route other public, economic contestations: the de-bate over slavery, for example.

*Maum Guinea* moves at two levels, as Victor alternates between chapters that forward the present-day narrative and chapters involving the slaves in a round of storytelling. The present-day events revolve around a dual romance plot. Virginia Bell and Philip Fairfax, young white lovers living on contiguous Louisiana sugar plantations, spend their days waiting calmly for their wedding to take place.[2] There is nothing to hinder their plans, as both families are delighted with the match. The other half of the novel's romantic quartet are Rose (Virginia Bell's waiting maid) and Hyperion (Philip's trusty valet), slaves on the adjoining plantations. Rose and Hyperion, like their masters, are deeply in love and have decided to marry. Their decision is not their own, however, since slaves are seldom permitted to marry whom they choose, especially if the chosen is from another estate. Philip's father refuses to allow the marriage. Just when this blow has landed on the unhappy lovers, a Mr. Talfierro arrives to call in a debt from Virginia's father, Judge Bell. The judge has no ready money, but he does have something Mr. Talfierro would take instead—the lovely Rose. Talfierro, a wealthy young bachelor, is immediately taken with Rose's mulatto beauty and wants her for his own. Virginia's father is reluctant to sell, though financial necessity eventually forces him to do so. Intercessions from Virginia and Hyperion do no good, and Rose is scheduled to depart the next morning. This is too much for Maum Guinea, a venerable old slave on the Fairfax plantation, who suggests that Rose and Hyperion run away; she even agrees to join them. The three fugitives take to the woods and secret themselves in a cave on the shore of a lake. As the remaining pages thin, however, the inevitable "happy" ending looms on the horizon. The fugitives are discovered, but Rose and Hyperion are finally allowed to marry. They live "happily ever after," though they do so as slaves, giving new meaning to that most reassuring of phrases.

Of course, any summary of the novel necessarily reduces its complexity, and this novel is nothing if not complicated. *Maum Guinea,* published as a Beadle dime novel in 1861, deploys a metaphorics of mirroring as its chief narrative strategy. On one level, Victor relies on the well-worn notion that the best art somehow "mirrors" everyday life—that it reflects social circumstances in textual form in order to teach a moral lesson. On a more complicated level, however, mirrors become metaphors within the novel. In this "slave romance" Victor attempts to cultivate a sympathy for the enslaved by showing the common humanity they share with their masters. The metaphor of the mirror becomes the mechanism through which Victor constructs parallel narrative spaces, as she sets in motion "black" plots that superficially resemble "white" plots. Although the circumstances of the two hopeful couples differ radically, it is Victor's main point that the love they share is made of basically the same stuff. The inability of her white characters to realize this, is meant to be an education for her readers, in the hope that they will make this crucial first step in the development of an antislavery sensibility. And yet, although *Maum Guinea*'s antislavery energies are apparent, their context always renders them suspect. In its most important moments the novel's plot works directly against the kind of empathic sensitivity that Victor wants to cultivate. Her reliance on the mirror as her central metaphor, though enabling some of her most effective antislavery passages, also serves to reflect, refract, and multiply the many tensions lurking just beneath the surface of this novel.

For Victor, the mirror metaphorically signifies the possibility for a cross-racial identification based primarily on recognition and sympathy. If the mirror is fractured—if this identification does not occur— then the institution of slavery remains comfortably intact. For only when slave owners look into a mirror (whether it be a mulatto half-brother or a symmetrical plot) and see nothing resembling themselves can the theoretical underpinnings of a slave economy stand firm. Although Victor strongly critiques the inability to identify with the sufferings of slaves, her narrative finally betrays her own complicity in this crisis of reflection. Victor's story ultimately breaks down when the narrative play of "self" and "other" becomes too extreme— when these two images can no longer reside within the same reflective and narrative space.

I recognize that my description of Victor's novel relies on the language of psychopathology. Part of what I hope to say about *Maum Guinea* and the larger lessons it offers concerns the psychological condition of narcissism. Victor's novel is useful to us because it makes whiteness visible as narcissism—as that psychological condition whereby a consideration of "the other" is first and foremost a consideration of "the self." Victor's decision to stage her novel as a series of mirrorings provides an ideal opportunity to witness whiteness as a state of pure self-involvement. The incoherences necessary to make such a self-involvement feasible bubble productively to the narrative surface.

*Maum Guinea* both consciously and unconsciously dramatizes the crisis of the mirror and locates the cause of this crisis in racism and slavery. As the novel draws to its happy conclusion, this "romance of slavery" comes to mirror much of the proslavery discourse of the day. Transracial sympathy not only does not require an end to slavery but in *Maum Guinea* is responsible for slavery as a continuing narrative necessity. Thus an understanding of *Maum Guinea* as mirror is only productive if we foreground the warping of its surface and concentrate on its unceasing tendency to deform and pervert that which it seeks to capture.

### Ambivalences

A look at *Maum Guinea*'s scholarly reception history—a history made up for the most part of random paragraphs in early- to mid-twentieth-century studies of plantation fiction—reveals a disturbing consensus about the novel. In *The Southern Plantation* Francis Pendleton Gaines describes *Maum Guinea*'s point of view as "emphatically abolition[ist]" (42). John Herbert Nelson calls the novel "a purely literary treatment of Abolitionist material" (85); Sterling Brown, in his landmark study *The Negro in American Fiction,* agrees that Victor's "stress is antislavery" (42). And George Fredrickson, in a more recent survey of white-supremacist ideologies in American society, calls *Maum Guinea* a "crude but vivid literary indictment of slavery" (*Black Image* 118).[3]

The little evidence that exists of the novel's political impact supports these scholarly appraisals of intent. Charles M. Harvey, writing in the *Atlantic Monthly* in 1907, claims that one of *Maum Guinea*'s biggest fans was Abraham Lincoln, who supposedly called it "as absorbing as *Uncle Tom's Cabin*" (39). Harvey also points out that an edition of the novel published in London around the same time as its U.S. publication had a noticeable effect on the British response to the American war: "[It] circulated by the tens of thousands in England, had a powerful influence in aid of the Union cause at a time when a large part of the people of that country favored the recognition of the independence of the Southern Confederacy" (43). As the coming war years would prove, the shift in English public and political opinion was essential to the eventual defeat of the Confederacy.

Lincoln's apocryphal association of *Maum Guinea* with *Uncle*

*Tom's Cabin* provides an interesting juxtaposition that may shed further light on the vexed question of political motivation. Whereas Stowe disclaimed any "literary" intentions in the making of her book, hoping only to "show the institution of slavery truly, just as it existed" (xx), Victor asserts just the opposite. In her author's introduction Victor writes, " 'Maum Guinea' has not been written to subserve any special social or political purpose. Finding, in the subject, material of a very novel and original nature, I have simply used what was presented to produce a pleasing book" (iv). Of course, this authorial disclaimer, much like Mark Twain's later "Notice" to the readers of *Huckleberry Finn,* can be seen as mere literary artifice, especially since Victor had written in the past that literature should only be tolerated if it served a larger social purpose.[4]

Despite Victor's suspicious claim to art for art's sake, those scholars who position *Maum Guinea* within an abolitionist literary tradition have a good deal of textual evidence to support them. The novel does indeed sustain an extended and multivalenced attack on the institution of slavery and on the human behavior (particularly on the part of whites) created by that institution. From a modern-day point of view, *Maum Guinea* is in many ways more effective in its antislavery assault than *Uncle Tom's Cabin,* for Victor, unlike Stowe, does not rely on an evangelical Christianity as her final frame of moral and juridical reference. Victor's most effective strategy is to show the utter failure of vision that slavery creates in the slaveholders, as her white characters never grasp the fundamental fact that their slaves have feelings and emotions akin to their own. As Melville had done five years earlier with his portrait of Captain Delano in "Benito Cereno," Victor forcefully represents racism as a cognitive dysfunction, a disorder preventing one from comprehending the outlines and demarcations of the immediate landscape. At some level Victor understands racism as a failure of vision, as a failure to see clearly, and thus to understand, one's reality.

Yet Victor was herself the product of a culture that inculcated such a failure of vision, and it should not be surprising that her representations of plantation life are distorted by the prejudices of her times. Just as Stowe's antislavery novel participates in and sustains certain racist stereotypes that had historically been part of a proslavery argument, Victor's novel is littered with offensive and derogatory ideas about black inhumanity. Her slaves, for example, are "as gay and free from care as a meeting of chattering apes in a Bornean forest" (16). But as Stowe's novel demonstrates, bigoted thinking does not necessarily make a novel proslavery. Stowe's attack on slavery is total, as not even the most "benevolent" of masters escapes her literary fusillades. Stowe could not imagine a form of slavery that would be acceptable to her. If we take Victor's novel into consideration, however, it becomes clear that Victor could imagine such a possibility, and it is this possibility that scholarly commentators on the novel have failed to contemplate. *Maum Guinea,* firmly embedded in a literary tradition that demands a "happy ending," leaves its two main slave characters in slavery at its conclusion—happily in slavery.

At the same time, however, *Maum Guinea* is surprisingly radical in some of its narrative gestures. Despite its dependence on minstrel caricatures of slave life, it grants to its primary black characters (actually mulatto characters) an unexpected degree of agency.[5] The novel's title character slashes a dog's throat with her knife in order to escape detection, and another slave trains his pistol on his supposedly benevolent master. The story of Nat Turner's rebellion is vividly and enthusiastically rehearsed, with almost no sympathy for the slaughtered whites. A mixed marriage between a white man and a slave not only takes place but becomes a crucial component of the novel's "happy ending." And the satire Victor aims at her white characters is surprisingly sharp, creating "white" caricatures to counter (at least in part) the novel's reliance on "black" caricatures. These and other elements demand that the novel be taken seriously as a progressive attempt to expose the absurd reasoning behind slavery.

In granting the novel's radicalism, however, we should not obscure its other meanings. The troubling fact remains that Victor leaves two of her primary slave characters cheerfully enslaved at the novel's conclusion. This ending is not simply a narrative hiccup, fundamentally at odds with the preceding pages. On the contrary, the ending is a congruent and reasonable piece of the novel's larger story. This "happy ending" becomes a narrative necessity within the novel's first twenty pages. For *Maum Guinea* to enact the type of happy ending common to the dime novel genre in which it is located, slavery must remain intact and, more importantly, morally acceptable. This narrative resolution of contradictory social fields and motivations can be understood as an example of what Fredric Jameson calls the "ideology of form." He writes, "The aesthetic act is itself ideological, and the production of the aesthetic or narrative form is to be seen as an ideological act in its own right, with the function of inventing imaginary or formal 'solutions' to unresolvable social contradictions" (79). *Maum Guinea*'s schizophrenic generic identity—a proslavery/antislavery "romance of fact"—suggests the difficulties in containing or diffusing the social conflicts that it narrates.

At some level, however, Victor's attempt to transform various and conflicting social codes into a coherent and palatable piece of fiction succeeded. The novel was immensely popular. Its narrative troubles and the social troubles embedded in antebellum America are not unrelated: it's possible that the latter explains the former. It is an understatement of absurd proportions to point out that the America of 1861 was highly conflicted, both as an idea and as a system of political governance and social organization. The novel's inability to escape its own incoherence partially explains its immense popularity, since the nation's many conflicts over slavery are superficially contained and resolved within this story that ends happily ever after. If *Maum Guinea* is a mirror, it reflects a war-torn society back to itself in a manner that provides some comfort and reassurance. By attacking slavery, yet leaving slavery intact, it allows a dissonant culture to voice its competing desires and motivations without requiring a concomitant social and political upheaval. The war that Stowe apocryphally started was left for Victor to diffuse.

### Selling Slavery

Readers of the antislavery *New York Tribune* would have seen, in the days leading up to *Maum Guinea*'s publication, a long series of notices announcing the dime novel that Beadle and Company hoped would be the literary stocking stuffer of the season. Many of the earlier notices hyped the novel by announcing its prepublication popularity: "To Newsdealers and the Trade: As most of the Trade and Newsdealers have already *doubled* (and some, even, have *trebled*) their standing orders for BEADLE'S CHRISTMAS STORY, we have deemed it advisable to postpone its publication day to Thursday, December 12" (6 Dec. 1861). Saying that *Maum Guinea* would surely be "the most popular and unique book of the year," the notice went on to mention that the third edition was already sold out—presubscribed before its actual release date. Not until five days later would the "appreciative and critical public" get their first taste of what this holiday offering had to offer: "Novelty of the Season: For Originality, Beauty, Humor, Pathos, and words to make the blood leap in the veins, it will find no equal among the books of a year" (11 Dec. 1861). When *Maum Guinea* was published on December 12, 1861, the *Tribune* carried seven separate advertisements announcing its arrival at the newsstands, the longest of which was taken directly from the "Publishers' Note" of the novel itself: "In presenting "Maum Guinea" to their readers, the publishers feel that no word of theirs is necessary to create an interest in its behalf. The peculiar and novel nature of the subject is treated with such power, pathos, humor and keen apprehension of character that it must stand out in relief as one of the most original and thoroughly delightful romances in our literature." The other six notices printed on this day were shorter, punchier, but no less enthusiastic on behalf of their product: "Be Sure to Get It!" "The Best Book of the Year!" "Everybody Will Read It!" "A Real Literary Treat!" and finally, "The Only Christmas Novelty!"

The next day's *Tribune* continued the publishers' fanfare, with a more extended notice of the novel's immediate popularity:

> "Maum Guinea." This name bids fair to become memorable in our literature. The character of that singular woman is a new creation, as startling and real as the state of the slave which it so wonderfully reproduces. Her "Children" are other slaves, each of whom has a life history of a character at once to enchain interest. As a romance of fact, it is one of the very best ever offered to the American public, and fully warrants all the encomium lavished upon it in all quarters. Its unusual sale is but in keeping with its merits. *Every one who reads it is intensely gratified.* It bids fair to find its way to the FIRESIDES OF AMERICA to a greater extent than any romance since the days of "Uncle Tom" and "Jane Eyre." (13 Dec. 1861)

Here we begin to see the intriguing set of terms on which Victor's novel was presented to the reading public. This oxymoronic literary offering, this "romance of fact," "reproduces" both the slave and her slavery. The novel becomes the situation it so vividly describes, as interest is not merely cultivated but "enchained." Thus the reader will put on the chains that it is assumed Maum Guinea will take off.

A look at the pages of the *Tribune* during these days before Christmas testifies not only to the publishers' zeal in hawking *Maum Guinea* to the public but also to their apparent success. Several notices directed specifically at news dealers outline revised publication schedules and provide a running commentary of the novel's rapid journey through various editions. Even taking into consideration the dual nature of these notices—both as announcements to news dealers and further advertisement for the novel as hot commodity—it seems that the publishers' efforts to make *Maum Guinea* the literary buzzword for the season had paid off. Although hard numbers are difficult to attain, most sources claim that *Maum Guinea* sold well over one hundred thousand copies in the United States alone and that foreign-language editions of the novel flourished.[6]

This brief narrative of the novel's publicity offers a glimpse into the thinking at Beadle and Company as to what kind of book they thought they had and to whom they intended to sell it. Absent any contemporary reviews of *Maum Guinea*, this trail of the publishers' pre- and postpublication hype may serve as the best means of gauging what this book meant in December 1861 and how its readers could be expected to have read it.[7] Eight months into a civil war, what emotional harp strings did Beadle and Company find it most expedient to pluck in selling this novel to an increasingly nervous wartime society? What specifically about Victor's novel could account for the popularity that it so quickly achieved?

### Marketing Abolition

First appearing on the literary marketplace in 1860, Beadle's dime novels were a pioneering force in the commodification of accessible and cheap literature in the mid–nineteenth century.[8] The early Beadle novels were four-inch-by-six-inch orange paperbacks of a hundred pages each. They usually sold for a dime a piece, though *Maum Guinea* was an exception to this rule; as a double issue (two hundred rather than one hundred pages), it sold for twenty cents. According to Albert Johannsen, these early works "gave fairly accurate pictures of the struggles, hardships, and daily lives of the American pioneers" and were "intensely nationalistic" (1: 4). Johannsen includes in his study a hierarchical listing of the various types of novels that the Beadle catalog included, ranking them from "greatest value" to least: early colonial and Indian stories; tales of the western encounters with "Indians"; "Westerns," which included stories of outlaws and adventurers; sea tales; stories of city life; and detective novels. Johannsen concludes with "love stories," which he imagines "should go at the bottom of the list" (2: 325).[9]

In *Mechanic Accents: Dime Novels and Working-Class Culture in America,* Michael Denning argues that the primary audience for dime novels was the working-class culture of factories and shop floors. For Denning, dime novels were the products of a newly developing mass culture industry and "can be understood neither as forms of deception, manipulation, and social control nor as expressions of a genuine people's culture, opposing and resisting the dominant culture" (3). Rather, "they are best seen as a contested terrain, a field of cultural conflict where signs and wide appeal and resonance take on contradictory disguises and are spoken in contrary accents" (3). Part of Denning's strength is his ability to take the love stories that Johannsen relegated to the bottom of his list and reimagine their importance in relation to the women and girls who were most likely to have read them. By doing so, he allows us to understand *Maum Guinea*'s fusion of a rather traditional love story with a less traditional political reform plot. As Johannsen's typology makes clear, novels of social and political reform did not often find a place in the Beadle canon. On the surface, then, it would seem that it is the "love story" aspect of *Maum Guinea,* not its more overtly political content, that gives it a home in the dime novel genre. Its plot of forbidden marriage is akin to other popular romances of the day in which young lovers overcome great odds to be together.[10] These stories often expressed and resolved class tensions, which tended to make them extremely popular among the working-class women and girls who read them. But what about *Maum Guinea*'s other main thread—the story of slavery and its abuses? How would a supposedly abolitionist plot play to the working-class culture that comprised the majority of Beadle's audience?

The question of the class dynamics of the nineteenth-century movement for abolition has been the subject of some controversy among historians. Often assumed to be a genteel preoccupation, recent scholarship has focused on abolition as a grassroots movement made up in significant part by the working class.[11] In *Abolitionism: A Revolutionary Movement,* Herbert Aptheker provides both the theoretical and anecdotal argument for a strong working-class participation in the antislavery reform movement. By demonstrating the northern capitalists' dependence on southern capital, Aptheker argues that the monied North would in many ways be a natural ally for the southern slaveholders. Accordingly, manufacturers and the merchant bourgeoisie "allied themselves with the immediate exploiters of the Afro-American people" (Aptheker 37).[12] Antiabolitionist mobs that swept the North in the winter just preceding the outbreak of the Civil War were often led, according to Aptheker, by "outstanding lawyers, merchants, and politicians" (49) and cheered on by leading newspapers. Leonard L. Richards confirms Aptheker's description of these mobs: "The typical anti-abolition mob consisted largely of 'gentlemen of property and standing'—lawyers, politicians, merchants, shopkeepers, and bankers whose careers were identified not only with the mercantile economy of preindustrial America, but also with the local political establishment" (149).

Abolitionists were of course aware of this hostility from monied northerners who themselves depended on the wages of slavery, and they therefore worked tirelessly to create an alliance with the "ordinary people"—that larger mass of folks who could add sheer numbers to their cause. This alliance was often predicated on a problematic but somewhat effective analogy between the bondsmen and bondswomen in the South and the oppressed workers of the North. The interests of capital, it was said, oppressed them both equally, and so a working-class affinity for the tribulations of southern slaves was urged as a natural step in the movement for the emancipation of white labor.[13] These theoretical justifications for labor/abolitionist solidarity bore real fruit. Radical abolitionist Thomas Wentworth Higginson remembered the alliance this way when he published his memoirs in 1898: "The anti-slavery movement was not strongest in the educated classes, but was primarily a people's movement, based in the simplest human instincts and far stronger for a time in the factories and shoe-shops than in the pulpits and colleges" (115). As Frederick Douglass had said in a speech at Salem, Ohio, in 1852, "[Abolition] is the poor man's work. The rich and noble will not do it. I know what it is to get a living by rolling casks on the wharves, and sweeping chimneys, and such like, and this makes me able to sympathize with the poor, and the bound everywhere. It is not to the rich that we are to look but to the poor, to the hardhanded working men of the country; these are the men who are to come to the rescue of the slave" (Blassingame 2: 396).[14]

## Reflecting Whiteness

As the preceding examples suggest, Beadle's advertising blitz for *Maum Guinea* appealed to several interests at once, all of which we can locate within the working-class culture where dime novels sold. The story of thwarted lovers; the tale of adventure and conspiracy; and finally, a story filled with the pathos of lives lived in slavery— these are the narratives that would indeed fulfill the publishers' promise that *Maum Guinea* "pleases all alike—old and young—male and female" (*New York Tribune,* 16 Dec. 1861). And despite the productive alliance between labor and abolition sketched above, residual and widespread working-class racism would not find itself challenged by Victor's novel. In fact, Victor's white-supremacist vision would simply serve as a further ground for a widespread appeal to the audience she intended to attract.

The white-supremacist worldview greets the reader from the start. In the introduction Victor establishes two primary ideas. First, she sketches her understanding of the real components of "Negro life" on the American plantation. "The native character of the black race under the Slave system," she writes, "is toned down rather than changed" (iii). What is this "native character"? According to Victor, the "negro type" is "superstitious, excitable, imaginative, given to exaggeration, easily frightened, improvident and dependent" (iii). These are the fundamental ingredients of blackness, according to Victor, and although the slave system has certainly shaped these characteristics, it has only lessened their intensity. Slavery makes the slave less superstitious than his or her African ancestor, but superstition remains one of those "idiosyncracies which distinguish the negro type in its native land" (iii).[15]

Importantly, Victor ends the first paragraph with an apparent awareness that representations of blackness are necessarily troubled by questions of perspective and subjectivity: "So differently do the negro character and the relation of slave and master impress different observers, that the philanthropic world is greatly at a loss for some settled opinion regarding the normal condition of the African in the drama of civilization" (iii). Immediately after this revelation, however, Victor goes on to assert that she has simply sought to depict the race "to the life" (iii), forgetting, as does Stowe, the problem of subjectivity. With this claim Victor moves into the second of her two major introductory ideas: the use of romance to represent "reality." She writes: "Seizing upon the Christmas Holidays as the moment when his exuberant, elastic nature has its fullest play, I have been enabled, in the guise of romance, to reproduce the slave, in all his varied relations, with historical truthfulness. His joys and sorrows; his loves and hates; his night-thoughts and day-dreams; his habits, tastes and individual peculiarities, I have drawn with a free, but I feel that it is a perfectly just, hand" (iii).[16] In fact, there is so much that is "real" in her novel "that it will scarcely be deemed a romance by those who read to be informed as well as to be pleased" (iii–iv).[17]

Victor's decision to stage her novel during the "Christmas Holidays," that time when the slave's "exuberant, elastic nature has its fullest play," reveals the dual and impossible nature of the novel she has written. Having argued that slavery simply tones down the native characteristics of "the black race," Victor chooses the holiday week as her interpretive window into the slave quarters. This week, a time on many plantations when the daily work of the slave is suspended, becomes the time when the slave is most fully him- or herself: "No work, no care, no punishment—nothing but eat and play; not for one day only, but for a week. They must enjoy themselves now enough to last them a whole year" (35). Victor is trying, in one sense, to write a novel about slaves free of their slavery. At the same time, however, she inserts into this novel stories of slavery's many cruelties, as the slaves gather each night around a fire to tell their various stories. Christmas week becomes a time when slavery is both "suspended" and vividly rehearsed, a time when the slaves spend their days exuberantly celebrating a roasted pig and their nights looking back at lives lost and families separated. Victor's narrative strategy proves her earlier (though now forgotten) point about subjectivity and slavery. She employs multiple narrative perspectives to tell the various stories of slavery. Her own voice—distinct from the voices of her storytelling slaves—becomes one of these competing narrative perspectives. And the perspectives must compete, since the stories they tell differ radically. The slaves tell of past trauma; Victor tells of present holiday cheer. Both are made to stand in for slavery itself, exposing both temporal and ideological confusion.

This incoherence—this inability of the novel to speak with anything resembling a monolithic voice—is actually built into Victor's central narrative metaphor.[18] The symmetry of the mirror, however attractive a narrative device it may be, can only obtain by obscuring the radically asymmetrical power relations that define the "black"/ "white" doublings in the novel. Although Hyperion's affair with Rose makes Philip's communications with Virginia more convenient, the letters would get sent with or without Hyperion's dutiful participation. Another slave could simply be ordered to do the job. Likewise, the union of Fairfax and Bell does not depend on the love their slaves have for each other. Though both Virginia and Philip would like to keep their trusty valet and waiting maid with them in their future household, their marriage is in no way linked to their slaves' prospects. Though anyone with the slightest knowledge of the power relations that prop up a slave economy would recognize the asymmetry of the supposed doublings in the novel, it seems important to state the obvious here in order to highlight the degree to which the metaphor governing *Maum Guinea* is flawed from the outset. Under slavery, black and white lives can never really resemble each other, and this is not solely because whites refuse to see that they share a common humanity with their slaves. The problem comes not with a basic lack of empathy but with the profound material differences that define the lives of masters as opposed to the realities of their slaves. There can be no real comparison. Paradoxically, it is this flaw that makes the novel a useful subject, as the metaphor Victor employs becomes her own narrative undoing. The metaphor of the mirror both holds together and fractures the competing threads of Victor's novel. It enables the novel's most effective antislavery passages while discrediting these passages when the mirror ultimately shatters. The mirror that Victor hopes will enable a transracial sympathy turns out to be not a transformative mechanism but the linchpin in a cyclical, closed, and ultimately narcissistic circuit of reflections.

Interspersed with the events of the novel's present are various mini-narratives, stories told by a group of slaves as they sit around meals and campfires. The idea comes from Maum Guinea, a mysterious mulatto woman "with a strange look in her eyes which might be sadness or might be hate, or both—nobody could read it" (11). The stories deal almost exclusively with the cruelties of slavery, with only an occasional minstrel interlude to break the drama. Here too Victor relies on doublings and mirrorings. The stories told, through their constant echoes and repetitions of one another, all begin to sound like a part of the same story—as in fact they are. Maum's narrative begins when Rose asks her to tell "us suthin 'bout *yerself,* Maumy, when you was a girl 'bout my age" (25). Thus Rose in effect asks for her own story, as she hopes to understand her own plight through the mirror of the life Maum Guinea has already lived.

Maum's story becomes the connective tissue linking the various tales of the past with Victor's story of the present. When Rose finds herself sold to Mr. Talfierro, Maum converts her despair into action, telling Rose and Hyperion to run away. At their request, she agrees to join them, providing Victor with the narrative opportunity to re-enact certain events of Maum's past as moments in Rose and Hyperion's present. As the three fugitives huddle in the cave, Maum tells the complicated story of her life under slavery and her struggle to rescue her daughter, Judy, from a similar fate. The story centers on Judy's marriage to a white sailor named Ephraim Slocum, who had been instrumental in Maum and Judy's escape.[19] Thus Rose becomes Judy, whom Maum has not heard from in years, and whose fate as a slave is unknown. The lake bordering the cave becomes the James River of Maum's story, the site where she first fell in love with her young master Dudley. Her flight with Rose and Hyperion refigures her attempt to rescue her daughter from the Dudley plantation, where she had been condemned to the same fate as Rose—that of being pimped by a financially strapped master.

Maum's willingness to repeat past plots is based, paradoxically, on her desire to avoid such repetition. For repetition, under the law of slavery, always involves death, separation, and despair. In fact, the novel's reliance on mirroring and repetition is itself a function of slavery as an overarching narrativizing structure. Under slavery the same things happen over and over: families are split, lovers denied, friends whipped and punished. The narrativizing function of slavery as a discursive system partially explains the repetition this novel depends on. We "know" slavery through discursive accounts of it, and this scriptedness can partially account for the repetitions and echoes that *Maum Guinea* enacts. Victor's strategy of "art" mirroring "life" and "black" mirroring "white" results in a series of narratives that reflect both one another and unwritten stories that have come before.

*Romancing the Slave*

In the days before their escape, Hyperion and Rose live, according to Victor, blessed lives, blending happily into the exotic landscape of Louisiana. As the two lovers exchange flirtations in the first chapter, Victor highlights their harmonious relationship to the natural world: "The rich sunshine of the South melted over the landscape, of which the figures of the speakers made at this moment a vivid and picturesque part" (7). According to Victor, "they seemed a natural part of the bloom and gorgeousness of the climate" (7).[20] The emphasis here is on Rose and Hyperion as natural components of the southern geography, at home in their slavery as the sun is at home in the southern sky.

The harmony of landscape and character is intensified in the novel's early chapters by the hope both pairs of lovers have of future marital bliss. Hyperion has received encouragement from Rose that his feelings are indeed reciprocated, and Virginia has accepted Philip's invitation to the upcoming Christmas ball. In short, the two suitors feel secure in their future happiness. Victor ingeniously represents the two men's happiness as mirror images of young love:

> Philip walked up and down the portico, thinking nothing, but dreaming every thing sweet and vague, the blood coursing through his heart to a music which thrilled every nerve—the music of his own hopes; though his step kept time unconsciously to the melody which floated from the direction of the stables, whither Hyperion had taken the horse. His valet was singing; though remarkable, even among the rich-voiced colored people, for the purity and power of his voice, it seemed to the young master as if it had never poured forth before so deep, unrestrained and joyful a strain. And perhaps it never had; for the colored man was dreaming too; and his memory was welling and full of the gold of somebody's smile— the toss of a crimson turban, the glitter of a pair of ear-rings, darting through all his visions. (10)

Here Philip and Hyperion momentarily lose their separate and antithetical identities, as Victor blurs the line between them. The music that thrills Philip's every nerve—music that the reader initially imagines as the metaphorical music of Philip's inner happiness—actually comes from Hyperion, who is singing happily near the stables. Hyperion's song is, as Victor represents it, the "music of [Philip's] own hopes" (10). Victor relies here on that standard trope of Eurocentric racism, in which the split between reason and emotion, culture and nature, is mapped from white to black bodies. Hyperion, allowed his unmediated expression of joy, makes Philip's reserve possible. The geography of the scene—Philip on the portico, Hyperion near the stables—further encodes the divisions that lie behind the false symmetry Victor imagines.[21]

Likewise, Rose's vision of the future is both dependent on and part of Virginia's marriage prospects. Dreaming of marriage to Hyperion, it is impossible for Rose to visualize this dream outside the reflection cast by her mistress: "They [Rose and Hyperion] would be married Christmas Eve, and then they would have a whole week to spend together—a whole week of regular honeymoon; and after that—why, they could see each other pretty often, and perhaps, before many months, they would belong to the same family, with a bride and groom to wait upon, and everything so nice and happy" (20). As Rose stretches her imagination, seeking the perfect picture of a future life, the picture she discovers is a life lived in slavery—lives owned by Virginia Bell and Philip Fairfax. Victor's obsession with mirrored relationships makes this scenario an inevitability. It is the symmetry that appeals to her, and this symmetry can only be realized within slavery, a system organized on the bedrock of asymmetry.[22] Thus, the narrative logic goes, Rose and Hyperion can only be truly happy within the very system that is determined to keep them apart. If the mirror has shown us the common degree of humanity existing between the two couples, it has also shown us the problem such an emphasis on commonality carries. Although Rose and Hyperion wish to be married "very much after the fashion of whiter and freer lovers" (29), Victor forgets that wishing does not make it so. Freedom and whiteness—concomitant terms both for Victor and for slavery—cannot be wished into being.

When, later in the novel, the long-awaited proposal from Philip is received and accepted by both Judge Bell and Virginia, Virginia's happiness spills over into Rose's life, as the young mistress indulges in the same "pretty dream" that had so occupied her servant. As she tells her waiting maid, "you shall be married the same evening. Yes, I've set my heart upon that, as one of the accessories" (101). This is not, however, the way she first greeted the news of her servant's desire to be married off the plantation, as Victor describes Virginia's petulant reaction to her waiting maid's hopes: "Miss Virginia had no idea of allowing her favorite maid to marry, and be having interests of her own, which might interfere with dressing her hair and humoring her caprices at all times" (21).

Thus Rose's "brilliant hopes had been blotted out, corn-colored tissue dress, gold ring, and all" (21), and an awareness of this loss brings Rose to an epiphany of sorts, as she realizes for the first time what it really means to be a slave. Again, Victor relies on a mirrored relationship between white and black lives to make her point: "During that half-hour, almost for the first time in her life, [Rose] wished she were not a slave—which was very unreasonable in her, for there are many free white people who can not marry whom they please nor when they please, nor have a silk tissue dress to be married in" (21).[23] In the instant that Rose becomes fully conscious of what it means to live life as a slave, Victor, playing to working-class anger and resentment, declares this consciousness the absurd product of irrationality. The mirror that initially established commonality between master and slave in order to cultivate sympathy for lives lived in slavery now discredits the justifiable anger that has finally reached the surface of Rose's life. Any temptation we may have to read Victor's comment ironically is soon tempered by this subsequent description of Virginia's "plight": "She was young, wealthy, beloved; ease and happiness were her birthright, and it would have been cruel for her to have been robbed of them thus early. She looked kind, too, and gentle; indolent, as a southern temperament is apt to be, but not ill-tempered. Her air was that of a person of refinement and intelligence above that of ordinary ladies" (22). With these two passages taken together, we can only assume that although Victor empathizes with Rose's unhappiness at not being allowed to marry, she refuses to blame this unhappiness on the institution of slavery. Slavery becomes simply another impediment to marriage, much like problems with the size of a dowry or passion thwarted by the incongruity of class. Here we have one of the earliest indicators of what we have suspected from the outset, as the problems inherent in Victor's central metaphor bubble to the surface. The two passages I've quoted here provide momentary glimpses into the lives and emotional states of the two primary participants in this drama, and it is obvious that the images are not symmetrical. Victor holds a mirror up to Rose's life, but the reflection no longer looks like her mistress. Instead, Rose now finds her despair ranked beneath some anonymous group of "free white people" (21). Victor's move here mirrors one of the many pro-slavery arguments of the time, which attempted to prove that blacks were better off under slavery than many poor whites were in their freedom. The narrative fracture troubling these passages exposes the problems with any proslavery ideology dependent on this kind of supposed symmetry. Although Victor continues to rely on doublings created through mirrored relationships, her narrative cannot faithfully follow the path of these reflections. Instead, the radical asymmetry of the Rose/Virginia "relationship" is here shown in full detail, as Virginia looks forward to marriage while Rose is made to realize fully her status as property.

This status is made nowhere more apparent than in the series of plot shifts introducing Mr. Talfierro, the "tall dark gentleman" (43) who happens to hold a five-thousand-dollar note from Judge Bell. As Victor portrays him, Talfierro is an elegant, wealthy New Orleans aristocrat, and when he sees Rose at a Christmas ball he declares her "a superb creature! The handsomest mulatto I ever saw" (43).[24] The knowledge of Judge Bell's pecuniary obligation to Talfierro, coupled with Talfierro's desire for Rose, makes it immediately apparent to the reader that Rose's inability to marry Hyperion is no longer her biggest problem. Talfierro wants her and is in a position to have her. This part of the plot unfolds in a conversation between Judge Bell and Colonel Fairfax, as the two lead a holiday hunting party. While expressing mutual satisfaction at the eminent union of their two houses, the two gentlemen move on to a discussion of the financial difficulties, leading to a confession of Judge Bell's financial obligation to Talfierro and of Talfierro's recent offer to cut four thousand dollars off of the five thousand he is owed in exchange for Rose. Bell admits to being sorely tempted by the offer, though he is reluctant to deprive Virginia of her favorite waiting maid. His reluctance is deepened by his awareness of Talfierro's purpose in wanting to acquire Rose: "I don't just like to sell that girl. She's very much attached to all of us, and she's so—so young—and—" (62). Judge Bell is unable to articulate his shame at pimping such a young girl, but the colonel is quick to dispel his friend's qualms: "We can't afford to humor the feelings of our negroes, Judge; it's a bad idea. They're a careless race, and don't suffer much from sentiment. I suppose Black Eagle, my pet horse, felt badly, when he was taken to strange pastures last year, but I was obliged to sell him. You know that the girl will, in all probability, be well treated, and have an easy time of it" (62). Victor's satiric distance on the colonel's opinions is obvious here and is a part of her larger effort to demonstrate the inability of the novel's white characters to imagine that their slaves feel as they do about such matters as love, family, and friends.

Yet in one sense the colonel's illogic is simply the next step in the process begun by Victor herself in the passage where Rose finally understands what it means to be a slave. No longer able to compare Rose's situation to that of Virginia, Victor had suddenly shifted her field of vision to include a nameless mass of, presumably, working-class whites. Like Black Eagle, this new standard of measure disrupts the symmetry that Victor has been forcing from the start. Although she clearly has some distance on Colonel Fairfax's attempt to compare Rose's plight to that of Black Eagle, she does not recognize his comments as a congruent piece of her larger narrative dilemma. Comparing people to horses depends on a logic similar to that which allows Victor to compare the free with the enslaved.

### Blood into Gold

Given the dilemma Talfiero's presence introduces, Victor makes him the mechanism by which we understand the limits of white sympathy when faced with financial reality, or, to borrow a phrase from Frances Harper, the "fearful alchemy by which . . . blood can be transformed into gold" (101). In a skillfully crafted scene staged in front of an actual mirror (as opposed to the novel's many metaphorical mirrors), Victor makes Talfierro a figure for Judge Bell's financial exigencies and provides the crucial link between the question of finance and Virginia's inability to see her slave's despair. It is New Year's morning, and we see Virginia admiring the many gifts sent by her parents and friends as best wishes for a successful marriage and a happy new year. The gift she is most pleased with (even more so than the guitar sent by Philip) is a pearl necklace sent by Talfierro. Whereas the reader is aware at this point of Talfierro's plans for Rose, Virginia is not; she can only murmur to herself that "Mr. Talfierro is such an agreeable gentleman—so tasteful and generous" (117). As Virginia admires herself and the new necklace in the mirror, Rose enters, having just found out that she has been purchased:

> "Look, Rose, what Mr. Talfierro has sent me," as she heard her waiting-maid enter, and caught a glimpse of her dress in the mirror. "Oh, I am so much pleased with it—it will be so pretty for the—the wedding," she continued, still looking in the glass at the fair reflection before her.
>
> It was not until she felt the skirt of her dress grasped strangely that she turned and beheld Rose crouching at her feet as if overwhelmed with terror, her eyes dilated, her lips parted, and trying in vain to gasp out an articulate word.
>
> "Save me! save me!" she presently sobbed or rather shrieked out. (117)

The movement of this passage ingeniously dramatizes the relationship between empathy and financial necessity that Victor makes the crux of the dilemma over slavery. We see Virginia admiring herself in front of a mirror, more beautiful than ever because of Talfierro's gift. She speaks to Rose as she catches a glimpse of her servant's dress in the mirror (the dress stands in metonymically for the slave, highlighting her status as commodity rather than person), but is unable to witness Rose's despair because she is "still looking in the glass at the fair reflection before her." Only when she turns away from the mirror—the site of Talfierro's beneficence and her own fair beauty—does she finally see Rose overwhelmed with terror. Whereas Rose's dress is allowed space in the looking glass, Rose herself only comes into true focus outside this reflective space. Thus Virginia's inability to see Rose results from her own narcissistic fascination with the fairer image she herself projects.

If we understand the mirror in this scene as the site of an attempted sympathy that requires an obsession with "self" before allowing for the possibility of an awareness of "other," then the movement in this passage sharply criticizes the novel's larger narrative strategy. The lines of sight and empathy demonstrate that so long as an awareness of the plight of others is predicated on a narcissistic obsession, that plight will remain unseen, or at least radically distorted. Rose is aware of this predicament, since she had thought to herself on another occasion that "it would be in vain to appeal to 'white folks' on common grounds of sympathy" (118). Rose's awareness is an astute one, though, ironically, it escapes Victor herself, which again shouldn't be surprising considering the line of argument I'm tracing here and its dependence on white narcissism as a trope for psychological disorder.

*Narcissism* was first deployed as a psychological category by Havelock Ellis in 1898, but was unpacked more fully by Freud in his 1914 work, "On Narcissism: An Introduction."[25] For Freud, narcissism was a transitional state between autoeroticism and an outwardly directed object-love, and it was healthy as long as it remained transitional. The term was derived, of course, from Ovid's story of Narcissus and Echo in book 3 of the *Metamorphoses*. Narcissus, a beautiful boy of sixteen, was so enraptured by the sight of his beauty in a pond that he was unable to make the outwardly directed connections that life depends on. As a result he died, and turned into an equally pretty flower. As the narrator says of Narcissus, "O fondly foolish boy, why vainly seek to clasp a fleeting image? What you seek is nowhere; but turn yourself away, and the object of your love will be no more. That which you behold is but the shadow of a reflected form and has no substance of its own" (155). For Freud, narcissists "are plainly seeking *themselves* as a love-object," a condition Freud finds most often "in people whose libidinal development has suffered some disturbance, such as perverts and homosexuals" ("On Narcissism" 88).[26] Although narcissism has come to signify several different ideas, for my purposes I understand it as a way of being that requires a consideration of others solely for the larger purpose of articulating and buttressing the ego, the self. In short, narcissism economically describes Victor's narrative/political strategy and similarly describes whiteness as the primary motivating factor of that strategy. Although Freud focuses most of his attention on "perverts and homosexuals," I want to add whiteness to that category of perversion (though without endorsing his views on the narcissism of homosexuals and women). Doing so allows us to see whiteness as a pathology, as an unhealthy way of living in the world. Risking anachronism, we can even attach something of a clinical diagnosis to it. The *Diagnostic and Statistical Manual of Mental Disorders,* published by the American Psychiatric Association in 1980, defines narcissism as follows: "A grandiose sense of self-importance or uniqueness; preoccupation with fantasies of unlimited success; exhibitionistic need for constant attention and admiration; characteristic responses to threats of self-esteem; and characteristic disturbances in interpersonal relations, such as feelings of entitlement, interpersonal exploitativeness, relationships that alternate between the extremes of overidealization and devaluation, and lack of empathy" (315). If we had to stop here, leaving this passage to define what we mean when we talk about whiteness, we could do worse.[27] By making this leap from *Maum Guinea* to a contemporary definition of a particularly controversial psychological category, I don't mean to attach specific diagnoses to specific people. I'm not claiming that Victor herself was a narcissist, nor am I making the slightly more credible claim that her character—Virginia Bell—was.[28] Rather, I'm using this contemporary definition to shed light on the flawed motivation behind Victor's narrative strategy, and I'm suggesting that this motivation indicates a larger ideological presence—whiteness, that "shadow of a reflected form [that] has no substance of its own," to borrow once again from Ovid. By having Virginia Bell and Rose—supposed mirrors of one another—play out this climactic drama within the reflective confines of a literal mirror, Victor economically and inadvertently reveals her own complicity in the narcissism she attaches to Virginia. That she can write lines for Rose that reveal an awareness of white self-interest without fully feeling the force of those lines offers an all-too-familiar example of whiteness as a failure of vision and understanding.

Of course, the reader is not surprised to learn that Virginia would rather look at herself in the mirror than witness her slave's plight. As she tells her father in a subsequent conversation, "It makes me unhappy to look at her" (121). And it is in this conversation with her father that she is made to see not only the financial necessity for Rose's sale but her own dependence on this transaction. As Virginia denounces the pearl necklace and wishes that Talfierro had never made their acquaintance, Judge Bell shows her the true nature of her dilemma: "He has not done such a bad thing for you, my dear. I am so pinched for money this season, that if he had not done as he has done, I don't see how I could have provided you with a suitable outfit" (122). Virginia responds, "Yes, I see; but I'm sorry for Rose" (122). And although her sympathy for Rose will remain, there is not much doubt that it is her trousseau, not her waiting maid's happiness, that is of more importance to her.[29] As Frances Harper wrote about whites involved in the slave trade, "instead of listening to the cry of agony, they listen to the ring of dollars and stoop down to pick up the coin" (101).

Hyperion, on hearing that Talfierro has acquired his fiancée, does not fare much better with Philip than Rose had with Virginia. When Hyperion tells Philip that Rose is to be sold, his master's response is cavalier: "Never mind, boy, there's as good fish in the sea as ever was caught. If they send Rose away, I'll keep a sharp lookout for some other pretty girl, that will suit you just as well" (78). Victor criticizes Philip's lack of empathy in what may be the novel's most overt antislavery passage: "He did not take [Hyperion's] case to heart, and judge it as he would have done his own—how could he? If he had done so, he would have pulled the key-stone from the foundation of the whole splendid theory of slavery" (78). Here Victor's tone leaves no question as to how we should read "splendid" in this passage. Victor dismisses whatever "reason" may lurk behind Philip's endorsement of slavery as an institution and consequently dismantles the theory that depends on this "reason." Victor lays bare the infrastructure of the slave system by dramatizing the inability of Philip and Virginia—two young people very much in love—to recognize that same love in others. Their failure to understand the slaves' situation is based on a very simple premise: they do not recognize Rose and Hyperion as fully human. But once again we are confronted with the novel's central dilemma. For if slavery depends on the idea that blacks are not human in the same sense as whites, *Maum Guinea* itself becomes a "key-stone" in that "whole splendid theory of slavery." Victor's alleged antislavery polemic loses its vitality and force with every movement of the plot.

The unraveling is nowhere more apparent than in the chapter called "The Fugitives." As Rose, Hyperion, and Maum hide in the cave, Judge Bell and Colonel Fairfax are left behind to ponder their recent losses. As the colonel puts it, "There's neither gratitude nor common sense in any of the race. . . . What did they want to cut up such a freak for?—leave comfortable homes, protection and plenty, for cold, hardships and poverty" (189). As the two masters curse the "baseness" of their "ungrateful" slaves, Victor intervenes to place the events of the chapter in perspective. She begins by taking the reader inside the troubled conscience of Maum Guinea. Maum is suddenly overcome by doubt, as she ponders her own ingratitude in helping Rose and Hyperion flee their "easy" slavery: "For what had they fled from comfort and plenty, from fire, food, kind masters, and easy service? Reckless, ungrateful, improvident creatures!" (130). Surpris-

ingly, given Maum's previous antiwhite hostility, her interior mono-
logue becomes a voice of antiblack chastisement, as Victor locates the
voice of the master within the mind of the slave. Maum conveniently
polices herself. Her self-incriminating doubt, which the reader is not
prepared for, is curious indeed until this passage takes its next surreal turn.

Moving away from Maum's inner musings, Victor shifts to what
is unmistakably her own voice, a voice laden with the intonations of
Judge Bell and Colonel Fairfax, the masters left cursing on the portico.
As she had done much earlier when Rose finally expressed indignation
at her life as a slave, Victor here intervenes to question the "reasoning
faculty" of the slaves. Referring to Hyperion she writes:

> That splendid reasoning faculty, developed to such a subtle de-
> gree of fineness in the brain of the pure-blooded white, had not as
> yet attained such power in this six-eight's mulatto-man. . . . Any
> one can read, at a glance, his want of wisdom and his wretched
> ingratitude; no one can blame the two gentlemen who denounce
> him with such harshness, as they stride up and down the portico,
> and wait for their horses to be brought by the first red streak of
> morning. What is most conducive to the financial prosperity of a
> nation at once becomes right—and what is best for the financial
> interests of these two individuals is, of course, right, and they have
> our sympathy. (131–32)

Maum's interior musings turn out to be a fraud, a polemic imported
from the author's own feelings on the question of slavery and financial necessity. This extended passage shows Victor's obvious desire to
play to both sides of the controversy over slavery.[30] The narrative conscience flits back and forth from master to slave, always eager to show
the reader that all opinions on the matter, even those based in passion
and irrationality, are at least understandable.

However, to acknowledge the strategic motivations behind
Victor's multivalent authorial voicings does not go far enough in
understanding this passage's peculiar location within a supposedly
antislavery romance. The intrusion of economic theory into the argument in favor of slavery—an intrusion that began with Virginia's dilemma over her wedding trousseau—marks a profound disruption in
the antislavery energies at work earlier in the novel. Whereas Victor's
earlier strategy had been to show the common degree of humanity

between master and slave—a common humanity that makes slavery a moral wrong—she now turns to an economic version of the "might equals right" argument. If slavery is an economic good for the country as a whole, then slavery is "right." It's that simple.[31] Though Victor had pointed out earlier that Philip's own "splendid theory of slavery" would crumble if he made the empathic leap from his own feelings to those of his slave, she neglected to point out that she had her own splendid theory waiting in the wings. With the move from sympathy as an antislavery force to economic strength as a proslavery rationale, the terms of both Victor's novel and her critique have changed radically. Victor's clever dramatization and critique of Virginia's complicity in the economics of slavery (Rose's happiness or the trousseau?) yields to the argument that slavery is an economic necessity. Since "ease and happiness were her birthright" (22), it was "right" that Virginia should have a beautiful trousseau for her wedding, and so Rose had to be sold. It is "right" that men like Judge Bell and Colonel Fairfax not be deprived of their property, and so the fugitives must be tracked down, captured, and returned to the masters. At a time of national crisis, Victor's novel, interested in the "good of the nation," makes this a narrative inevitability. The consequences of this shift from moral necessity to an economics of pragmatism will become apparent at the novel's conclusion.

### Merry Christmas

The search party, now including Maum's son-in-law Slocum, discovers the fugitives, and it is revealed that Philip has purchased Rose from Talfierro to placate Virginia. The happy ending begins to unfold, but its terms seem confused. As Philip tells Rose, "You're mine, now, Rose" (211), the reader cannot help but wonder whether Talfierro has simply been replaced by yet another white male owner of Rose's body. But Philip's ownership is only important to the extent that it enables him to confer ownership on his soon-to-be wife. Virginia will be Rose's true owner, though Virginia's own relationship to her future husband will of course resemble yet another relationship of property. Lost in this complicated series of transactions is Hyperion. He will be allowed to marry, though his bride will belong to another. He himself is still property.

At this point Captain Slocum emerges from the shadows and begins another series of revelations. When Maum cries out for information about her daughter, Judy, Slocum tells her that "Mrs. Slocum is well and hearty, I thank you—a good wife, and the mother of three of the—purtiest babies'" (212).[32] According to Slocum, the only thing that really clouded the couple's happiness was Judy's concern for her mother. Slocum had written to the Gregory plantation, and on hearing that Maum had been sold, Judy "cried and grieved" (213). Slocum promised his wife that as soon as he had "time and means" he would search for his mother-in-law, though "years slipped by, and there was always something to prevent" (214). Only when Slocum sees that Judy's concern has begun to wear on her "mind and health" does he go south in search of his mother-in-law. The rest of Slocum's story is already known to the reader, except for Philip's rather sudden decision to buy Rose himself. As Slocum tells it, "[Philip had] made up his mind to purchase the girl, himself, and thus secure the smiles and gratitude of his lady-love, as well as a nice attendant for his future wife" (214). Why this decision had not been arrived at sooner is left a mystery, as is Slocum's troubling admission that "years slipped by" before he could find the time to locate Maum, whose daughter was grieving for her daily. At any rate, Slocum wraps up his story by telling his mother-in-law that he has purchased her: "you're my Maumy, now, Guinea. I've got the deed for you in my vest" (214). Looking at a picture of her daughter with her grandchildren, Maum's heart finally bursts, "and with sobs and tears, she fell upon her knees and thanked the Lord for all his mercies" (215).

Once the revelations are concluded only two paragraphs remain, an epilogic glance into the future. We are told that the next summer Philip and Virginia, an "extremely happy new-married couple," traveled to the North to visit the "mansion of Captain Ephraim Slocum" and to see "the pretty wife of whom he was so proud" (215). They find that Judy is indeed "the marvel of beauty her mother's fondness had painted her" and that "no prettier children ever laughed around the lap of a grandmother than those who frolicked in the light of Maum Guinea's wordless affection" (215).[33] Questions remain, however. For example, what are the circumstances of Maum's life in New York City? Given Slocum's inability to disclose his wife's racial status (see note 19), can Maum exist in anything like a public relation of kin? If she lives with her daughter and son-in-law (and we aren't told that she does), must she assume the facade of servant in order to keep guests from understanding her true relation to the Slocums? Do her grandchildren, who are passing for "white," even know that the person they are frolicking around is actually their grandmother? And would the answers to these questions explain that curious phrase, "wordless affection"? It seems that the North, that site of Maum's "happy ending," is nothing more than a sort of racial "closet," where Maum must "pass" for a "house nigger" in order to be around the family that she spent her life trying to make possible.[34] Her assumption of this constructed identity—the ultimate in "black" roles—facilitates Judy's passing. The family is together, but only on Slocum's terms.

The novel's final paragraph is even more troubling: "Mr. and Mrs. Fairfax brought their valet and waiting maid with them to the North; they felt secure in the strong ties of gratitude which bound the couple to their service—the laughing, brilliant, animated couple married the same night as themselves—Rose as happy in her pink tissue, as her mistress in her pearly satin—who had no farther thought of deserting those who had made life to them now seem like a long CHRISTMAS HOLIDAY" (215). The "strong ties of gratitude" are not the only ties that bind, however. Although any attempt to locate the events of this novel within a contemporary chronology is necessarily conjectural, it is reasonable to assume that the novel's present is sometime between 1850 and the time of its writing in 1860–61. If this is the case, the Fugitive Slave Law, which was passed as part of the Compromise of 1850, would provide yet another tie that binds the slaves to their masters on the visit north.[35] Despite their desperate attempt to flee slavery just a few chapters earlier, Hyperion and Rose are still slaves. The only change is that slavery has now become the site of their unblemished happiness, a place of joy and contentment that they would be foolish, even crazy, to flee.

The capitalization of the words "Christmas Holiday" in Victor's text shouts their importance, forcing the reader to wonder what a lifelong Christmas holiday might look like. The tenuousness of the "good times" on the plantation has been obvious from the very beginning of *Maum Guinea*. The present-day events of the novel occur during one week out of the year, a time when dancing and feasting replace toil and labor as the norm. The slaves know their joy is limited, and it is perhaps this knowledge, according to Victor, that gives their holiday hijinks such intensity. Just as we knew it would be, by the novel's end the holiday season is over. As Victor writes with only two chapters to go: "The holiday life of the negroes on Colonel Fairfax's plantation, was exchanged for the toil which was to occupy them until Christmas came again" (203). With only fifty-one weeks to go until their next week of happiness and joy, the slaves settle back into their slavery. As the novel ends, so does its governing fiction. The novel could pretend that slavery was not real, as long as slavery was not its temporal setting. With the Christmas holiday over, *Maum Guinea* has nothing to do but conclude, since its governing terms no longer exist.[36]

But according to Victor's last line, at least two of her characters do get to live forever in the terms of slavery's holiday suspension. Rose and Hyperion are blessed with the holiday season as their own "eternal return." The events of this novel—itself a metonym for the Christmas holidays, since it must end when the holidays end—become Rose and Hyperion's continual present. The dances, the pig roasts, the coon hunts, these form the substance of Victor's happy slavery. To the extent that this novel is the narrative of holiday week on the slave plantation, it becomes the life that Rose and Hyperion are blessed to repeat over and over again.

But what kind of a blessing is this? If Rose and Hyperion are destined to repeat the events and the emotions of this novel, it is important to remember just what these events and emotions were. In addition to the dances and celebrations, we saw cruel and uncaring masters, slaves sold as sexual property, lovers denied the right to marry, grueling flight from untenable circumstances, thoughts of suicide, and families separated. The stories told within the novel's larger narrative only add to this list of cruelties: babies sold away from their parents, beatings, murder, bloody insurrection. Though we know these last events only as stories, the stories are told during the Christmas holidays, and the depression inspired by the telling becomes a large part of this novel's holiday mood.

So slavery becomes once again a discursive system, littered with repetitions and mirrorings of cruelty. If Rose and Hyperion's life together is to be a repetition of slavery as the text of *Maum Guinea,* we know that such a repetition will inevitably involve death, separation, and despair. As readers of plantation novels, we know that these are the plots that black couples married under the law of slavery are doomed to repeat. Without knowing she was doing it, Victor writes into the last two words of her novel the nightmare that we as readers know must await any couple in slavery. This "happy" ending tells the truth all too well.

Yet though I want to insist on the role of genre in the construction of this warped ending, I don't want to absolve Victor of her eager participation within that genre or of her failure to rise above it. Might it be possible to end an antislavery romance written in 1861 on different terms? Fortunately, we have a ready counterexample to *Maum Guinea* in Harriet Jacobs's *Incidents in the Life of a Slave Girl,* published in the same year as Victor's novel. By looking briefly at the ending of Jacobs's narrative, we can get a clearer sense of the generic possibilities available to Victor, and the possible reasons that she was unable to avail herself of them. The most famous line from *Incidents* can get us started: "Reader, my story ends with freedom; not in the usual way, with marriage" (302). As many critics have noted, this rather simple statement economically exposes the difficulty of writing black female lives within the generic confines of a sentimental fiction dependent on the codes and values of whiteness. As Valerie Smith puts it, by making this pronouncement Jacobs "acknowledges that, however much her story may resemble superficially the story of the sentimental heroine, as a black woman she plays for different stakes; marriage is not the ultimate reward she seeks" (xxxvi). If we think of this line in the context of *Maum Guinea*'s denouement, its truth becomes crystal clear. Jacobs's syntax suggests an oppositional relationship between the subjects on either side of her semicolon: freedom and marriage. This is precisely the case in Victor's novel, where marriage simultaneously obliterates the possibility of freedom and, more ominously, makes that possibility no longer a moral necessity.

Just a few lines after this antithetical juxtaposition of freedom and marriage, Jacobs goes even further to trouble the terms of the happy ending she finds herself narratively a part of. Her freedom having been bought for her against her wishes, Jacobs expresses her gratitude to her benefactress this way: "But God so orders circumstances as to keep me with my friend Mrs. Bruce. Love, duty, gratitude, also bind me to her side. It is a privilege to serve her who pities my oppressed people, and who has bestowed the inestimable boon of freedom on me and my children" (303). Without ignoring the very real advantages of this "boon of freedom," I want to highlight how Jacobs rhetorically undermines the terms of this freedom, casting significant doubt on its material existence. Jacobs is *bound* to Mrs. Bruce's side; she *serves* this woman who *pities* her; freedom has been *bestowed* on her. Within the space of these two sentences, Jacobs challenges the happiness of this generically happy ending. Where Victor claimed Rose and Hyperion's "strong ties of gratitude" as a powerful inducement to remain in slavery, Jacobs at least hints that these ties are a form of slavery themselves. Jacobs's ending is far more satisfying than Victor's, precisely because Jacobs was able to subvert the terms of that happy ending she felt compelled to enact.[37] Jacobs's reference to the ties that bind contains the awareness of the literal fact of that metaphor; Victor's remains oblivious to it. This difference is crucial and signals the mutability of genre in the right hands and the right sensibility.

Though Victor's novel can be said to have failed in quite a few ways, those failures are ultimately what make it useful to us. *Maum Guinea* renders contradiction coherent at a time when the nation itself was yielding up its ideological limitations and givens. By 1861 the attempts of a decade earlier to forestall disunion had unraveled. The social and political chaos of the late 1840s, which centered on the debate over slavery's westward expansion, had been superficially contained by a series of compromises. A decade before the publication of Victor's novel, the Compromise of 1850 and the Fugitive Slave Law had chiseled together a delicate peace, a temporary stay against disunion. These legal texts can be seen as fictions that attempted to hold irreconcilable differences within the same solution. A decade later, the fiction was unmasked. The nation's competing narrative threads could no longer exist within the same narrative space. The Union, its fictional underpinnings exposed yet again, tore asunder.

Within this context, *Maum Guinea* makes a great deal of sense. It holds conflict and contradiction together in ways that apparently made for a compelling read in 1861, and it does so as the nation itself was giving up all pretense that such a thing was possible. What was no longer politically viable was still a narrative possibility. Working-class racism could exist comfortably with labor abolitionism; moral arguments against slavery refused to stand in the way of economic arguments in favor of slavery. The final result? Antislavery energies are contained and diffused by a happy Yuletide slavery. These contradictions—glaring from a distance—would not have announced themselves as such to a contemporary audience. Paradoxically, Victor's novel, which she hoped would mirror a cultural reality, did just that.

America's so-called Negro problem has always been, at the same time, a theological problem. W. E. B. Du Bois put this clearly when, in 1913, he called the Church "the strongest seat of racial and color prejudice" (*Crisis* 334). "The Negro problem is the test of the church" (*Crisis* 335), he wrote, and since American Christianity "was the bulwark of American slavery" (*Crisis* 334), it is hard to imagine that Du Bois was very optimistic about the outcome of this test. As he writes in *Darkwater* (1920), "A nation's religion is its life, and as such white Christianity is a miserable failure" (36). Du Bois does allow himself a touch of optimism, however, when, in the *Crisis* essay, he muses on the historical interrelation between religious racism and American science. "Even the rock of 'Science,'" he writes, "on which the white church rested with such beautiful faith, hoping to prove the majority of humanity inhuman, . . . even this Rock of Ages is falling before honest investigation" (*Crisis* 335).

Although the rock of science may have been crumbling in 1913, sixty years earlier it was just beginning to form. In "The Claims of the Negro Ethnologically Considered" (1854), Frederick Douglass launched a sustained attack against the midcentury vogue of American ethnology—the scientific school of so-called racial difference. Armed with a theory of multiple creations—polygenesis—the ethnologists offered a new weapon to the arsenal of proslavery discourse, one that attempted, in Douglass's words, to "read the Negro out of the human family" ("Claims" 295). The theory of polygenesis proved tremendously attractive to proslavery theologians, for it sketched a world in which some "human families" were better descended than others. Some could trace themselves back to Adam and Eve, and those who could not were then biblically constituted as appropriate material for slavery. The ethnologists offered scientific sanction for a biblical theory of slavery at a time when the tension between science and religion was on the rise. Scientific "discoveries" often contradicted biblical "truth," creating a double bind for so-called Christian slaveholders and their apologists. The ethnologists offered one way out of this double bind by giving theological racism a biblically acceptable narrative of polygenesis.[1]

In the years following Douglass's essay, scores of American scientists and theologians returned to the biblical scene of the Garden of Eden as the setting for their racist imaginings of "the Negro's" place (or more accurately, lack of place) in the human family. In so doing, they found a black presence at the scene of the temptation, a black man where the snake should have been. Their concerns with the question of so-called racial purity made this black man's proximity to Eve the cause for alarm. Recently collected in *Anti-Black Thought, 1863–1925: "The Negro Problem,"* edited by John David Smith, these Eden revisionists offer a window into how science and religion mediated and shaped white America's attempt, during the latter half of the nineteenth century, to rid itself once and for all of "the Negro." Like Charles Jacobs Peterson and Metta V. Victor, the writers I discuss in this chapter were dedicated to crafting stories about race that they hoped would become racial truths. The theoscience that resulted from their attempt has a great deal to tell us about the shaky and often surreal infrastructure of whiteness as a form of racial, sexual, and intellectual anxiety. As Anna Julia Cooper trenchantly observed in 1892, "Some developments brought to light recently through the scientific Christianity . . . may lead one to suspect the need of missionary teaching to 'elevate' the white race" (204).

### The Credit of the Bible

As Ethiop (William J. Wilson) wrote in "What Shall We Do with the White People?" (1860), midcentury white theologians were "wholly absorbed in cutting and trimming theological garments to suit their various patrons," patrons who were most often invested in upholding the tenets of white supremacy (61). Douglass made a similar point regarding the dubious entanglement of antiblack science with conventional Christian theology. In "The Claims of the Negro" Douglass foregrounds the fundamental biases at the heart of so-called scientific objectivity. "It is the province of prejudice to blind," Douglass writes, "and scientific writers, not less than others, write to please, as well as to instruct, and even unconsciously to themselves, (sometimes,) sacrifice what is true to what is popular. Fashion is not confined to dress; but extends to philosophy as well" ("Claims" 298). With characteristic sarcasm, Douglass dismisses "all the scientific moonshine that would connect men with monkeys" and calls for the nation's moral growth to keep up with its alleged "increase of knowledge" ("Claims" 291, 292).[2] As Frances Harper would assert some years later, with perhaps too much optimism, "Ethnologists may differ about the origin of the human race. Huxley may search for it in protoplasms, and Darwin send for the missing links, but there is one thing of which we may rest assured—that we all come from the living God and that He is the common Father" (220).

As Douglass recognizes, however, it is not simply "prejudice" that produces faulty science, but prejudice mixed with a misappropriation of biblical authority. The power of the Bible in the war over the racial past produced one of the central ironies in this debate, since Douglass, through his Christian faith, proceeds from assumptions and goals similar to those of the ethnologists he was debunking. He realizes that the question of the unity of humankind will in part be decided by what "reflects the most glory upon the wisdom, power, and goodness of the Author of all existence" ("Claims" 293). "The credit of the Bible is at stake," he writes, and "the value of that sacred Book . . . must be materially affected, by the decision of the question" ("Claims" 293).

Douglass's allegiance to the Bible puts him in the rather strange company of the negrophobic Charles Carroll, whose writings were dedicated to proving that the Negro was a "beast." "Inasmuch as my views of the negro were based upon the Bible," Carroll writes, "I realized that it was necessary to show that the scriptures were in absolute harmony with the sciences at every point" (*Tempter* xv). Though Carroll's goal of a perfect harmony between science and religion might seem overly optimistic, the force of white racism was capable of making the most discordant of notes blend perfectly. In a culture eager to prove the Negro's inferiority and inhumanity, this harmonizing would be less difficult than might be imagined.

The science we are talking about here was of dubious shape and intention. Ethnology, called by Ephraim Squier in 1849 the "science of the age" (385), was largely a hodgepodge of anthropology, Egyptology, and craniology. It was designed to investigate, in Squier's words, "the superiority of certain families over others" and "to what extent they may assimilate with, to what repel each other, and how their relations may be adjusted so as to produce the greatest attainable advantage to both" (386). Beginning with Dr. Samuel Morton's *Crania Americana,* published in 1839, scientists transformed an American obsession with physical difference into a science of so-called racial difference. With an eye to hair, lips, foreheads, and feet, these scientists articulated a theory that equated morphological characteristics with mental and emotional possibility. These men legitimated with science what could be called the commonsense racism of their cultural moment.

Yet the theory of polygenesis that grew out of this science seemed to radically question the Mosaic account of creation found in Genesis. How could polygenesis possibly be accepted in a theologically dogmatic society—one like the South, which, for all its interest in the latest scientific theories, always judged those theories against the presumed greater authority of biblical truth? The tension between science and theology that so concerned Du Bois and Douglass characterized and ultimately shaped much of the nineteenth-century debate over racial difference and slavery. At issue was a complicated struggle for various forms of sanction and accreditation, as thinkers like Josiah Nott, Louis Aggasiz, Samuel Morton, and Joseph DeGobineau struggled to navigate their way through a maze of conflicting authority. Science and religion became the Scylla and Charybdis of the "race question" in mid-nineteenth-century America. Ethnologists gleefully waged war against the parsons, yet worked in constant fear of the parsons' very real cultural power. Sometimes happy in their roles as martyrs to "truth," these scientists were continually frustrated by the power of the Church.[3]

And in terms of the larger argument over slavery, the power of the Church functioned in anything but a straight line. As William Stanton has argued, in the days before the war the South's religious dogmatism denied it a scientific justification for its slaveholding (194). Had southern plantation owners fully accepted the theory of polygenesis, their argument in favor of slavery could have been supported by the cold "facts" of science. But to accept these facts would have meant to deny the literal truth of the Genesis story, and, in the long run, the South's refusal to do so denied it very little.

For if science offered one way to support the enslavement of blacks, religion, if examined in the "proper light," could offer another. What the South lost in its reluctance to embrace new scientific "evidence" of racial difference and so-called black inferiority it made up for in the stories of the Bible, where one could find such rich nuggets as Noah's strange curse on Canaan, the Flood, the destruction of Sodom, and other stories of biblical apocalypse. In the often surreal narratives of nineteenth-century biblical scholarship, these stories, with all their misreadings, bear the brunt of supporting the antiblack, proslavery theorists in their theopolitical quest for racial purity.

But it was not just to Canaan and his troubled family that these theorists turned for their evidence of black inferiority. Rather, they started "in the beginning," at the story of the Fall. From as early as 1860, various writers located their racist polemics in the heart of the Garden, at the site of Eve's temptation. Devoting countless pages to minute exegeses of the tempter's true identity, these authors, with various permutations on the theme, arrived at a reading of the temptation in which the "serpent" was either an ape or a human, often black, and usually male.

This rereading accomplished at least two significant things. First, if the tempter was a black man, then obviously black men existed either contemporaneous with or prior to Adam and Eve. The proponents of polygenesis had made this a narrative necessity. Second, and in my view more importantly, this reading of the temptation of Eve worked to buttress hysteria over the issue of miscegenation or, in the nineteenth-century parlance, amalgamation. If Eve's tempter was a black man (or a black woman), then original sin was not located in her eating of the apple but in her far more grievous crime of heeding the seductive words of a black tempter. Thus miscegenation becomes the reason for the Fall, just as it was interpreted to be the cause of subsequent biblical apocalypses. By locating a black tempter in the Garden of Eden, antiblack theorists created a richly textured and narratively dense web of proslavery theology and fueled the postwar fires of amalgamation hysteria. Just as *Uncle Tom's Cabin* functioned as a midcentury appeal to save a slave-ridden and thus destruction-bound nation, these theorists of the Garden constructed their own allegorical entreaty, one that showed the nation on the same path that previously led to the Fall, the Flood, and various plagues by fire and locust. Amalgamation, miscegenation, intermarriage, integration— these were the contemporary sins that would surely seal the nation's doom.[4] In the following pages I examine a few of the most important moments in this period of biblical exegesis, paying particular attention to how the concerns and fears of the postwar South found themselves projected back to the Garden—back to the mysterious relationship between Eve, "our" great white mother, and that darker force, capable of bending her desires to his own.

The story of Adam and Eve, like much in Genesis, is remarkably condensed. A great deal happens in a few words, which accounts in part for the torturous interpretive history of this and other Mosaic accounts. As Elaine Pagels argues, "from about 200 B.C.E. (before the common era), the story of creation became, for certain Jews, and later for Christians, a primary means for revealing and defending basic attitudes and values" (xix). It functioned as a sort of morality primer. Boiled down to its central themes, the story of the temptation and subsequent Fall revolves around issues of knowledge, nudity, desire, power, and blame. The link between these themes is often tenuous and surprising. Why, for example, is an awakening into the knowledge of Good and Evil signified solely by Adam and Eve's sudden awareness of their nudity—of their bodies ("and the eyes of both were opened, and they knew that they were naked" [Gen. 3.7])? This sudden and shameful nakedness carries the symbolic whole of Adam and Eve's new life, a life filled with the knowledge not only of supreme goodness but of its attendant evil. Their awareness of their bodies functions as a metonym for the fallen world, and thus their fall from godliness.[5]

Just as nudity is complicated in this scenario, so is desire, which flows in circuitous ways in the Garden. The colloquy between Eve and the Serpent, who "was more subtil than any beast of the field" (Gen. 3.1), eventually tends toward a realization of Eve's true desire and her decision to act on it. Tempted with the forbidden fruit, Eve sees that the tree in the middle of the Garden is one "to be desired to make one wise" (Gen. 3.6), and she no longer hesitates. But the decision to act on her desire—a desire implanted in part by the serpent's suggestion—results in a rerouting of that desire, since part of God's curse for Eve's transgression is that Eve's "desire shall be to thy husband, and he shall rule over thee" (Gen. 3.16). The serpent awakens Eve to one kind of desire, only to begin the chain of events that eventually deflects this desire into its ultimate complicity in a patriarchal system of control.

Finally, there is the question of blame and counsel. When God asks Adam why he has broken his commandment, Adam effects a double displacement of blame: "And the man said, The woman whom thou gavest to be with me, she gave me of the tree" (Gen. 3.12). Adam is the innocent victim both of the woman and of God. Likewise, Eve responds to God's question with another displacement: "The serpent beguiled me" (Gen. 3.13). These displacements of responsibility have to do with heeding the counsel of others—of acting on suggestion. Adam's primary sin, after all, wasn't the eating of the apple but the fact that he "hearkened unto the voice of thy wife" (Gen. 3.17). And by analogy, Eve's sin involved not only her seizing of the forbidden fruit but her willingness to be led by the serpent and the ease with which she was beguiled.

Taken together, these various themes combine to form a widely instructive fable. To know the good from the bad is to know the clothed from the naked. To act on simple hunger and desire results in shame. The path of a purely selfish desire leads to the curse of a mandated desire, one that becomes a force in the field of power and control. Eve and the serpent obviously occupy similarly disreputable positions; through their give-and-take of temptation and yielding they cause the Fall itself.[6]

Seen in this light, this brief story was indeed ripe for the needs and uses of those nineteenth-century theologians who returned to it. Eve's transgression of divine law—a metonym in this case for a feminine violation of male sanction—results in the covering of bodies and the construction of the patriarchal family unit. Although gender and sexual politics are clearly on display here, a question remains as to where these scholars found the racial subject matter they also needed for their story to be complete. How did they get from the "subtil serpent" to the more insidious and seductive Negro?

To answer these questions, it's useful to think about the various associations that have clung to the serpent figure over the centuries. At the heart of these associations is the question of gender. According to Henry Kelly, in the Rabbinic tradition "the Eden serpent was thought to have been very *male,* since it actually lusted after Eve" (302). This belief, coupled with the phallic connotations traditionally associated with the serpent, at least partially explains the traditional gendering of the serpent as male (as does the heteronormativity that seems to demand a male/female relationship at the site of the temptation). The serpent's maleness and concomitant lust for Eve played a large role in the religious lore surrounding the temptation. For example, the writer of the Apocalypse of Moses, dramatizing the temptation from Eve's perspective, emphasizes the lustfulness at the heart of the encounter: the serpent "poured upon the fruit the poison of his wickedness, which is lust, the root and beginning of every sin, and he bent the branch on the earth and I took of the fruit and I ate" (qtd. in Tabick 161). Likewise, the Talmud shows that "the serpent came to Eve [and] infused filthy lust into her" (qtd. in Tabick 161). This infusion of lust further encodes the phallic power and intention associated with the serpent.[7]

It's worth mentioning, however, that the serpent's representational genealogy isn't entirely male. According to Kelly, around 1170 C.E. "a new tradition was born, that of the maiden-faced serpent in the Garden of Eden" (308). This female serpent was most likely born in response to the notion that Eve would have been most easily beguiled by a familiar image, one similar to her own (Kelly 308). The fact that the serpent was "maiden-faced" further emphasizes Eve's pre-Fall innocence. But this wasn't the only logic behind the regendering of the traditionally male serpent. Given the serpent's associative evil and treachery, cultural misogyny made the link from serpent to woman a facile one, as did the rather commonplace linkage of images of women with that of the scorpion, another traditional symbol of treachery (Kelly 313). Kelly quotes the author of the *Ancrene Riwle,* who offers this Solomonic insight: "The man who grasps a woman is like one who grasps a scorpion" (qtd. in Kelly 313). Similarly, the *Ancrene Riwle* describes the scorpion as "a type of worm that is said to have a head something like a woman's but behind this it is a serpent. It puts forth a fair countenance and flatters with its head but stings with its tail" (qtd. in Kelly 313). More recent representations of the serpent as female can be found on the doors of Notre Dame and the ceiling of the Sistine Chapel (Kelly 319).

While we will have cause to return to this notion of the symbolic embodiment of feminine treachery, I want to emphasize for now the assumed maleness of the serpent in both Christian and Jewish traditions. The most important aspect of this serpentine masculinity is its association with brute and degenerative lust. This is nowhere more apparent than in the following passage from the writings of Philo of Alexandria, a Greco-Roman Jewish philosopher and theologian. According to Philo, the serpent is

> a fit symbol of pleasure, because . . . it is an animal, without feet, sunk prone upon his belly, secondly . . . he takes clods of earth as

food, thirdly . . . he carries in his teeth the venom with which it is his nature to destroy those whom he has bitten. The lover of pleasure is exempt from none of these traits, for he is so weighed and dragged downwards that it is with difficulty he lifts up his head . . . he feeds not on heavenly nourishment . . . but on that which comes out of the earth . . . which produces drunkenness, daintiness and greediness. These . . . make a man a glutton, while they also stimulate and stir up the stings of his sexual lusts. . . . His aim is not to sate his hunger, but to leave nothing that has been set out undevoured. (qtd. in Tabick 160–61)

Like his hunger, the serpent's sexual appetite is all-devouring.

I quote this passage at some length because it offers a convenient link back to the question of racial identity that nineteenth-century thinkers attached to the Eden serpent. The terms of this categorization—unthinking sloth, brute sexual appetite and threat—were precisely the terms applied to black men during the white hysteria spawned by the changing power dynamics of Reconstruction. The notion of the black man's never-satisfied and ever-increasing sexual desire proved to be the primary force behind late-nineteenth-century Jim Crowism, as well as the brutal reign of lynch law. Antiblack theologians understood that if this notion could be granted biblical sanction, then the fluctuating tide of racial extremism in the years during and after Reconstruction would have found a new and compelling gravitational force.

### Trouble in the Garden

Primary responsibility for the propagation of this racist Eden mythos belongs to a Nashville publisher named Buckner Payne, who in 1867, under the pseudonym of Ariel, published a pamphlet with the descriptive title, *The Negro: What Is His Ethnological Status? Is He the Progeny of Ham? Is He a Descendant of Adam and Eve? Has He a Soul? Or Is He a Beast in God's Nomenclature? What Is His Status as Fixed by God in Creation? What Is His Relation to the White Race?*[8] In his efforts to prove that "the Negro" is (and always has been) a beast, Ariel reawakened the controversy over polygenesis, claiming disingenuously that his work had nothing to do with politics. Harrison Berry, a black respondent to Ariel's work, got to the heart of the matter when he wrote that "it is too apparent to be doubted that the whole fabrication is founded on the interest of the great diabolical slave power, making the enslavement of the Negro justifiable on the hypothesis of his being a beast" (8).[9]

Because Ariel's argument figures so prominently in the larger debate, it's worth pausing to summarize its main components: (1) Noah's curse did not make Ham a Negro; (2) since Noah and his wife were both white and "perfect in their genealogy," and since Adam and Eve were also white, it is impossible that either pair could be "the progenitors of the kinky-headed, black-skinned negroes of this day" (45); (3) this being the case, the Negro was of necessity created prior to Adam, along with "the other beasts and cattle" (25), and is "a *beast* in God's nomenclature; and being a beast, was under Adam's rule and dominion, and, like all other beasts or animals, has no soul" (45). Ariel's Adam-like naming of the Negro as a beast depends on his translation of the original Hebrew term for "men." Genesis 4:26 describes a time when men "began . . . to call on the name of the Lord," and Ariel makes much of the word *began* here. Since Adam, Cain, Abel, and Seth "were all the men that were of Adam's race that were upon the earth at that time" (28), the "men" who suddenly began to call on the name of the Lord "were negroes—the *men* so named by Adam when he named the other beasts and cattle" (28). This linguistic sleight of hand allows Ariel the distinction that his theory requires, one separating the race of Adam from the race of "men."

Ariel's ultimate conclusion is that the tempter in the garden "was a *beast*, a *talking* beast" (45). The commerce between Eve and the Negro beast—stated but not unpacked by Ariel—stands as the Ur-sin, the first cause of the Fall. And it stands at the root of Ariel's story. Shifting from biblical exegesis to contemporary diatribe, Ariel concludes by reminding the reader that "a man can not commit so great an offense against his race, against his country, against his God, in any other way, as to give his daughter in marriage to a negro—a *beast*—or to take one of their females for his wife" (48). If the country continues to engage in this practice, warns Ariel, then it can expect the same fate faced by the antediluvians: "The states or people that favor this equality and amalgamation of the white and black races, *God will exterminate*" (48). The South may have lost the war, but in Ariel's optimistic view, its real troubles were just beginning.[10]

As the Ariel debate proceeded, its terms became somewhat more lucid, though no less surreal. One of the more interesting and strangely compelling responses to Ariel's work is *Caliban: A Sequel to "Ariel"* (1868), written under the pseudonym, appropriately enough, of Prospero.[11] Prospero begins by demonstrating Genesis's account of not one but two primary creations, a fact proving that "there were men upon the earth before Adam" (4). Prospero achieves this by pointing out what he calls the lexical distinction between the Hebrew word for *God* (Elohim) and the Hebrew word for *Lord* (Jehovah). According to Prospero, a record of the work done by Elohim is found in Genesis, chapters 1 and 2, through verse 6; Jehovah's efforts are documented in Genesis 2.6–25. Thus in Prospero's view there were two creations: the man and woman created in Genesis 1, whose chief occupation seems to be the maintenance of animals, and the man and woman created in Genesis 2, who are to be primarily engaged in agricultural pursuits, as their task is to keep the garden. But who exactly were these pre-Adamites? With the help of "modern science" (8), Prospero gives the following answer: "The preadamites were Mongols and Negroes, together with their mixed progeny. Created male and female, and in many pairs, they multiplied rapidly, exterminated the wild beasts, and replenished the earth with beings of their own species, penetrating into every land" (8). Having confirmed the presence of Negroes and Mongols before Adam and Eve, Prospero can brush aside the "superstitious" reading of Genesis in which a serpent tempts Eve and instead posit that "the tempter was a preadamite, perhaps a negro" (15). And though this "perhaps" seems to qualify his statement, Prospero's subsequent association of the tempter with a "witch-doctor" all but erases that qualification: the temptation "presents a vivid picture of an African medicine-man, or conjurer, with his 'grey dissimulation,' whispering his diabolical temptation into the ear of unsuspecting Eve" (15). Significantly, Prospero eroticizes the scene; the proximity required by the whispering presents a picture of preconjugal small talk.

Prospero's account of the temptation is certainly more explicit than Ariel's, but it does not approach the miniromance sketched by A. Hoyle Lester in *The Pre-Adamite, or Who Tempted Eve?* (1875). Lester's description is explicitly sexual and grants to Eve an agency often denied her in other accounts. Lester's Eve can be seen as an example of what Jonathan Ned Katz calls the "newly heterosexualized woman," with "heterosexual" meaning, in this sense, a male/female erotic attraction freed from reproductive imperatives (90). As Katz points out, in the nineteenth-century men were considered to be "more heterosexual" than women (32). Richard von Krafft-Ebing's *Psychopathia Sexualis* (first published in English in 1893), which normalized heterosexuality as a healthy, different-sex eroticism (one not necessarily tied to reproduction), viewed men as more heterosexual than women because they were "more aggressive and violent in [their] wooing" (qtd. in Katz 31). In contrast, if a woman "is normally developed mentally, and well bred, her sexual desire is small. If this were not so the whole world would become a brothel and marriage and a family impossible" (qtd. in Katz 31). The "new woman" of the 1880s, however, represented a departure from earlier distributions of lust (Katz 90). As women began to claim their own erotic agency, they became, according to writers like Krafft-Ebing, more heterosexual. They also became, not surprisingly, more of a threat. Lester's Eve is an early manifestation of this newly heterosexualized—and thus newly sexual—woman.

Lester begins by establishing a context for Eve's transgression, one in which she is portrayed as a bored and frustrated woman on the loose. Eve had become "wearied with the monotony that daily surrounded her. . . . The presence of Adam had no doubt become irksome, and his voice, for the time, had ceased to fill the aching void that agonized her tender heart" (22). Lester describes Eve's subsequent wandering in the language of sexual desire. She wanted to "explore the farther limit of her territorial domain, she wandered far along meandering brooks, and plucked strange flowers to while away the slow-fleeting moments, and slaked her thirst at gushing fountains where she dreamed no mortal had yet partaken thereof" (22). Eve's quest here is certainly sexual (the slaking of thirst at gushing fountains, for example). But hers, as portrayed by Lester, is a sexual desire imbricated with her craving for the exotic, the different. She seeks the "farther limit." She plucks "strange flowers." The eroticism of this passage is deeply entwined with its exoticism, setting the stage for Eve's ultimate encounter with the tempter, who in Hoyle's account is a Mongol, belonging "most assuredly to the highest order of the inferior races" (22).[12]

Eve, "innocent and unsuspecting," meets a "stranger," who is taken with her naked beauty. Eve bends her "attentive ear" in "enchanting conversation" with this "son of perdition," who came to her in "manly form, stately and erect" (22, 24). According to Lester, Eve and the tempter "met often and lingered long in some solitary shade by rural founts" (25). The temptation was not an isolated moment but rather resulted from a courtship of sorts, a much more gradual seduction:

And this gay deceiver spoke of the germ in the human heart where affection springs, . . . and of love with its operations on the tender heart, and said, Partake of the forbidden fruit: "Then shall your eyes be opened, and ye shall be as gods, knowing good and evil."

Eve, poor woman, yielded to the evil machinations of this seductive deceiver. She rose from the mossy couch a wiser but a fallen creature, and returned to the presence of her lawful companion disrobed of virtue, that precious jewel, the brightest ornament of her sex. (25)

This encounter, which Lester describes as "intercourse or intimacy," resulted in the birth of Cain, that "mongrel offspring" (26).

What interests me most about the above passage is the slippage between the tempter's command to "partake of the forbidden fruit" and Eve's subsequent rising from the "mossy couch." Nowhere in this passage is the Tree of Knowledge mentioned, where the "forbidden fruit" allegedly hung. This silence leads us to a syntactic discovery: the tempter's command results not in the eating of the apple but in sexual intercourse. In this account, the forbidden fruit literally becomes the Mongol's penis. The implicit story told by Ariel and others of "black" sexual seduction is here made explicit.[13]

### Engendering Temptation

The zenith of the pre-Adamite/tempter theorizing was reached in 1902 with the publication of Charles Carroll's mammoth *The Tempter of Eve; or, The Criminality of Man's Social, Political, and Religious Equality with the Negro, and the Amalgamation to Which These Crimes Inevitably Lead*. With seventeen chapters, nine illustrations, and a total of 503 pages, Carroll's work was the most extensive to be written on the subject. *The Tempter of Eve* was published by the Adamic Publishing Company, a St. Louis religious press, and it followed by two years Carroll's more widely known work, *The Negro a Beast*, published by another St. Louis firm, the American Book and Bible House.[14] Although little information exists concerning the circulation and reception of *The Tempter of Eve,* anecdotal accounts suggest that *The Negro a Beast* was widely circulated, particularly in the South. Writing in the *North American Review* in 1905, Edward Atkinson called *Beast* "the most sacrilegious book ever issued from the press in this country" and claimed that it was "securing a very wide circulation among the poor whites of the Cotton States" (202). In *Christian Reconstruction in the South* (1909), H. Paul Douglass tells of being offered Carroll's *Beast* through a door-to-door subscription campaign. Douglass attributes an unfortunate popularity to Carroll's book: "During the opening years of the twentieth century it has become the Scripture of tens of thousands of poor whites, and its doctrine is maintained with an appalling stubbornness and persistence" (114). This popularity was so disturbing to a group of Texas Baptists that they passed a resolution at their convention in 1902 condemning Carroll and urging "our ministers, teachers, and membership everywhere to expose and denounce the insulting and outrageous book, now circulating in the South" (Womack 3).

Although *The Negro a Beast* brought Carroll a certain notorious fame, he saw *The Tempter of Eve* as his crowning achievement, a grand summation of his views on Negro inhumanity.[15] Those views were absolutely congruent with a large cross section of public opinion on the "race question" at the turn of the century—particularly in the South. As George Fredrickson has argued, the period from the 1880s to around 1910 can be seen as struggle between two different strains of Southern racism: the negrophobes and the accommodationists. The negrophobes, who tended to dominate Southern opinion on the matter, saw blacks as a degenerating population, the inevitable victims of Darwin's "struggle for life."[16] This view depended on an image of the Negro as "beast," and it was this image that both of Carroll's works intended to document and propagate.

In pre-Adamite theory Carroll found the perfect path to such an image, as did others. As Forrest Wood notes, two works by Carroll's contemporaries adopted similar strategies: William Campbell's *Anthropology for the People: A Refutation of the Theory of the Adamic Race Origin of All Races, by a Caucasian* (1891) and Alexander Harvey Shannon's *Racial Integrity and Other Features of the Negro Population* (1907).[17] Further, Carroll provided himself with a degree of scientific respectability by citing selected passages from Alexander Winchell's

*Preadamites, or, a Demonstration of the Existence of Men before Adam* (1880). Winchell, a professor of geology and paleontology at the University of Michigan, provided Carroll with an accredited scientific grounding for his racist theology.[18]

*Tempter* adds new fuel to the pre-Adamite fire in two interesting ways. Although Carroll concurs with many of his predecessors in casting a Negro in the role of the tempter, he makes an intriguing revision in the drama of seduction, further highlighting the dangers of this imagined commerce between white and black in the garden. In addition, Carroll stands outside the previous antiblack theorizing by reason of his identity—he was, by some accounts, a black man. I want to leave this second distinction in suspension until the conclusion of this chapter.

The primary point of interest in *The Tempter of Eve* concerns the identity of the tempter promised in the work's title. Calling the numerous theories previously advanced on the question "more or less absurd," Carroll catalogs the various versions of the story, discrediting the notion of the serpent as an agent of the devil and the theory that the tempter was "an orang" capable of speech, also in the service of Satan (400). Since Carroll refuses to acknowledge that such a "Satanic Majesty" even exists (a product, he says, of the "grossest ignorance and superstition"), he insists that the tempter was an independent agent acting purely in the interest of coercing Eve into a violation of Divine law (402).

And who was this tempter? Who would have such an independent motivation? Like others before him, Carroll believes that the tempter was indeed a Negro. Unlike his predecessors, however, Carroll's tempter is "a *negress,* who served Eve in the capacity of maid servant" (402). Through a cunning work of verbal fiat, this Negress "instilled into [Eve's] mind distrust of God; engendered in her heart discontent with her position; and aroused in her nature the unholy ambition that she and her husband 'be as gods'" (404). According to Carroll, the Negress's clear status as an animal or beast required a duty in Adam and Eve "to control it in common with the rest of the animals" (405). Instead, "Eve accepted the negress as her counselor, and allowed the negress to control her" (405). The eating of the forbidden fruit was the couple's "second offense"; their first was accepting "the negress as their counselor," an act in which "they necessarily descended to social equality with her" (405–6). This chain of events, concludes Carroll, "reveals the startling fact that it was man's social equality with the negro that brought sin into the world" (406).

It is important to remember, however, that this "social equality" is not itself the ultimate sin. Rather, it simply makes possible (or even inevitable) the "most infamous and destructive crime known to the law of God": amalgamation (406). It is this possibility that Carroll's regendering of the tempter seeks to avoid, at least at the level of representation. We have seen the anxiety produced by the imaginings of Eve's encounter with a black man in the garden, and we have seen the various narratives that result from this anxiety, ranging from Ariel's relative silence on the issue to Prospero's more explicit depiction of sexual intercourse. Carroll avoids what Robert Young calls "the implicit politics of heterosexuality" (25) (and the corresponding implication that Eve has sexual desire) by substituting a cunning black woman for the oversexed black man. Blackness still stands in for seductive evil, but the terms of the seduction, and thus its meaning, have been changed. By shifting from the male/female scene to the female/female scene, Carroll neatly sidesteps the reproductive (i.e., amalgamationist) implications of the temptation.

Carroll's decision to include a visual representation of the temptation scene (see figure 1) offers another possible explanation for his view of the tempter as a woman.[19] This illustration literalizes the temptation scene far more graphically than the discursive versions of Carroll's predecessors. Its primary emphases are on the stark white/black contrast and the participants' nudity, a nudity always assumed in the accounts of the temptation but seldom rendered graphically. Eve's femininity is obvious, though hidden from the viewer by a rather surprising shock of hair that flows down her front. This hair, meant to hide breasts and genitalia from the viewer, does nothing, however, to cloak Eve's body from the tempter, as the partial appearance of Eve's left breast makes clear. The hair preserves the reader's modesty—not the tempter's, and not Eve's. In contrast to Eve, the tempter's gender is less obvious, and thus less in need of cover (a need rendered doubly unnecessary by "the Negro's" supposed lack of modesty). There is nothing very "feminine" about the tempter's appearance. The lines are straighter, in contrast to Eve's obvious curves, and there is the appearance of facial hair. The artist has attempted to bestow breasts on the tempter, but the effect is closer to that of well-developed pectorals.[20]

Figure 1. Eve and Her Tempter.

In short, the presence of this illustration in the midst of Carroll's argument accomplishes two things. The decision to illustrate graphically the temptation scene foregrounds a nudity that simultaneously requires the absence of black masculinity. What can be rendered in words (Prospero's version, for example) becomes more dangerous as a visual—in fact, becomes impossible. And so the visual representation requires the erasure of black male sexuality. However, the picture does not fully accomplish the goals that Carroll's argument requires. The narrative move from male tempter to female tempter, accomplished in words, does not succeed visually. It is as if the lingering vestiges of black male sexual threat resurface in the tempter's inability to appear female in the same way as Eve. Absent actual male genitalia, the tempter still appears male here, further encoding the historical conflation of blackness with maleness.[21]

On second look, however, it becomes apparent that male genitalia are not really absent from the illustration. The tempter's left forearm, protruding from the pelvis, stands in for the absent black penis. Its angle and size suggests semitumescence; the shape of the hand further signifies the absent presence of the glans. On third look, yet another transformation occurs. The tempter's left fist, the head of the penis, decidedly resembles the head of a snake—a serpent. What we have, then, is a triple conflation. That which Carroll works so hard to separate ultimately resists such disentangling. Attempting to show us a black female tempter, this illustration cannot do so without reinscribing the forcibly removed black penis, an inevitable return of the repressed. Further, this black male sexual threat—which in other accounts replaces the "absurd" notion of "serpent as tempter"—here becomes indistinguishable from the threat of snakes. The black woman whose very existence allows the picture disappears from it entirely, leaving only the cultural residue of black male sexuality: the protruding black penis, the soon-to-strike, yet somehow alluring, snake.[22]

The quick slippage from female to male is made possible by the rather surprising discontinuity between Carroll's tempter and the prevailing image of the black female during the nineteenth century, the "Hottentot Venus." Known primarily for her abnormally large buttocks and genitalia, the image of the Hottentot Venus crystallized white fears of black female sexuality as simultaneously pathological and corrupting, and did so primarily through the visual language of sexual difference. The fact that Carroll's tempter is far removed from this conventional iconography of black female lasciviousness further demonstrates that his interest in this black woman is to some extent a dodge—a cover for his greater interest in the sexual temptation of black masculinity. Giving us this "mannish" female tempter rather than the exaggerated, pathological, and more easily recognizable femininity of the Hottentot, Carroll keeps black masculinity relatively intact and retrievable.[23]

However, although the female tempter disappears from the scene, I do not want to suggest that the threat she represents isn't real. Black masculinity was not the only guise in which blackness produced defensive contortions in the white imaginary.[24] Taking a speculative leap, I want to attach a historical identity to Carroll's unnamed and menacing female tempter. By doing so, the values at stake in this representational/racial crisis will become clearer. Carroll's work appeared in historical proximity to the writing and activism of Ida B. Wells, perhaps the most famous and effective antilynching activist of the 1890s. Wells, an African American woman, achieved national prominence in 1892 when she published a letter in her own newspaper, the *Free Speech,* questioning the always assumed linkage between interracial rape and lynching. Wells attacked this linkage by granting (or more accurately, returning) to white women an agency denied them in what Robyn Wiegman has called the "rape mythos."[25] In an editorial that brought death threats against her, Wells offered the tabooed suggestion that alliances between white women and black men were rarely the result of force: "Nobody in this section of the country believes the old thread bare lie that Negro men rape white women. If Southern white men are not careful, they will over-reach themselves and public sentiment will have a reaction; a conclusion will then be reached which will be very damaging to the moral reputation of their women" (Wells, *Selected* 17). She put it more explicitly in an expanded version of this initial editorial: "White men lynch the offending Afro-American, not because he is a despoiler of virtue, but because he succumbs to the smiles of white women" (Wells, *Selected* 19).[26] Thinking the author of the editorial to be Wells's male business manager, J. L. Fleming, the Memphis *Scimitar* suggested that it was the "duty of the whites to tie the author to a stake, brand him on the forehead and perform a surgical operation on him with a pair of shears" (qtd. in Tucker 117). The Memphis *Commercial* wrote, "There are some things the Southern white man will not tolerate," such as "the obscene intimations" of this editorial (qtd. in Tucker 117). The *Scimitar*'s assumption of male authorship is both interesting and revealing, but for now, I simply want to highlight the visceral reaction that Wells's views brought forth. Why such a reaction? In part, Wells's work against lynching carried with it an implied acceptance of miscegenationist alliances, of voluntary sexual alliances between white women and black men. What lies at the heart of the hysterical male response that greeted

Wells's editorial is what Jacquelyn Dowd Hall calls "an uneasiness over the nature of white women's desires," an uneasiness that lynching and antimiscegenation laws attempt to mask (Hall, "Mind" 336). The strength of Wells's antilynching writing lies in her awareness of this uneasiness, and of its almost bottomless depth. As she writes in *A Red Record* (1895): "With the Southern white man, any mesalliance existing between a white woman and a colored man is a sufficient foundation for the charge of rape. The Southern white man says that it is impossible for a voluntary alliance to exist between a white woman and a colored man, and therefore, the fact of an alliance is a proof of force" (Wells, *Selected* 145). This statement suggestively returns us to the illustration included in Carroll's work. What are the real dynamics at work there? We begin with a black woman offering the fruit of knowledge to a white woman. If we emphasize the sameness of gender rather than the difference of race, we can see this moment as a potential feminist alliance that transgresses racial boundaries. The fruit of knowledge offered by the tempter suggests an entrance into the kind of public activism exemplified so clearly by Wells. We hear echoes of Carroll's fear in his disgusted claim that "Eve accepted the negress as her counselor" (405), "counselor" signifying not merely a shifted power dynamic but a new relationship of tutelage. In this reading, Wells brings politics to white women, and the result is an alliance that threatens both patriarchy and white supremacy.[27]

In an important sense, however, the fear that Wells's antilynching campaign might contaminate white women by inviting them into the political arena was radically misplaced. As Hazel Carby has argued, very few white women responded to the social critiques and activism of Wells, or to her sister activist Anna Julia Cooper (Carby, "Threshold" 270).[28] Rather, as Marjorie Spruill Wheeler has shown, white women came to political activism primarily through the suffrage movement. And in the South, white suffragists consistently deployed a rhetoric that worked *against* black/white feminist alliances by suggesting that the enfranchisement of white women would be the easiest cure for the "Negro problem," since this swelling of the ranks of white voters would counteract those black men enfranchised under the Fifteenth Amendment. Though the strategy ultimately failed, leading suffragists such as Rebecca Latimer Felton and Jean Gordon hoped that white racial fear might be the key to opening up the polls to white women, and in order to exploit this fear they consistently worked against the kind of reform pursued by Wells and others. Responding to the phenomenon of lynching, Felton said that "if it needs lynching to protect woman's dearest possession from the raving human beasts—then I say lynch: a thousand times a week if necessary" (Wheeler 103).

The suffragists' "southern strategy" can be traced to their awareness of what Wheeler calls "the historical association in the minds of white Southerners between advocacy of the rights of blacks and feminism" (111). The suffragists' failure to win the vote through their appeal to southern racism can be read as their inability to overcome this historical linkage between feminism and the postwar struggle for black civil rights. The South associated white female activism with the same type of threat to whiteness that African Americans represented, and this association was too strong and too entrenched to yield much ground during a period of significant racial anxiety.

In fact, the illustration accompanying Carroll's text makes this point clearly. Despite the shortage of real alliances between black and white women, the mere hint of such an alliance triggers a contortion in the fields of phallic power and authority. The presence of Wells and others as politically active black women causes the illustration to change shape, so as to represent more accurately the psychic threat at work. The illustrator's inability to represent a black woman without suggesting the contours of black male sexual threat has its analogue in the *Scimitar*'s assumption that the writer of the offending editorial must be a black man. The threat of castration (remember the "operation" and the "pair of shears"), which is intended to diminish the potency of black masculinity, actually endows the figure of Wells with that masculinity. This transmogrification is similar to that which enables what Wiegman calls the "lynch scenario," whereby castration actually depends on "an intense masculinization in the figure of the black male as mythically endowed rapist" (83). Castration is only necessary when its antithesis—the overly endowed phallic Negro—has secured a troubled home in the white male imaginary.

This "intense masculinization" accurately describes the graphic change from black woman to black man witnessed in the illustration accompanying Carroll's text. The double miscegenation of the scene (black woman/white woman; black man/white woman) calls forth a similarly doubled response. Out of this scene come the dual possibilities of transracial feminist alliances and transracial sexual alliances.

Both threaten the core of white supremacy, with its foundation in patriarchy. Just when Wells, whose antilynching activism implied an implicit approval of transracial sexual relationships, offers this forbidden knowledge, Eve disappears. In her place is the black man whom Wells allegedly wanted Eve to meet. The thing Carroll fears most from Eve's proximity to the proamalgamationist Wells comes into being before his eyes.

As the illustration demonstrates, distinctions insisted on and verbally enacted do not always behave themselves. Whereas Carroll sees history as one long conflict between God and man over "man's social, political, and religious equality" with the negro" (228), it is possible to see *The Tempter of Eve*—and all of those tracts and pamphlets that precede it—as one long attempt to both document and erase black male sexual threat from the white nation's collective unconscious, from that primal scene in the Garden of Eden.

### Identity/Identification

The attempted erasure of black masculinity brings me back to the question of Carroll's identity. Historical information concerning Carroll's identity is sketchy at best.[29] Carroll slips in and out of blackness, depending on the source. For example, Eric Sundquist describes him as a mulatto; Joel Williamson labels him a "black man." George Fredrickson and Forrest Wood make no mention of Carroll's race, leaving the assumption that he was white. John David Smith, editor of the collection that reprinted *The Tempter of Eve,* also provides no biographical information on Carroll and seems to assume that Carroll was white. M. B. Thompson, a black respondent to Carroll's work and Carroll's contemporary, also operates on the assumption that Carroll was white. Finally, Monroe Work's generally reliable *Bibliography of the Negro in Africa, and America* does not list Carroll as either a Negro or a mulatto.[30] In a picture of the author facing the title page of *Tempter* (see figure 2), Carroll appears to be a white man. But given the fact that appearance tells us very little about racial identity—especially as it is defined by the law—this picture cannot be said to solve the puzzle. Whether Carroll was black, white, or some combination of the two, I cannot assert with any assurance.

What I can do, however, is use my inability to locate Carroll along either side of the color line as an opportunity to say a few things about

Figure 2. Charles Carroll.

the kind of reading I have been engaged in, and its limits. When able to fix an author's identity as white, I seem to have no problem reading outward from that identity and working from assumptions that it supposedly provides. Presumably, I could do the same thing if I decided that Carroll was indeed black. For example, I could position him as a representative of the so-called self-hating negro, completely co-opted in mind and spirit by those whites whom he hopes to imitate. If I decided that he was a mulatto, I could argue that his fear and hatred of amalgamation amounts to nothing more than a theoretical attempt to jettison that part of himself that he sees as contamination. As a third option, I could suggest that Carroll's surreptitious strategy is to create blackness as a thing of cunning and power. By constructing this phantasmic figure of black power, Carroll ironically challenges whiteness as a site of knowledge and control. The "negro as beast," then, becomes a prototype for the Black Arts Movement of sixty years later, a character in search of a Baraka play.[31] Were it not for the overall tone of Carroll's massive work, this argument might be worthy of further consideration. As it stands, however, it does not ring true. My discomfort with all these readings raises questions about my obvious comfort in reading outward so confidently from whiteness as an identity. Is whiteness so neatly packaged that it comes with a clear list of ingredients and instructions? Well, yes and no. Carroll ventriloquizes whiteness as ideology, regardless of his skin color. Yet he becomes invisible within the hyperscriptedness of blackness as a false series of neat and legible categories. Not knowing where to "place" him, we don't quite know what to do with him.

And so I want to shift the emphasis from Carroll's identity to his identification, foregrounding the power of whiteness as ideology rather than skin color.[32] Although a white skin may make the ideology more useful to one, it is not necessary. As a way of seeing, a myth of power, an entire social structure, whiteness works precisely because of our inability to "read" Charles Carroll—our inability to contain him by easy categorization. In contrast to the popular wisdom that whiteness can only exist within a clearly readable, binary structure (a wisdom I want to complicate rather than discredit), I am suggesting that absent such a structure its power actually intensifies in proportion to its invisibility. Unable to locate whiteness in or on the body of Carroll, we are left with the realization that it works best as unattached abstraction, as that which flows through us without staying in any one place for too long. Like a fugitive, it knows to keep moving.

The dilemma that Carroll represents—both as racial ambiguity and theologian—extends far beyond the moment of his writing. Asked to discuss the subject of miscegenation twenty-three years after *The Tempter of Eve* was published, W. E. B. Du Bois wrote that "the question of the extent to which whites and blacks in the United States have mingled their blood, and the results of this inter-mingling, past, present and future, is, in many respects, the crux of the so-called Negro problem" (Du Bois, *Against* 96). The mingling of blood that Du Bois cites stands at the heart of the Garden, constituting the phantasmic prehistory of the specifically American mingling he addresses.

The scene that Carroll cannot bring himself to witness becomes his obsession, the crux of his problem.

But it is finally America's problem. In *Playing in the Dark,* Toni Morrison argues that "the fetishizing of color" undergirds much, if not all, of America's literary aesthetic (80). For Morrison, canonical American literature depends on the "thunderous, theatrical presence of black surrogacy—an informing, stabilizing, and disturbing element" of a specifically white literary imagination (13). By black surrogacy Morrison means the unacknowledged but never silent Africanist presence that fuels so many white imaginings of the so-called American experience. The classic American themes of freedom, autonomy, and individualism, Morrison argues, are in fact anything but free, autonomous, or individual. Rather, they only exist in the absent presence of their counterparts—slavery, for example—and thus are wholly dependent on blackness for their place at the center of white America's literary musings about itself.

If Morrison is right in her insistence on a "dark, abiding, signing Africanist presence" (5) in the American Eden (and I believe that she is), then of course there is a black tempter in the Garden. The nation could not imagine itself without him—or her, if we remember the illustration Carroll's argument depends on and the nervously disappeared threat of black female autonomy it represents. In the hands of Carroll's illustrator, we witness the birth and simultaneous death of the female tempter. Like a hazy hallucination, continually morphing in response to the needs and fears of the viewer, the cunning Negress never really stood much of a chance. The political threat she posed to Carroll's sense of white patriarchy was real, but it could not approach the visceral reaction guaranteed in the white imaginary by the "erect" and "stately" (to borrow Lester's adjectives) form of black male flesh. Given Carroll's cultural moment, the picture of Eve and the temptress is somehow off. There is something missing that the culture requires. And in the blink of an eye, the snaking black penis returns, and the picture is complete. With the return of the repressed, the harmony of form and content is restored. Not wanting to see a naked black man in the garden, Carroll lacked other options. The black man was there, in the beginning.

*Chapter Four*

# Charles Chesnutt and the Masturbating Boy: Onanism, Whiteness, and *The Marrow of Tradition*

Restless, grasping, unsatiated . . . —Ethiop (William J. Wilson)

On June 16, 1875, four days before his seventeenth birthday, Charles W. Chesnutt made the following entry in his journal: "I received yesterday a book for which I sent weeks ago. It is called 'The Sexual System and its Disorders.' The largest part is about venery and masturbation, really a bad habit. And if the dear Lord will help me and keep me in my good intentions I will break myself of it. God help me!" (*Journals* 64).[1] I quote this passage not to belabor the obvious—that the young Chesnutt was a masturbator—but to establish in the future author's own words the anxiety created by the various antimasturbatory discourses of the late nineteenth century. A "really bad habit," Chesnutt calls it, and he wasn't alone in thinking it so. It's hard to tell if he was able to keep to his word, though an entry of about three weeks later casts significant doubt on the success of his pledge. Missing his girlfriend Josie, Chesnutt writes, "I love the girl. . . . Here is a lock of her hair! I kiss the lock of hair and press it to [my] bosom[.] Would it were she!" (*Journals* 68). Seemingly lost in his reverie, Chesnutt stops abruptly: "What a fool I am, sitting here [blotted word] I thought I was more of a man than that" (*Journals* 69). Unmanned by whatever that blotted word might be—and we can only guess, really—Chesnutt is unable to finish his stream of thought and substitutes a few stanzas from a poem by Robert Burns instead, the poetic equivalent of a cold shower. And in the first line of his entry two days later, he writes simply, "I have made up my mind to try and do right, and to get religion if I can" (*Journals* 69).

With the publication in 1901 of his second novel, *The Marrow of*

*Tradition,* Chesnutt revisited, if only obliquely, the guilty pleasure of his earlier days, projecting onto the character of Tom Delamere the youthful desires he had himself struggled against. As a reader of self-help literature in his early years, Chesnutt was familiar with, and persuaded by, the antimasturbation sermons of his day. As a mature artist, he tapped that discourse and bent it to his own purposes. Through his implicit portrayal of Tom Delamere as a sexually degenerate and dissipated remnant of the white aristocracy, Chesnutt challenges the sexual integrity of white masculinity at the turn of the century and, in so doing, revises the white-supremacist mythos of black male sexual threat and white female victimization. Chesnutt shows the threat to whiteness to be situated primarily at the site of white masculinity, thus reversing the terms of representation established by countless late-nineteenth-century writers and popularized by Chesnutt's contemporary Thomas Dixon Jr., who made black sexual assaults on white womanhood his signature leitmotiv. Dixon's *The Leopard's Spots* shows whiteness threatened by black male sexual assaults on white womanhood. Chesnutt reroutes the energy of this alleged threat, revealing whiteness to be its own worst enemy. Countering the hysterical racism of his moment, Chesnutt redirects the public gaze from black male sexual threat to white male sexual degeneracy, recasting "the Negro as Beast" with "the white man as Masturbator." If Chesnutt could show white men acting outside a procreative economy, committing the sin of Onan at the site of a crumbling aristocracy, then whiteness would be revealed as a narcissistic and ultimately impotent cultural force.[2]

Although the terms of this revision are certainly specific to Chesnutt, it's useful to see him as something of a representative figure. The plot of *Marrow* exemplifies a strategy employed by other black writers who attempted to disrupt the literary economy of whiteness at the turn of the century. This strategy usually involved working within the parameters of popular fiction while trying to redirect popular (i.e., white) needs, fears, and anxieties. Like Frances Harper, Pauline Hopkins, and Sutton Griggs, Chesnutt found himself stuck between a rock and a white place. These and other African American writers wrestled with a difficult and central question: How is it possible to intervene in the literary economy of whiteness without simultaneously becoming invested in that economy? Chesnutt offers a striking example both of the possibilities and of the pitfalls of such an intervention and, in the process, complicates any easy assumptions about what it means to oppose the structures of whiteness versus what it means to inhabit those structures. In other words, although Chesnutt's novel obviously stands apart from the white-supremacist writings discussed in previous chapters, we shouldn't let this obvious difference create or rigidify a binary map of the ins and outs of whiteness. One isn't either in or out of whiteness; rather, one always exists in some relation to it.

Chesnutt reveals the inherent impotence of whiteness primarily through his portrayal of the novel's chief villain, Tom Delamere, the grandson of an elderly remnant of Wellington's most honored aristocracy. In Chesnutt's hands, Tom's grandfather represents the best of southern honor and chivalry, at least so far as such traits can extend in a slaveholding class. Tom, however, represents another type: the fallen and degenerating aristocrat. Tom wiles away his days waiting for an inheritance, gambling and losing far beyond his means, and drinking to the point of unconsciousness. Even worse, in order to pay off his gambling debts, he robs an elderly white female friend of the family and in the process causes her death. He commits the robbery while in blackface (minstrelsy being his one real talent), thereby displacing blame for the deed onto Sandy, a loyal servant of the Delamere family whom Tom particularly resembles when corked up. After the robbery Tom goes on an extended fishing trip, leaving Sandy at the mercy of a bloodthirsty lynch mob.

As if this isn't enough degeneracy for one white man to carry, Chesnutt pushes the point by calling Tom's masculinity into question at every opportunity. Though Chesnutt calls Tom the "handsomest young man in Wellington" (16), the compliment turns out to be rather backhanded. As Chesnutt writes, "No discriminating observer would have characterized his beauty as manly. It conveyed no impression of strength, but did possess a certain element, feline rather than feminine, which subtly negatived the idea of manliness" (16). So that we don't miss the point, Chesnutt later compares Tom's degeneration to "that of a well-bred woman who has started on the downward path" (165). The fact that "Delamere" is French for "of the mother" seals the deal.

The terms of this degeneration, dependent as they are on Tom's questionable masculinity, are central to Chesnutt's larger point about the declining value of whiteness as a cultural commodity. In *To Wake the Nations,* Eric Sundquist points out this "feminization" of Tom

Delamere and briefly discusses its role in Chesnutt's representation of white villainy (431). In so doing, however, he fails to notice a related and intriguing fact, one to which I intend to apply some pressure. Put simply, Tom Delamere is a masturbator.

How do we know this? When suspicion about the identity of the murderer finally shifts from Sandy to Tom, old Mr. Delamere makes a thorough search of Tom's room, looking for evidence. Breaking open a locked drawer in Tom's bureau, he finds what he is looking for: "Thrown together in disorderly confusion were bottles of wine and whiskey; soiled packs of cards; a dice-box with dice; a box of poker chips, several revolvers, and a number of photographs and paper-covered books at which the old gentleman merely glanced to ascertain their nature" (222). What interests me most about this montage of nineteenth-century debauchery are the last items—the cryptically described photos and paperbacks. We don't have to work too hard to reach the same conclusion that Mr. Delamere quickly reaches: Tom collects pornography. And though Chesnutt refuses to name the practice that accompanies such a collection—particularly when the collection is found in the bedroom of a twenty-one-year-old single male—I think we're well within our interpretive license to assume that Tom is guilty of that nineteenth-century vice, onanism. Tom is a spiller of seed.[3]

This scene of the room search and subsequent discovery can be viewed as a stock scene, one repeated again and again in various genres, but particularly in novels of detection and vice.[4] It reveals more than "evidence" of a crime; rather, it reveals the identity of the room's inhabitant. Behavior adds up to more than the sum of its parts, as Tom Delamere becomes a type of person rather than a simple series of behaviors or desires. This formulation echoes an oft-quoted passage from Foucault: "The nineteenth-century homosexual became a personage, a past, a case history, and a childhood, in addition to being a type of life, a life form, and a morphology, with an indiscreet anatomy and possibly a mysterious physiology" (*History* 43). Although I'm not categorizing Tom as Foucault's new creature, the "homosexual," Foucault's main point about identity applies equally to "all those minor perverts whom nineteenth-century psychiatrists entomologized by giving them strange baptismal names" (*History* 43). For Chesnutt, Tom is a type of person; the materials found in his room attach themselves to its occupant in a way that signifies beyond his actions (murder, for example) to his or her identity (racist, say, or masturbator).

The association of reading materials with various forms of villainy gets repeated again and again in late-nineteenth-century literature. In *Traps for the Young,* New York City vice officer and moralist Anthony Comstock tells of a twenty-one-year-old man (Tom's age, by the way) who was arrested "for sending most obscene and foul matter by mail" (28). The nature of this material can only be guessed, since Comstock refuses to elaborate. The young man asks to visit his room to change clothes before he's taken away: "While in his room, and up to the moment of the finding of a pile of . . . vile five-cent story-papers in one corner, he had been perfectly cool and stolid. When these were discovered, he started as though a nest of adders had been opened and said with great feeling, 'There! that's what has cursed me! That has brought me to this'" (Comstock 28–29). We don't have to accept the young man's logic (is he speaking the truth or merely tapping a cultural prejudice as a way to redirect blame?) to note the connection between this scene and the one involving Tom. Cheap fiction becomes, in both cases, the proof of guilt.

Nor do we need to know the exact nature of Tom's "paper-covered books" to make the claim I'm making. The mere presence of paperbacks in Tom's room casts a variety of suspicions on him, particularly given the nineteenth-century fear of "the evil book"—of dangerous reading. In his widely read *The Student's Manual* (1857), the Reverend John Todd devotes a whole chapter to reading, in which he warns against "bad books": "These are to be found every where," he says, and he entreats his "young readers never to look at one—never to open one. They will leave a stain upon the soul which can never be removed. I have known these books secreted in the rooms of students, and lent from one to another" (146).

If Todd's warning about the "stain" that results from bad books doesn't sufficiently connect his bibliophobia to antimasturbatory discourse, the fact that he includes a passage on the evils of masturbation in the middle of his chapter on reading certainly does. As G. J. Barker-Benfield points out, Todd's section on masturbation is in Latin and includes his lament for those masturbators who have come to "premature death, some in academic halls, some very quickly after leaving college, and some having graduated with honors" (170). The association of masturbatory degeneracy with the ivied halls of academia widens the connection between literacy and autoeroticism, whereby not just "bad books" but any reading whatsoever leads to this most pernicious of sins.[5]

The terms of this relation between literacy and sexual degeneracy become clearer in the following passage from Comstock's work, in which he issues an injunction to those who would do right by their children: "It is manly and speaks of moral courage for the right, for you to enter a dignified protest against the dissemination of this literary poison" (42). Though Comstock is speaking specifically of five- and ten-cent paperbacks, his emphasis on the "literary" as a type of poison is certainly suggestive, as is his use of the word *dissemination*. Literature becomes a type of fluid that can enter one's body through its dissemination. Bad books become both an incitement to spill semen and the semen itself.[6] This double bind defines not only the erotiphobic tenor of Todd's and Comstock's writing but its inherent homosocial fascination, as writing and reading enact a sexualized commerce between male authors and male students and between those boys who pass these books from one to another in their ivy-halled academia. The added texture of homosexual possibility can be seen as yet another reason for the vigorous attacks on masturbation itself, which is, after all, a fundamental and widely popular example of same-sex sexual commerce.

In the case of Tom's collection of pictures and books, I am interested in what we may learn if we linger over this admittedly parenthetical moment in Chesnutt's novel. I would be content to leave it in parentheses if Chesnutt did not, time and time again, establish solid connections between the novel's racial subject matter and its preoccupation with a so-called proper masculinity, which foregrounds how *Marrow* enacts a deliberative conversation about the nature and shape of both sexual and political manhood. This preoccupation crosses and recrosses the color line. In the white romance plot, the reader, like Clara Carteret, is faced with the conflicting choice between Tom Delamere and the young newspaper editor, Lee Ellis. Which version of white masculinity is to prevail? In the novel's re-creation of the Wilmington violence of 1898, the reader is offered conflicting paths of black male resistance to white racism: Josh Green, the militant and violent insurgent, or Dr. Miller, the voice of reason and accommodation. Which "type" of black masculinity can be counted on to save the day? And in the story of Major Carteret's attempt to ensure the future of the white aristocracy through a male heir, Chesnutt links impotence with whiteness in a way that finds its parallel in Tom's masturbatory degeneracy. By raising these questions of a so-called proper masculinity in the dual context of Tom Delamere's downward spiral and Major Carteret's desire for a male heir, Chesnutt stages his version of black literary uplift on the increasingly enfeebled bodies of white men. Whether this setting is the best backdrop for such a project is a question I return to in my conclusion.

## White Manhood

The linkage between masturbation and degeneracy has a long and hoary history. As a moral and scientific discourse, its inception can be established with the publication in 1700 of *Onania: or, the Heinous Sin of Self-Pollution, and All Its Frightful Consequences.* This work, which went through multiple editions in several languages, spawned others, from Daniel Defoe's *Conjugal Lewdness, or, Matrimonial Whoredom* to Samuel Tissot's Latin work, *Onanism: A Dissertation on the Maladies Brought on by Masturbation,* which was quickly translated into English, German, and Italian. Although these works were printed and popular in America, masturbation phobia didn't reach its zenith in the States until the nineteenth-century proliferation of guidebooks for the young—primers designed to help adolescents (particularly male adolescents) navigate that tricky terrain into adulthood. Todd's *The Student's Manual,* with its Latin lecture on the evils of masturbation, was the most popular of these guides. The Latin was necessary, presumably, to avoid causing the very thing being lectured against.[7]

That this antimasturbatory discourse occurred under the name of Onan is actually the result of a serious and possibly willful misreading. According to Genesis, Onan's older brother Er, who had just married Tamar, "was wicked in the sight of the LORD," who therefore slew him (Gen. 38.7). Onan was then commanded by his father to marry Tamar so that he may "raise up seed to thy brother" (Gen. 38.8). The command accords with Levirate law, which required that a man must help the wife of his dead brother conceive (Taylor 57). Onan, however, was apparently uncomfortable with his prescribed role: "And Onan knew that the seed should not be his; and it came to pass, when he went in unto his brother's wife, that he spilled it on the ground, lest that he should give seed to his brother. And the thing which he did displeased the LORD: wherefore he slew him also" (Gen. 38.9–10). As this passage shows, Onan's sin wasn't masturbation, but coitus interruptus—the refusal to carry through with his father's procreative injunction.[8]

Why was masturbation so dangerous? In the third edition of his *Studies in the Psychology of Sex* (1920), Havelock Ellis lists the commonly accepted by-products of a masturbatory lifestyle. They include "insanity, epilepsy, numerous forms of eye disease, strange sensations at the top of the head, neuralgia, asthma, cardiac murmurs, acne and other forms of cutaneous eruptions, eyes directed upward and sideways, intermittent functional deafness, redness of nose, warts on the hands in women, and hallucinations of smell and hearing" (249–50). Although Ellis doubts that masturbation is the only cause of these tribulations, he does state that there is "good reason to believe that some of them may be the results of masturbation acting on an imperfectly healthy organism" (250). The specific symptoms that Ellis catalogs were often conflated under the more general diagnosis of "degeneration," which could signify physical, mental, and moral deterioration (MacDonald 429). In 1887, for example, an American cleric warned young men and women that masturbation "debilitates the physical constitution by a wasting of the vital power, it impairs the mental faculties, it corrupts the moral nature, it sears and petrifies the conscience" (Spence 444). Writing a few decades earlier, a French doctor called masturbation "a disease that degrades man, poisons the happiness of his best days, and ravages society" (Lallemand ii). And in 1870 an American doctor wrote that masturbation is "a habit more pernicious to the intellectual man (setting aside the physical disabilities resulting therefrom), than any other habit to which he is usually addicted. Tobacco and alcohol are not so potent to rob man of all the high prerogatives of manhood, as this humiliating, self-abasing vice" (Gardner, *Conjugal* 69–70). I quote these examples at some length because of the richness of their rhetoric, a rhetoric that sounds strikingly similar to the language of white racism and fear at the turn of the century. Masturbation "ravages society"; it deprives one of the "prerogatives of manhood." These two phrases, especially considered in the context of Chesnutt's writing, bear specifically racial coding. The language of American racism, particularly in the 1890s, focused on a different type of sexual threat—the "burly black brute"—whose favorite activity, it seems, was ravaging. And these "prerogatives of manhood," it must be pointed out, were prerogatives of white man-

Chesnutt admits to having read and been influenced by it, it also economically dramatizes the connection between anti-onanism and that late-century crisis of American masculinity suggested by Gardner's phrase, "prerogatives of manhood." As Eric Sundquist has argued, the last decades of the nineteenth century witnessed what could be called a new cult of southern masculinity, a renewed cultural focus on heroic white male bodies born in direct response to the perceived loss of white male power. As Sundquist argues, by the early 1880s the South had developed a "ceremonial celebration of southern heroes" that worked to replace the white manhood cut down during the war (*To Wake* 425). The emphasis was specifically on the re-creation and reimagining of a rapidly waning southern virility. Staged through speaking tours by the likes of Jefferson Davis, veterans' parades, festivals, and reunions, the "new South" dedicated itself to reifying a lost masculinity that came to stand for the energy and hope of a white southern future (Sundquist, *To Wake* 425). That Chesnutt chose to emphasize Tom Delamere as an example of degenerate white male sexuality reveals his strategic sense of how white masculinity was currently being constructed and the burdens it was being asked to carry.

These burdens assumed graphic shape in Abbey's work. By reversing the terms of sexual threat, Chesnutt not only removed white women from the equation but in so doing wrote black men out of the "Negro as beast" narrative.[10] By transferring the burden of purity and procreativity to white men, Chesnutt created a new "beast," the white, impotent, sexual degenerate. Illustrations accompanying Abbey's text reveal the graphic power of this new threat, a power Chesnutt hoped would erase from the public's eye that previously more visible threat of the leering black rapist. Chesnutt textualized Abbey's graphic representations of the "monster masturbator" (see figure 3), to borrow a phrase from Jonathan Katz (45), so that they may view in the public imagination with those bestial Negroes popularized by Dixon, Page, and countless others. These images of lifeless, shriveled-up white men shift the terms of the conversation about white health. Chesnutt focuses his attention not on white women as the last bastion of white moral and physical integrity but on white men as the carriers of whiteness in its liquid forms: blood and semen. Although writers like Dixon tended to emphasize the former, thus laying the burden on white women, Chesnutt, with his emphasis on

16-year-old masturbator, left;
21-year-old abstainer, right.

50-year-old masturbator, left;
70-year-old abstainer, right.

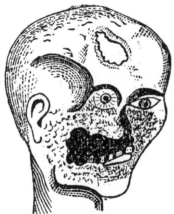

## Ulceration.

"Ulceration," resulting from
a lack of sexual integrity.

Figure 3. From *The Sexual System and Its Derangements,* Dr. E. C. Abbey (1875).

various forms of male impotency, found a way to shift the terrain of racial generation so that white men became the primary burden bearers.

The shift I'm describing can be better understood if we first remember that the force of white racism in America, especially in the late nineteenth century, depended on an obsession with the miraculous properties of blood—its imagined ability to shape and define not only a distinct identity but a specific kind of person. As Richard Dyer writes, "In [white-supremacist] discourses, all blood and genes carry mental properties, but, invisibly, white blood and genes carry more intelligence, more spirit of enterprise, more moral refinement" (*White* 24). Blood—a fluid and thus transferable property—holds the key to racial identity and therefore must be guarded with extreme care. In his 1906 work, *The Color Line: A Brief in Behalf of the Unborn,* William Benjamin Smith asks a fundamental question: What, at this moment of white racial crisis, does the South stand for? The answer, according to Smith, is simple: "She stands for *blood,* for the 'continuous germplasma' of the Caucasian Race" (5).[11]

In this war over blood, Smith, Dixon, and others located the weakest defense at the site of white womanhood and thus insisted on the family as the most necessary of social forms. The "instinct of the family," Smith writes, "with its imperious and uncompromising demand for absolute female chastity," is the only bulwark against racial mongrelization (9). If a white man degrades himself through sexual contact with a black woman, the offense is "individual and limited" (10). "For the female dissolute," however, "there is no forgiveness," for the offense of the woman is "general, and strikes mortally at the existence of the family itself" (10). As long as white women remain within the protection of the family, be it as mother, daughter, or wife, whiteness can breathe easier.

Writing against the racist assumptions of this siege mentality, Chesnutt offers a way to think through its reversal, astutely positioning white men as the weak link of racial integrity. For if blood is the tenor of American racism, then semen is its vehicle. Dr. Augustus Gardner, an admirer of John Todd and author of the 1872 volume *Our Children,* defined sperm as "the purest extract of the blood" and "the concentrated powers of [man's] perfected being" (*Our* 162). In his *Treatise on the Nature and Treatment of Seminal Diseases,* Homer Bostwick called semen "the very cream and essence of the blood" (81).

And Dr. Abbey, Chesnutt's primary authority on such matters, referred to chronic masturbators as those whose "life-blood [was] fast ebbing away" (2). Given this view of semen as the crystallization of corporeal power, and given Tom's status as masturbator, the seed he's busy spilling isn't mere fluid, but rather the essence of whiteness.

### Procreative Economies/Racial Economies

That whiteness is the dwindling quantity here—specifically aristocratic whiteness—is made clearer by Tom's inability to play his proper role in *Marrow*'s rather thin romance plot. Early in the novel the reader learns of an unspoken but widely known engagement between Tom Delamere and Clara Carteret, an engagement approved of and wished for by both families. Chesnutt adds the requisite rival for Clara's affections in the person of Lee Ellis, a young newspaper editor of no particular breeding, but a hard worker. Tom's degeneration first becomes an issue when his behavior—mainly card playing and drinking—is brought to the attention of Mr. Carteret, Clara's half-brother and the leader of the local campaign for white supremacy. Carteret lectures Tom on "the danger of extremes, and the beauty of moderation" (93). Tom is so shaken by this lecture and the possibility that his vices may become widely known that he begs Clara for an earlier wedding date than previously intended. As he tells her, "My home life is not ideal,—grandfather is an old, weak man, and the house needs the refining and softening influence of a lady's presence. I do not love club life; its ideals are not elevating. With you by my side, dearest, I should be preserved from every influence except the purest and the best" (101–2). The hastening of sexual union that Tom suggests would get the approval of many anti-onanists of the eighteenth and nineteenth century, who often prescribed marriage as the best cure for the spiritual and physical evils attendant on self-pollution (MacDonald 425).[12] Tom's particular vices make marriage a greater necessity. Since only a woman can save him from his sins, Clara and Mr. Carteret consent to a shorter engagement.

This new arrangement, however, is not to last long. Scheduled to meet Tom at a seaside resort, Clara and her party are unable to locate him. Sent in search of him, Ellis finds Tom in the following unfortunate position: "Sprawling on a lounge, with flushed face and disheveled hair, his collar unfastened, his vest buttoned awry, lay Tom

Delamere, breathing stertorously, in what seemed a drunken sleep. Lest there be any doubt of the cause of his condition, the fingers of his right hand had remained clasped mechanically around the neck of a bottle which lay across his bosom" (146). But Chesnutt's "seemed" and "lest there be any doubt" actually raise further doubt as to the cause of Tom's condition, particularly given the argument I am pursuing here. Although alcohol is the explicitly named culprit, this picture of Tom also suggests what the anti-onanists referred to as post-masturbatory lassitude. The flushed face and general dishevelment, not to mention Tom's right hand still clasped around the neck of a bottle, suggest a young man both in urgent need of the marriage he has prescribed for himself, but also someone unfit for such a marriage. Though Ellis gallantly hides Tom's condition from Clara, the evening becomes the turning point in their relationship and is largely responsible for Clara's eventual cancellation of the engagement. The union that the families hoped would ensure and revitalize the future of Wellington's white aristocracy is not to be. If we remember that Onan's sin wasn't masturbation but coitus interruptus—the refusal to carry through with his father's procreative injunction—Tom's inability to couple with Clara Carteret is even more significant. Like Onan, Tom thwarts the procreative urge.

Tom's inability to play by the rules of both social and literary convention—his inability to enter the procreative economy required by both the culture and the novel form—gets mirrored in other ways in the novel, further building Chesnutt's case against white masculinity. The tenuous position of white masculinity is nowhere more apparent than in the novel's preoccupation with the male heir born to the Carterets, named Theodore Felix, but called Dodie (Chesnutt wastes no time in stressing the diminution of the white family line). During labor Mrs. Carteret's health is very weak, and the opening chapter carries the scent of "death and funeral wreaths" more than it does the hope of new birth (1). Despite Chesnutt's ominous foreshadowing, however, Dodie somehow manages to get born, becoming the catalyst for a renewed pride in "race, class, and family" (28). Dodie is, to put it simply, the novel's great white hope—quite a burden for a baby to bear. And before the first chapter closes, Chesnutt raises serious questions about Dodie's fitness for the job. Old Mammy Jane, the family's loyal black servant, discovers a mole under Dodie's left ear and reads this immediately as an omen of evil to come. "Had the baby been black," Chesnutt tells us, Mammy Jane "would unhesitatingly have named, as his ultimate fate, a not uncommon form of taking off, usually resultant upon the infraction of certain laws, or, in these swift modern days, upon too violent a departure from established social customs" (10). Jane is thinking, of course, of lynching, which Chesnutt euphemistically renames "judicial strangulation" (10). That Dodie should be born into such a narrative, even if its author is Mammy Jane's superstition, casts significant doubt on his future status as upholder of white purity. Within the novel's first pages, Chesnutt suggests the possibility of white racial slippage, as a narrative reserved for blacks gets associated with Dodie, the great white hope.

As it turns out, Dodie's journey through the novel is precarious indeed. He comes close to strangling on a piece of his rattle, and he almost gets dropped out a window. More importantly, the novel ends with his life in grave danger, the victim of a critical case of croup.[13] Because of the race riot that Carteret's campaign for white supremacy has instigated, the only doctor available to treat Dodie is Dr. Miller, a black doctor who has lost his own son in the violence. Though Miller initially refuses his services, he eventually agrees to help, consenting to his wife's wishes. The novel ends with the suggestion that Miller has arrived in time to save Dodie.

This cluster of events economically encapsulates Chesnutt's agenda. Upon Dodie's feeble shoulders depends the future of white masculinity, and thus the future of the Carteret family line. If Dodie dies, Mr. Carteret is denied an heir, and since the doctor has already told him that his wife cannot bear another pregnancy, such an event would render him, at least figuratively, impotent. This contingency is bound up in the dangerous proximity of his whiteness to the novel's various forms of blackness. Dodie's mole carries with it the taint of color, and Carteret's absolute dependence on Dr. Miller for the salvation of his family's white future signifies the even greater dependence of whiteness on blackness. White manhood, then—both its present and its future—is threatened by racial slippage and sexual nonprocreativity.

The crucial question, however, concerns the nature of the relationship between these two threats. Returning to Tom Delamere, the similarity between his dilemma and Mr. Carteret's becomes instructive. Both characters suffer the erosion of their procreative possibility, but Tom's case offers a better opportunity to understand how Chesnutt stages the downward spiral of the white aristocracy through the push and pull of race and gender. Although I've discussed what I'm calling Tom's masturbatory degeneracy, I haven't yet explored its relationship to his only real talent—"coon impersonations" (96). His talent for blackface minstrelsy has him in large social demand. As I've already mentioned, it is a talent that almost allows him to get away with murder. My question is this: what is the relationship between Tom's ability to "become" black and his *in*ability to enter the procreative economy of whiteness? If we return to the scene of Tom's room, we find that both of these aberrations are written into the identity of the place where Tom lives. Having already discovered the suspicious pictures and paperbacks, the nail in Tom's coffin is delivered when Mr. Delamere discovers a wrapper from a package of burnt cork. In the same interpretive and discursive space, then, we find evidence of Tom's sexual depravity as well as his ability to "become" black.

Chesnutt's comparison of Tom to a "well-bred woman who has started on the downward path" (165) provides a good place to tease out this connection between sexual and racial degeneracy. Chesnutt obviously links Tom's downfall to what could be called an erosion of "the gender line," that demarcation signaling the territorial break between masculinity and femininity. In the same passage, however, Chesnutt references a more famous turn-of-the-century border marker, the color line, and in so doing helps us understand the link I am trying to establish here between Tom's sexual degeneracy and his slippage toward blackness. "Delamere had made rapid headway" toward the bottom limit of social depravity, Chesnutt tells us: "Having hitherto played with sin, his servant had now become his master, and held him in an iron grip" (165). The language of servant and master in this passage is broadly instructive and bears a significant relation to the rhetoric of masturbatory degeneracy. Chesnutt may in fact have remembered this rhetoric from his reading of Dr. Abbey so many years earlier. Referring to masturbation, Abbey writes, "practiced usually with a total ignorance of its dire consequences, it soon obtains a *complete mastery* over him and he is a *chained victim* more miserable and abject than the galley slave" (11–12). Having "played with sin," Tom finds himself in the position of servant, far from his ancestral and racial heritage of mastery. And since, as Abbey's language demonstrates, the categories of servant and master are themselves racially the way to America's racial future. *Marrow*, like Hopkins's *Contending Forces* (1900), stages a contest between various possibilities of black leadership. These novels self-consciously constitute themselves as literary conversations about black political responses to white racism at the turn of the century.

Of course, literary uplift was not without its own political valences. The work of uplifting the race was an admittedly bourgeois project and depended on Progressive-era notions of civilization and hierarchy. As Kevin Gaines has argued, this dependence brought with it a certain complicity in racist and imperialist agendas. For Gaines, Hopkins represents "the dilemma of black writers torn between the desperate aspiration for the status of respectability, a strategy which tacitly endorsed prevailing assumptions of racial and social hierarchy, and the struggle to articulate an autonomous and oppositional racial group consciousness" (449–50). Gaines's point about Hopkins applies equally to Chesnutt, who found himself in this same difficult position between respectability and protest, between middle-class strivings and under-class anger. It is a point that the African American novelist Sutton Elbert Griggs makes in *The Hindered Hand; or, The Reign of the Repressionist* (1905), a literary response to Dixon's *The Leopard's Spots*. In this novel, Earl Bluefield, a black man who represents a "militant" response to white racism, becomes suspicious of his friend Ensal's commitment to his race once Ensal falls in love and contemplates marriage. As Griggs writes, "Earl had all along rejoiced in Ensal's determination to remain unmarried, fearing that family life might add to his conservatism" (50). From Earl's point of view, marriage not only cements one's entry into middle-class respectability but simultaneously divorces one from the radical edge of racial struggle.

This tension gets played out in *Marrow* as a contest between the antithetical characters of Josh Green, the working-class militant, and Dr. Miller, the middle-class accommodationist.[15] When Green and his men turn to Miller in hopes that he will lead their response to the white mob, Miller offers pragmatic counsel: "Keep quiet, boys, and trust in God. You won't gain anything by resistance" (282). "My advice is not heroic," he continues, "but I think it is wise" (283).[16] Though "every manly instinct urged him to go forward and take up the cause of these leaderless people," Miller opts for a different kind of manhood, one defined by strategic accommodation rather than violence (282). After the riot, Chesnutt himself weighs in on the question of black resistance, offering the following interpretation of the events: "The negroes of Wellington, with the exception of Josh Green and his party, had not behaved bravely on this critical day in their history; but those who had fought were dead, to the last man; those who had sought safety in flight or concealment were alive to tell the tale" (316). That Green ends up dead while Miller is left to act heroically at novel's end would seem to signal Chesnutt's answer to the question he has posed for himself: what kind of blackness—or more specifically, black masculinity—is most constructive at this moment of violent and deadly racism? [17]

Yet Chesnutt's conclusion is not without a healthy dose of ambivalence. We should remember that Miller's heroism is in the service of the novel's great white hope. His decision to help save baby Dodie suggests a rebirth of the white future so jeopardized throughout the novel. Though Chesnutt leaves Dodie's fate in doubt, the suggestion remains that Dodie will indeed survive, thereby enacting the antithetical fate of Miller's own son, who is dead by novel's end.

I do not mean to suggest that Chesnutt is unaware of the ironies involved in Miller's dilemma here. In fact, Chesnutt stages this scene so as to wind the situation's irony to its highest pitch, allowing Miller a mastery over the Carterets at the very moment in which he ensures the future of the Carteret name. However, the novel's ending does tell us something about the class politics of black uplift that is related to my earlier reading of the novel's dependence on an anti-onanist discourse. Miller's middle-class strivings depend, both at the level of politics and narrative, on the death of Josh Green. In order for Miller's choices to be the proper ones, Josh's choices must be punished. Likewise, Miller's assumption of the only kind of black masculinity left standing at novel's end depends on the previously demonized masculinities of Major Carteret and Tom Delamere, both of whose manhood is called into question precisely because of its potential nonprocreativity. Although I don't take issue with Chesnutt's demonization of these bigoted white characters, the terms of that demonization may ultimately backfire, since they are embedded in the same middle-class assumptions that keep Miller and other blacks locked out of both social and political power. Defined against the normative influence of middle-class whiteness, Tom Delamere and Dr. Miller are both in trouble.[18]

The double bind Chesnutt has created is made painfully clear when

Miller's own manhood is called into question at the very moment he becomes black manhood's last, best hope in the novel. The novel's ending enacts a reversal, as Major Carteret is finally assured of his procreative status as the upholder of whiteness while Miller is suddenly denied his procreative role as father through the death of his son. The white-supremacist violence shifts the burden of impotence from Carteret to Miller, from white to black.

Thus the issue of procreative sexuality gets complicated both by the politics of black uplift and by the violence of white supremacy. Although the masculine future of whiteness is called into question throughout the novel, it is the masculine future of blackness that ends up dead. That Miller is the only black man left standing in Wellington at novel's end is a hollow victory for everyone but himself and Major Carteret, who needs him to save his son. Chesnutt, I think, was aware of that hollowness, but was compelled by other forces to enact it nonetheless.

And what were these other forces? Namely, Chesnutt's hope that he could make novel writing a tool of political and social change. It is at the site of this lifelong goal that *Marrow* can be said to have failed. Having earlier adopted Stowe's *Uncle Tom's Cabin* and Albert Tourgée's *A Fool's Errand* as examples of racial novels that had a significant social impact, Chesnutt set out to achieve the same. "If I do write," he told his journal in 1880, "I shall write for a purpose, a high, holy purpose, and this will inspire me to greater effort" (139). This "high, holy purpose" was the white uplift I mentioned earlier. The difficulty of that project may have sealed its failure at the moment of its conception. William Andrews has accurately described the dilemma Chesnutt faced: "Notoriety as a black polemicist in literature, a 'protest' writer against racial injustice, would not open the doors of the popular magazines and publishing houses further to him. Somehow Chesnutt had to adapt his most original but most potentially controversial subject matter, the caste system in the South, to the exigencies of the genteel white literary market. Somehow he had to make his revisionist point without sounding like a controversialist" (93). Yet in the exact same literary climate an overtly racist writer like Thomas Dixon Jr. was able to conquer that "genteel white literary market" while deliberately courting the very controversy that Chesnutt had to eschew. And Stowe, Chesnutt's model of fifty years earlier, had made the same kind of conquest with an antiracist appeal that the nation did not necessarily want to hear. Of this trilogy of racial writing, all intended for and directed at the largest audience possible, Chesnutt's was the only work not to find that audience. As Andrews argues, this failure can at least partially be explained by the difficulty of the project he set for himself: transforming the morality of American whites, suggesting future paths for American blacks, all within the confines of pleasant, noncontroversial literature.

Although Andrews's point certainly offers one way to understand Chesnutt's commercial failure, there may be an even more intrinsic cause at work, one based in the principles of middle-class uplift that Chesnutt dedicated himself to. This type of moral uplift required an appeal to certain "universal" values—justice and honor, for example. Chesnutt's problem was that such an appeal depended on the same normative codes of middle-class America that worked to exclude him from that American franchise. To elevate white America meant to reinforce (albeit unintentionally) the kind of whiteness that has no room for blackness, since blackness would always be defined as something fundamentally outside the normative necessity of the white middle class. The values Chesnutt held dear—both as a hopeful citizen of an American democracy and as a black artist hoping to achieve widespread commercial success—ultimately became his undoing.

Ironically, Chesnutt weaves this dilemma into the novel itself, and he does so in a way that clearly reveals the costs of relying too much on the white middle class. Included in the novel's diverse array of black characters are Mammy Jane and her grandson Jerry, both of whom have pledged their devotion and loyalty to the Carteret family. Chesnutt draws these characters as minstrel throwbacks to an earlier time, dedicated to achieving what power they can by currying favor with whites at the expense of other blacks. As Mammy Jane gushes to Major Carteret, "I's fetch my gran'son' Jerry up ter be 'umble, an' keep in 'is place. An' I tells dese other niggers dat ef dey'd do de same, an' not crowd de w'ite folks, dey'd git ernuff ter eat, an' live out deir days in peace an' comfort" (44). Chesnutt critiques such a position in the simplest way possible: he kills off both Mammy Jane and Jerry in the white-supremacist violence that ends the novel. Further, he emphasizes that their sycophantic relationship to the white middle class buys them no protection whatsoever. Jerry dies in a hale of gunfire, waving a white handkerchief as his flag of surrender and calling out to Major Carteret for protection. Carteret never hears Jerry's voice. As Chesnutt writes, Carteret "had just become aware that a negro was being killed, though he did not know whom" (307). Chesnutt's point is clear: Jerry's allegiance to whiteness—his faith in the white flag of black surrender—gets him nothing but death.

Although I do not mean to suggest that Jane and Jerry are analogs for Chesnutt himself—Chesnutt's critique of these characters is too strong to make this a real possibility—I do think that their doomed allegiance to white middle-class values has something to tell us about Chesnutt's own relationship to those values. As a novelist Chesnutt is far removed from the turban-headed figure of Mammy Jane or the shuffling and mumbling Jerry. Yet like these characters Chesnutt imagines that the white middle class can somehow ensure the future of blackness. His faith as a novelist lies in the middle ground as a place from which to launch a revolution in racial thinking. But the middle ground, by definition, can have nothing to do with revolution. Revolution does not happen at the center.

This tension can productively return us to Chesnutt's specific relationship to anti-onanist discourses, especially if we foreground the anti-onanist project as yet another kind of uplift. Chesnutt's literary project of black and white uplift has its earlier moment in Chesnutt's adolescent uplift, where he vowed to stop masturbation so as to avoid the plagues enumerated by Dr. Abbey. The sixteen-year-old Chesnutt learned from Abbey that only those who avoid masturbation could become the "divines, statesmen, legislators, judges, scientists, agriculturists, mechanics [and] thinkers" of tomorrow (Abbey 8). The avoidance of self-abuse was the first step in a young man's journey up—up into the middle class, up into the annals of great and important men.

This journey was complicated, of course, by Chesnutt's status as a black man living in a white-supremacist culture, which raises an important question about the racial politics of Chesnutt's adherence to Dr. Abbey's advice. Was there a racial valence to Abbey's version of middle-class uplift? To get at this question, we might ask who Abbey and other anti-onanists imagined their audience to be. Were they writing to white boys, black boys, or both? Although race is never mentioned in Abbey's pamphlet, the pictures that accompany the text show white people exclusively. Abbey's refusal to explicitly engage the question of racial identity may result from a strange sense in which the question was already answered before it was asked, especially if we consider for a moment how race and sexuality play off of one another to establish identity. Although antimasturbatory rhetoric was obviously intended to stop young men and women from masturbating, it was more generally intended to desex these adolescents, to halt their entrance into a sexualized society. This rhetoric, then, was one piece of a larger Victorian logic, whereby sexuality was meant to be strictly procreative, and anything that broke the bounds of procreativity was dangerous and menacing. And what kind of sexuality was more dangerous and menacing to late-nineteenth-century middle-class whiteness than black sexuality? In fact, the phrase "black sexuality" is redundant, since in the white-supremacist culture I am describing blackness is always already sexual, whether it takes the shape of the ravenous black woman or the lustful and overpowering black man. In our attempt to map the unspoken racial logic of anti-onanist discourse, we can imagine this attempted desexing as, at the same time, a whitening, an attempt to rescue white youth from the overflowing sexuality attached to blackness. Books like Dr. Abbey's, without specifically saying so, hoped to introduce young men into two interrelated structures: the narrative of middle-class uplift and success, and whiteness as an untainted, nonsexual procreative contract.

Tom Delamere's behavior violates the various moralities that make whiteness a successful disciplinary force. Yet by demonizing Tom, Chesnutt oddly locates himself within that disciplinary force and, in so doing, threatens the political project that *Marrow* was intended to serve. Anti-onanism, a discourse of uplift meant for fine, upstanding white youth, was borrowed by this fine, upstanding black youth — borrowed twice in fact, once as a teenager and again as a novelist. In both cases it can be said to have failed. Although there is no evidence in the first instance, I remain skeptical. In the second, it is simply a fact that *Marrow* never achieved the sales Chesnutt hoped for. This failure took a noticeable toll on Chesnutt and may have been largely responsible for his increased efforts in nonliterary pursuits. As he put it in a letter to his publisher, "I am beginning to suspect that the public as a rule does not care for books in which the principal characters are colored people, or with a striking sympathy with that race as contrasted to the white race" (Chesnutt, *"To Be"* 171). Chesnutt admitted that there may be better ways to help his people than "writing books about them which the public does not care for" (*"To Be"* 171).

In these moments of self-doubt, Chesnutt glimpsed his own participation in what must have seemed like an increasingly masturbatory literary economy. As a young man Chesnutt decided on fiction writing as a way to lead himself and his country to a greater racial justice, to a greater American society. Unfortunately, Chesnutt never found an audience at the time of his writing.[19] He was left alone with his imagination, which certainly contained the seeds of a brighter future. What he lacked was a culture fertile enough to make those seeds generative and productive. Chesnutt failed in his ultimate goal but, in so failing, gave future generations a brilliant and biting picture of whiteness as a pathology—curable, but mortally close to the brink. Dodie's dilemma at the novel's conclusion—gasping for breath, but awaiting the curative power of Dr. Miller—is simultaneously whiteness's dilemma. That Chesnutt may be rushing to the aid of both is the novel's final irony.

## White Heterosexuality

I've referred throughout this chapter to the "procreative economy of whiteness," and I've consciously resisted other language—in particular, language that would describe whiteness as not only a procreative economy but a heterosexual economy. Why this resistance? Isn't procreation merely standing in metonymically for something like a newly emerged turn-of-the-century heterosexuality, and, if this is the case, why not call this thing what it is: white heterosexuality? In closing this chapter I want to attempt an answer to this question.

When Chesnutt wrote *Marrow*, sexual behaviors and the names for those behaviors were very much up in the air. As I pointed out in the introduction, *heterosexuality* as a term made its textual debut in the United States in 1892, and it did so as both perversion and norm. For Kiernan it signified deviancy; for Krafft-Ebing it began to take on its modern shape as the standard by which sexualities and persons are regulated and judged. This slippage occurred amid a shift away from a purely procreative justification for sexual desire and toward something like Freud's pleasure principle, where heterosexuality signals the destination of sexual maturation, the healthy state that defines other states as immature, sick, perverse. The shift was subtle; as Katz writes, "a different-sex erotic ideal was slipped silently into modern consciousness" (67).

*Marrow* stands at the heart of this liminal period, this era of the anxious and conflicted birth of heterosexuality. Tom Delamere represents the public face of a transition. He is clearly perverse; he's incapable of entering a procreative economy, and he channels his sexual desire with contempt for that economy. He represents a move from procreation to pleasure, where the pathways of sexual desire become less constrained, less responsible, less productive.

Chesnutt understands that this shift has consequences for the maintenance of whiteness. Contrary to my suggestion in chapters 1 and 2 of an analogous relationship between whiteness and heterosexuality, here I want to suggest that *Marrow* shows whiteness to be threatened by the newly emergent heterosexuality. If heterosexuality signifies a newly defined, normalized eroticism—one liberated from procreative imperatives—it breaks the allegedly closed circuit of white reproduction. It locates desire outside family, race, and nation. In other words, white heterosexuality necessarily risks contamination. Through the complicated pathways of nonprocreative desire, it opens whiteness up to nonwhite pollution. So when Richard Dyer describes heterosexuality as "the cradle of whiteness" (*White* 140), he gets it only half right, missing some of the ambivalence that characterizes the relationship between these two structures of desire. Chesnutt, by contrast, helps us understand that ambivalence, how whiteness seeks not only to cradle heterosexuality but to expel it, to abject it. The nervous relationship between whiteness and heterosexuality becomes more explicit in the next chapter, where we will see what happens when a male/female procreative standard becomes something else—becomes, in fact, the homoerotic imperative of a new white nation.

# Chapter Five

# White Sex: Thomas Dixon Jr.
# and the Erotics of White Supremacy

They [whites] are obsessed with sex and discuss it interminably, with
long dissertations on their moods and reactions, complexes and subli-
mations. Life to them seems to be one perpetual psychoanalytical clinic.
This appears to the Negro observer as a sure sign of sexual debility. . . . It
is difficult to imagine a group of intelligent Negroes sprawling around a
drawing-room, consuming cigarettes and synthetic gin while discussing
their complexes and inhibitions. — George S. Schuyler

The self-same thing they will abhor
One way, and long another for.
— Samuel Butler's *Hudibras,* quoted
by Kelly Miller in "As to the
Leopard's Spots, an Open Letter to
Thomas Dixon, Jr."

White supremacy is a fleshy ideology; it's very much about bodies.
An obsession with skin color is only the most obvious manifestation
of this. Put simply, for all its fascination with color, white supremacy is
perhaps equally driven by its fascination with sex. Black female bodies
are sites of ungovernable lasciviousness. White female bodies become
sexual territory to be displayed, fought over, and protected. Black
male bodies, sometimes disguised in the white imaginary as female
bodies, hold multiple fascinations as sexual threat, sexual perversion,
and objects of unspeakable desire. And white male bodies, for all their
apparent invisibility, depend absolutely on the bodies of others to feed
the various systems that their invisibility maintains.

To flesh out these abstractions, think about rape and lynching.

Both have been ritualized instruments for the maintenance of racist and masculinist domination. White men, so the story goes, must protect their virginal white women from burly black brutes. Black men must be lynched in order to deter others. The lynching, of course, can become the arena for a ritual of sexual fascination and revulsion—what Young calls the "ambivalent double gesture of repulsion and attraction" (115)—as castration offers the socially sanctioned opportunity for white men to traffic in black male genitalia. A fleshy ideology indeed.

As this example makes clear, white supremacy can be usefully understood as a homosocial network (or, to borrow a suggestive coinage from Dana Nelson, a "homopolitical" network)—one in which white men engage in forms of sexual and sexualized commerce with other white men and black men over the bodies of white women.[1] My goal here is to get a clearer sense of the sexual negotiations involved in the maintenance of white supremacy by focusing on those instances in Thomas Dixon Jr.'s *The Leopard's Spots: A Romance of the White Man's Burden—1865–1900* (1902) in which the homosociality of racial desire and hatred is most transparent. At almost every turn in the plot, Dixon finds himself narratively dependent on white women and black men in positions of exchange. In the novel's obsession with alleged black sexual crimes against white women, white men use these women as a battleground for their complicated skirmishes with black men. In the novel's larger allegiance to the conventional romance plot, a white woman is given from white man to white man in marriage, a move that ultimately consolidates white male political power at the expense of both white women and black men, dramatizing the extent to which white supremacy is more properly understood as white-male supremacy. In *The Leopard's Spots,* then, the campaign for white supremacy and racial purity takes place over and through the bodies of these marginalized mediaries, transitional phrases in the clumsy syntax of patriarchy and racial domination.[2]

*Swordplay*

Dixon's novel begins as the remnants of the Confederate army make their way back to their homes and families. One soldier who won't be returning, however, is Colonel Charles Gaston, who was killed in an assault against Yankee forces near Richmond. Returning in his stead—and as his proxy—is his loyal slave Nelse, who had promised the colonel that he would deliver his personal effects to his wife and son. One item that Nelse delivers to the now-widowed Mrs. Gaston is the colonel's sword: "When the boy was asleep in the nursery adjoining her room, [Mrs. Gaston] quietly closed the door, took the sword of her dead lover-husband in her lap, and looked long and tenderly at it. On the hilt she pressed her lips in a lingering kiss" (12).

This exchange of the sword—from Colonel Gaston, through Nelse, and to Mrs. Gaston—is already densely textured with images of power, sexuality, and racial bodies. The sword, after all, had been used to slay Yankees in a war to preserve southern institutions, one of which, of course, was slavery, the very system that considered Nelse property. But as it turns out, Mrs. Gaston isn't the designated recipient of the sword; young Charlie Gaston is, as his now-dead father explains in a letter to him: "My Darling Boy: I send by you Nelse [*sic*] my watch and sword. It will be all I can bequeath to you from the wreck that will follow the war. This sword was your great-grandfather's. He held it as he charged up the heights of King's Mountain against Ferguson and helped to carve this nation out of a wilderness" (13). The sword, then, makes its journey through a four-generational line of white male descent over and through the bodies of Nelse and Mrs. Gaston. It does so in the service of nation building and white supremacy, aiding first at the birth of an American nation, and now the beginnings of an Aryan nation.[3]

Of course, the sword isn't just a sword—either in defense of homeland on the battlefield or being gently caressed and kissed in Mrs. Gaston's lap. The phallic imagery is inescapable and revealing. As Gayle Rubin has argued, the phallus can be seen as a "set of meanings conferred upon the penis" (190), "a symbolic object which is exchanged within and between families" (191). Rehearsing this Lacanian narrative, Rubin continues: "In the cycle of exchange manifested by the Oedipal complex, the phallus passes through the medium of women from one man to another—from father to son. . . . It is an expression of the transmission of male dominance. It passes through women and settles upon men" (192). Rubin's (and Lacan's) linkage of this transfer of male authority with the crisis of the Oedipal complex is significant here, given Dixon's rather intense treatment of mother/son bonds in the novel. After his father's death, young Charlie Gaston's

sole dream is to fill his father's role as constant companion and pro-
tector of his mother. The frequency with which he kisses his mother's
eyes and lips is striking. For Mrs. Gaston, the blurring of roles has
already occurred, as she emerges from her delirium and imagines that
Charlie is in fact her dead husband: "'Dearie, I knew you would
come,' she murmured. 'They told me you were dead; but I knew
better'" (30).[4]

It is also significant that in Dixon's novel the sword passes not only
through a woman but through a black man. This is particularly fitting,
since the sword symbolizes both patriarchal and racial domination.
That Dixon requires Nelse for this transfer of authority from father to
son will acquire thematic importance later in the novel when Charlie
grows up to be the leading racist demagogue in the state, a position
that lands him in the governor's mansion by novel's end. That he first
secures his "manhood" through the agency of a black man provides
an early indicator of the ways in which this manhood will be exercised later.

The specifically racial context of this transfer overdetermines the
Lacanian framework that Rubin offers, reorienting its flow of power
and control. As I demonstrate later in deploying Eve Sedgwick's
notion of homosociality in a specifically racialized setting, this triangular dance with the sword doesn't merely effect the "transmission
of male dominance." Rather, it effects the transfer of white dominance, gendered male, thereby excluding both Mrs. Gaston and Nelse,
who have no real narrative function in Dixon's novel once this transfer
is complete.

As the transfer shows, white male political power is effected only
through the forced participation of white women and black men in
positions of exchange. These homosocial exchanges, and the erotic
iconography that enables them, suggestively dramatize the historical
workings of white male racial desire. *The Leopard's Spots* can be usefully
seen as a fictional exegesis of certain theoretical assumptions that, all
too often, remain at the level of abstract assertion. We know, for example, that race and gender are interdependent categories. We know
that the battles fought over racial domination are simultaneously
struggles to preserve various patriarchal systems of organization and
control. But behind these theoretical commonplaces lie much more
complicated schemes. Gaps remain that must be accounted for. *The
Leopard's Spots* is important precisely because it helps us identify and

fill in these gaps, to make real the assumptions that guide our critical thinking.

But it also helps us take these assumptions a crucial step further. Dixon's novel is, when all is said and done, a story about white racial desire. In this sense, following Sedgwick, it's helpful to see desire as the name for a structure, an "affective or social force, the glue, even when its manifestation is hostility or hatred or something less emotively charged, that shapes an important relationship" (*Between* 2). For Dixon, white desire—with all its contradictions and instabilities—becomes the narrative eros, the novel's primary erotic site. The energy generated there circulates in various directions, but finally between white men, as they contest for and around the bodies of white women and black men. The question that concerns me here is a version of one that Sedgwick has already asked: "What does it mean—what difference does it make—when a social or political relationship is sexualized?" (*Between* 5).

What Dixon's novel requires, however, is a reorientation of this question, one that simultaneously exposes its limits as well as its potential. As Susan Fraiman has suggested, Sedgwick's primary focus on homosociality as a way to live same-sex desire in a radically homophobic culture often elides the ways in which the homosocial can function absent desire as its primary energy. As Fraiman puts it, "Men's ties to each other are frequently characterized not simply by uneasy desire but also by political domination, on one side, and resistance to that domination, on the other—that race and racism, for example, cross and complicate relations between men so that the erotic, while undoubtedly present, may no longer be the predominant affect or agenda" (68).[5] In Dixon's novel the "predominant affect or agenda" is the creation and maintenance of white supremacy. Homosociality, fueled by hatred but more often than not rendered as same-sex eroticism, is ultimately what makes that white supremacy possible.[6]

To reshape Sedgwick's question, then, or more accurately, to provide its antecedent: before asking what difference it makes "when a social or political relationship is sexualized," we must first ask what the terms of the "social" and "political" are. And if the answer is that the social and political are defined primarily by race—as they are in Dixon's novel—the sexualization of these relationships will depend not so much on relations of gender but on relations of color. As with Rubin's use of Lacan, race overdetermines the triangular framework we're working within, thereby exposing the centrality of race to sexuality as a system of control. For as Fraiman again reminds us, "women are often at the nexus of male struggles that, however, eroticized, are more fully explained in terms of attempts both to enforce and to oppose white supremacy" (69). *The Leopard's Spots* offers an ideal opportunity to explore the twists and turns of triangulated desire in a culture in which race is never not an issue.

### Sex into Politics

Equipped with sword, young Charlie Gaston grows up to be a handsome man, widely renowned for his oratorical prowess. This reputation earns him an invitation to memorialize the Confederate dead at Memorial Day celebrations in Independence, North Carolina, about one hundred miles from his own home in Hambright. Dixon stages the Memorial Day activities as a festival of flowers, women, and "that oldest religion of the ages, the worship of the dead" (212). The events building up to Charlie's speech metonymically describe a different kind of buildup—one overtly sexual. In this chapter, called "The One Woman," Dixon literalizes the white-male romance with white supremacy by highlighting the erotic appeal behind the worship of fallen men.[7]

Charlie is met at his hotel by a procession formed in his honor, consisting of "two long rows of beautiful girls holding great bouquets of flowers" (211). As Charlie approaches, "this long double line of beauty and sweetness opened, and escorted gravely by the oldest General of the Confederacy present, [Charlie] walked through the mile of smiling girls and flowers. Behind him tramped the veterans, some with one arm, some with wooden legs" (211). After this contingent of phallic-limbed men penetrates the long avenue of flower-bedecked southern belles, "the double line close[s]" behind them (211). Here, Dixon tells us, "was the throbbing soul of the South, keeping fresh the love of her heroic dead" (211). Sexual penetration, laden with nationalist desire, is the key to racial memory.

When the time comes for Charlie's speech, his oratorical energies flow in response to this reverence for the Confederate dead. He is overtaken by visions of "his father's straight, soldierly figure, . . . and with him all the silent hosts that now bivouacked with the dead" (212). His voice "was penetrated and thrilled with thought packed until it burst into the flame of speech" (212). About fifteen minutes into his speech, however, his inspiration shifts, as he discovers in the crowd "the face of the One Woman of all his dreams" (213). This is Sallie Worth, about whom Charlie had been told in advance by his match-making guardian, Mrs. Durham. From the moment he spots her, "every word that he uttered was spoken for her" (213). Yet although Charlie's primary inspiration shifts from dead white men to Sallie Worth, the basic components of that inspiration remain the same. His romance with the dead, which had initially animated his speech, finds new form in Sallie, who "sat as still as death, . . . her fluted red lips parted" (213). Thus Sallie Worth, by novel's end to be Charlie's wife, first appears to him as the passive image of the death he is eulogizing. At the height of his oratorical frenzy appears this vision of Sallie, who somehow symbolizes everything that his speech implies: the reverence for a South that no longer exists, the worship of young dead men.

Charlie's speech, which marks the beginning of his political ambitions, blurs the political in interesting ways. An eroticized fusion of nostalgia and romance, its plea in defense of the Old South depends primarily on sexual energy. More specifically, it is sex itself, from the moment Charlie and the veterans penetrate the South's "throbbing soul," to the moment when Charlie himself is "penetrated and thrilled" with the thought of dead men, and finally to Charlie's vision of Sallie, "still as death," but waiting in eager expectation. Even before Charlie becomes a leader of the party devoted to rescuing North Carolina from "negro domination," we see the intermingling of sex and racial nostalgia, male action and female passivity.

As this chapter gives way to the next (interestingly called "The Morning of Love," reversing the love of mourning we've just witnessed) it becomes clear that for all the novel's sexual imagery, sex itself is a site of great anxiety in Dixon's narrative. In various ways, *The Leopard's Spots* shows us that Charlie's anxiety is imbricated with Dixon's own, that Dixon is anxious over feminine power or, more specifically, the release of this power in overtly racialized contexts.[8] In this context, it's worth noting the narrative sleight of hand that brings about the return of one of Stowe's most memorable characters, Simon Legree. Dixon's working title for the novel was actually *The Rise of Simon Legree,* and though the title changed, this character from Stowe's novel figures prominently in Dixon's reconstructed South. Too smart to make Legree an antiblack hero (the force and currency of Stowe's representation would make this close to impossible), Dixon instead capitalizes on Stowe's demonization of Legree, making him even more degenerate than before. His political allegiances, of course, have shifted, as Legree, who even in Stowe's novel hailed from Vermont, now works for and represents carpetbagger corruption. If the reader wonders how Legree was able to make this transformation undetected, Dixon provides a succinct, though very telling, explanation: "He shaved clean, and dressed as a German emigrant woman. He wore dresses for two years, did house work, milked the cows and cut wood for a good natured old German. He paid for his board, and passed for a sister, just from the old country" (85). To put it mildly, this passage is densely textured. Although Legree is obviously racialized here, Dixon does so in a doubly coded fashion, exposing the proximity between Legree as German and Legree as "black threat." Late in the novel, for example, Reverend Durham, Charlie's friend and adviser, warns a preacher from Boston of the "possible day when a flood of foreign anarchy threatens the foundations of the Republic" (337). "Against that day," Durham continues, "we will preserve the South!" (337). Thus the South must remain racially pure so that it can redeem a nation moving toward mongrelization. Although Legree's German-sister routine certainly stands in for this northern mongrelization, the threat he represents to "the Republic" is no different from the threat blacks represent to the South. Dixon economically casts Legree—now an outcast from the South—as both foreign and internal threat to the nation's racial life.

To account for Legree in drag raises another matter. On the surface, by putting Legree in a dress, Dixon further demonizes him by calling into question that most sacred of properties, his masculinity. Cross-dressing suggests a sexual kink for Dixon, which, when coupled with Legree's newfound German roots, casts him beyond the pale. It's worth mentioning, however, that Dixon isn't totally opposed to so-called sexual kinks, as a rather surprising eruption of sadomasochism late in the novel makes clear. In an exchange between Sallie Worth and Mrs. Durham, Sallie jokingly refers to her father's belief that Charlie "will try to whip me in five years" (432). Mrs. Durham responds, "Yes, he will whip you, but they will be love licks and you will cry for more" (432). In this context, Legree's cross-dressing offends less because of its sexual transgressiveness than because of its association with the female. Legree's demonization isn't fully accomplished until he is simultaneously tainted by foreign ethnicity and demasculinization. He becomes a condensed site of Dixon's racialized anxiety over female sexuality.

This anxiety spills over onto Charlie, who, during his courtship of Sallie, is deeply troubled by her love of dancing, a love Charlie most certainly does not share.[9] Charlie's refusal to attend a dance that Sallie has organized causes an early crisis in their relationship. On the surface, his refusal results from pride and is connected to issues of race and class. Admitting to his lack of a proper suit for the ball, Charlie tells Sallie that he "can't afford to buy one for this occasion. I couldn't be nigger enough to hire one, so that's the end of it" (251). Charlie may be poor, but he's still "white" as long as he refuses to play the role of someone able to afford finer clothes. Connected to the issue of attire, however, is a more fundamental reason for Charlie's refusal to enter the ballroom: "If I could only dance, I assure you I'd try to fill every number of your card. Not being able to do so, I simply decline to make a fool of myself" (252). Tortured by the vision of Sallie dancing with other men, Dixon shows Charlie to be fully aware of what he is missing: "He knew the dance was a social convention, of course. But its deep Nature significance he knew also. . . . that it was the actual touch of the human body, with rhythmic movement, set to the passionate music of love. This he knew was the deep secret of the fascination of the dance for the boy and the girl, and the man and the woman" (341). Thinking of Sallie in the arms of another man, Charlie "never knew how deeply he hated dancing before" (252). Although jealousy supplies one reason for his feeling, his admitted inability to dance suggests a more complicated picture.

Charlie is, to put it bluntly, the archetypal early-twentieth-century heterosexual man. Jonathan Katz describes a basic conflict at the heart of the newly emerged heterosexuality, one in which the flesh and the spirit wage an unresolvable battle. As Katz puts it, "The heterosexual ideal displays, from its inception, a fundamental tension. Heterosexual affirmation encounters a basic conflict between the pleasures of the flesh and the yearning for a pure, fleshless spirit. The sexual in the hetero ideal was a troublemaker from the start" (30). Dixon portrays Charlie as the poster boy for this tension: "His whole life had been dominated by this dream of an ideal love. For it he had denied himself the indulgences that his college mates and young associates had taken as a matter of course. . . . He had kept away from women. He had given his body and soul to the service of his Ideal, and bent every energy to the development of his mind that he might grasp with more power its sweetness and beauty when realised. Did it pay? The Flesh was shrieking this question now into the face of the Spirit" (343). Charlie is paralyzed by the heterosexual ideal, by its irreconcilable longings toward pleasure and purity.

Given Charlie's tortured inner debate over the relative merits of physical and "spiritual" love, and given the role we've already seen Sallie play in Charlie's burgeoning political career, it's worth asking where sexuality appears in this novel and what kind of sex it seems to be (or more accurately, what kind of sex it doesn't appear to be). Charlie cannot participate in "the rhythmic touch of the human body" (252) when it is shrouded in the "social convention" of dancing. He can, however, call up and respond to sexual energy in his political oratory, as his speeches become the repository for the desire thwarted by Charlie's inability to dance.

The novel, in effect, demands this transfer of (hetero) sexual energy into the realm of politics, where it can fuel a different kind of fire. With this move, the shift from specifically heterosexual energy to something more like Sedgwick's notion of homosocial desire is fully enacted. The shift is enabled by Allan McLeod, who is to become Charlie's chief political adversary, as well as a romantic threat to Charlie's aspirations in the direction of Sallie Worth. A protégé of General Worth's, McLeod has long been an intimate of Sallie and works throughout the novel to secure her hand in marriage. Despite Sallie's indifference to McLeod, Charlie is clearly worried over this possible rival.

In one of his frequent periods of despondency over his hopes with Sallie, Charlie visits Reverend Durham for advice. The lines between romantic and political rivalry blur considerably when Durham counsels Charlie on the proper course to be taken. Durham tells him that it's fine for women to despair over thwarted love, since for a woman such as Sallie "love is the center of gravity of all life" (308). With "normal men," however, things are different. As Durham puts is, "The center of gravity of a strong man's life as a whole is not in love and the emotions, but in justice and intellect and their expression in the wider social relations" (308).[10] One almost feels in Durham's words a deliberate pull away from heterosexuality—away from those sexual energies that deplete one's masculinity. Charlie immediately seizes on this advice, vowing to "fight this coalition of McLeod and the farmers every inch" (308). His romantic rivalry with McLeod seamlessly becomes a political rivalry. Charlie must quit thinking about Sallie and think instead about politics. Given the mechanics of this transfer, it makes sense that the political arena becomes the site of the novel's sexual confrontations and relations. The linkage of sexuality to Charlie's white-supremacist political future becomes a staging ground for homosocial exchanges in which women are given from men to men in the service of political consolidation, and on behalf of white rule.

### Black Dick

Before looking at the second of Charlie's two main speeches in the novel, the one that finally wins him Sallie's hand in marriage, I want to focus briefly on Dixon's treatment of white women as threatened commodities—as needing white male (and consequently phallic) protection against black sexual terror. We can see this most clearly in the case of Tom Camp, a poor white man whose daughter Annie is engaged to marry a man by the name of Hose Norman. Within minutes of the couple being pronounced "man and wife" (125), the wedding party is interrupted by a gang of "Negro troopers" who carry Annie away as "Hose's mountain boys" come to the rescue waving pistols (126). Though Tom succeeds in knocking down one of the black terrorists (he takes off the wooden leg he acquired during the war and uses it as a club), the rest of the gang carries Annie into the woods.[11] An urgent colloquy between Hose's boys and Tom Camp leaves no doubt as to the price affixed to the woman in this system of exchange between men: " 'What shall we do, Tom? If we shoot we may kill Annie?' 'Shoot, men! My God, shoot! There are things worse than death!' " (125). The boys shoot, and a bullet hits Annie in her temple, leaving "a round hole from which a scarlet stream was running down her white throat" (126). The men carry Annie back to the cabin and lay her "across the bed in the room that had been made sweet and tidy for the bride and groom" (127). Dixon's eroticization of Annie's wound—it suggests the imminent loss of her virginity that the black troop both interrupted and allegedly intended—makes it fitting that her bleeding body is carried to the bridal bed. And the troopers' entrance only minutes after the solemnization of the wedding vows creates the perfect juxtaposition through which to examine the sexual politics of this abduction scene. Although Dixon asks the reader to imagine the black men as potential rapists, it's actually the white men who shoot Annie through the skull. It is the collective discharge of their guns that creates Annie's wound, a wound obviously suggesting her loss of virginity. Tom's order to shoot and the wound that results suggest not black sexual assault but incest, the inverse of and defense against miscegenation.

Yet the timing of the scene points out a black usurpation of white male privilege, as Hose, whose name is significantly phallic, is denied his legitimate role as deflowerer. The entrance of the black troops simultaneously disrupts the narrative of white heterosexual union and produces the rape narrative, which seems to require that union as a necessary first step in the attempted sexual assault that follows. According to the narrative logic, the attempted rape can only occur once Hose and Annie are wed, suggesting that the victimization of Annie isn't truly significant until it is simultaneously a crime against Hose, whose woman has been taken from him. For Dixon, Annie signifies only in relation to her conflicted status as dead bride—both to Hose and, more generally, the white male South. Although I don't mean to conflate rape with sex, in Dixon's portrayal the scene isn't sexualized until the entrance of the black troopers. Despite Hose's name, Annie's wound doesn't occur until blackness comes knocking.

As Tom attempts to comfort the boys who fired the bullets, however, he paints a picture not of death but of salvation: "It's all right, boys. You've been my friends to-night. You've saved my little gal. I want to shake hands with you and thank you. If you hadn't been here—My God, I can't think of what would 'a happened! Now it's all right. She's safe in God's hands!" (126). Annie's martyrdom, which precipitates a rebirth of the Ku Klux Klan, becomes the excuse for a new wave of white terrorism of blacks, and the clear signal to white women is that they must fear not only the potential black rapist but also the avenging white mob that may find it necessary to sacrifice them in the name of racial purity.[12]

The narrative deployment of the feminine corpse is Elisabeth Bronfen's subject in *Over Her Dead Body: Death, Femininity and the Aesthetic*. For Bronfen, "death and femininity serve as ciphers for other values, as privileged tropes" (xi). This is clearly the case in Dixon's novel, where the imagined violation and eroticized death of Annie function purely in the service of other narrative energies: namely, the revitalization of white manhood and white-supremacist fervor. According to Bronfen, the martyrdom of feminine bodies serves a dual purpose, enabling "the production of art and the re-establishment of order" (xii–xiii). While alive, Annie's existence as threatened white commodity threatens whiteness itself; as a violated corpse, she no longer threatens the order of whiteness and instead buttresses that order by rallying the white troops.

Dixon's focus on death as an honorable alternative to rape by a black man dramatically underscores the extent to which women in this novel function solely as signifiers in exchanges between men. These exchanges are both ideological and erotic, as the ideological becomes a site of a differently directed erotic energy. Annie Camp is not a woman; rather, she stands in for such abstract notions as "the South" or the quintessence of "Southern womanhood." In either case, her character exists as an idea, not a person. Lying at the root of his portrayal is a displaced erotics, a transference of heterosexual desire in which racial domination becomes the narrative eros, as white women are denied bodies while the bodies of black men are forced to work overtime.

Not content with one scene of supposed black sexual villainy, later in the novel Dixon again offers Tom Camp's family as the site of racial assault. Flora Camp, the daughter Mrs. Camp gave her husband to take the place of Annie, is allegedly raped by a friend of Charlie Gaston, a black man named Dick (described in the novel's "List of Characters" as "an unsolved riddle").[13] Though we do not witness the rape itself, Dixon shows the reader the battered body of Flora, her skull crushed in with a rock. As with Annie, the rape is signified indirectly through a trickle of blood: "Down her little white bare leg was still running fresh and warm the tiniest scarlet thread of blood. It was too plain, the terrible crime that had been committed" (371).[14]

It's interesting that Dixon stages both these assaults at the site of the Camp family, primarily because the Camps occupy a clearly visible class position within the novel's array of white characters. Distinguished from the formerly aristocratic Gastons, but friendly to them, the Camps represent that degree of whiteness existing in closest proximity to blackness. Dixon seems to suggest that the black assault on whiteness will happen first at this border territory, this liminal state between border-transgressing blacks and the "best" that whiteness has to offer. The Camps, then, occupy the front line in the war to preserve the unsullied future of whiteness. It's therefore less than a coincidence that Tom Camp is the most virulent racist in the novel.[15]

Within this context, Dixon's restaging of sexual assault—a repetition almost exact in its details—recalls Freud's notion of repetition either as the return of something that has been repressed or a mechanism through which one achieves mastery over a painful circumstance.[16] It's useful to see Dixon's narrative technique as an instance of the second possibility. Dixon as author seeks control over the trauma of his characters, a trauma not limited to this specific instance, but part of a larger anxiety over whiteness as a stable property, an anxiety that Dixon certainly shares.

The anxiety over whiteness takes its more specific shape in Dixon's concern over black male genitalia. That Dixon offers Dick as the "rapist" in the assault on Flora shows a revealing conflation of black men with actual genitalia. (*Dick* as slang for *penis* had currency in American usage as early as 1888.) [17] As Frantz Fanon has written in an oft-quoted passage, this conflation reveals a white psychopathology in which "one is no longer aware of the Negro but only of a penis; the Negro is eclipsed. He is turned into a penis. He *is* a penis" (170). Given his name and the crime of which he is accused, Dixon's description of Dick as "an unsolved riddle" highlights, to an almost ludicrous extent, white male anxiety over black male sexuality. That Dixon goes to the trouble of naming his black male rapist "Dick" reveals the extent to which black men were felt as sexual threats not only by white women but by white men, who felt it necessary to respond in kind.

In the wake of Annie's death, for example, Reverend Durham seeks to comfort Tom Camp over his loss by telling him that "your child has not died in vain," since "a few things like this will be the trumpet of the God of our fathers that will call the sleeping manhood of the Anglo-Saxon race to life again" (128). This "sleeping manhood," yet another phrase carrying phallic connotations (or in this case antiphallic connotations, given its slumber) does not remain asleep for long.[18] Only twenty pages pass before the South's "sleeping manhood" takes the form of white-sheeted and hooded vigilantes organized under the banner of the Ku Klux Klan (an image of white racial erection if ever there was one). Anglo-Saxons respond to "Dick" with one of their own—an erection for an erection. Worried over myths of black sexual prowess, white men respond to black sexual threat with arousal. To protect their women from black "Dick," that "unsolved riddle," they must themselves be hard.[19]

If we think back to the first sexual assault of the novel, where Hose Norman and his mountain boys fight off the black troopers, Dixon's hand shows more clearly still. Annie's new husband is interestingly named. "Hose" carries a phallic association that, when coupled with "Norman"—suggesting as it does the hyperwhiteness of Scandinavia —combines to create an apt composite for Dixon's purposes.[20] These two assaults, taken together, reveal the story Dixon is primarily concerned with, as he pits Norman Hose against black Dick. Remembering Rubin's description of the phallus as "a set of meanings conferred upon the penis," we can see this clash of male genitalia as an ideological struggle, one in which Dixon's concern over the protection of white female virginity leads to his imagining of male/male arousal.[21]

This imagined male sexual contest over the bodies of white women exposes the intimate connection between male domination and racial power. In Dixon's view, the ultimate issue is one of "racial absolutism" (336), a state only achievable through male control over female sexuality. In a conversation late in the novel between Reverend Durham and a preacher from Boston, Dixon establishes the stakes being played for. In response to Durham's statement that his only goal is to establish and maintain absolute segregation in the South, the preacher suggests that the battle is already lost, since "evidences of a mixture of blood" (336) already abound. Interestingly, Durham dismisses this evidence as the lingering effects of "the surviving polygamous and lawless instincts of the white male" (336). Since these instincts are on the wane, he argues, the only threat to "racial absolutism" comes from the black man, who, through an accumulation of wealth and culture, may someday "be allowed freely to choose a white woman for his wife" (336). He continues, "The right to choose one's mate is the foundation of racial life and of civilization. The South must guard with flaming sword every avenue of approach to this holy of holies. And there are many subtle forces at work to obscure these possible approaches" (336). Once again we encounter one of the novel's many swords, this time wielded in defense of the "holy of holies," a phrase occupying a rather vague syntactic position within Durham's sentence. On one level, it simply refers back to "the right to choose one's mate." At the same time, however, given the syntactic proximity of the "flaming sword" and the "avenue of approach," the "holy of holies" becomes the very "thing" being fought over: female genitalia.²² In defense of this genitalia—for Dixon the key to racial integrity—stands, of course, the white phallus, trying hard to fight off the "many subtle forces" working to admit greater access to white female sexuality. And what might these "subtle forces" be? Female autonomy, for one. As Michael Rogin puts it, "The sword guards the female genitalia not only to protect the white woman from the black phallus but also to keep her from acquiring a phallus of her own" (176). Although the "right to choose one's mate" is the key issue, it's not a right that extends to women. For if it did, the possibility would be raised that it's not simply "the lawless instincts of the white male" that threaten racial integrity but the possibility of white female desire for black men, a desire that would render the "flaming sword" of the white South no longer so necessary.²³

Absent this white female desire, however, and given the increasingly better behavior of white men, the only avenue available for the contamination of whiteness is the black rape of white women, which explains its centrality both to Dixon's narrative and to more general cultural imaginings and deployments. In "'The Mind That Burns in Each Body': Women, Rape, and Racial Violence," Jacquelyn Dowd Hall argues that during the latter half of the nineteenth century rape became a more overtly political weapon than it had been during the days of institutionalized slavery. Whereas the white plantation owner's unrestricted sexual access to his black slaves was a cornerstone of the patriarchal plantation system, in the years following the war the idea of rape was to become a central image in a political discourse devoted to reinforcing a white male power that had to some degree been subverted by the South's defeat. The freedmen's newfound right to a position of power within their own families threatened that power formerly exercised exclusively by white men.

Hall sees lynching as a story men told themselves about the social and psychological ordering of their lives. The story casts them in the role of avenging hero, restoring to them a power that was rapidly slipping away. With this power comes an erotic twist, as lynching worked to call forth the apotheosis of frail, victimized Womanhood, forced into the public eye as a symbol both of sexual contamination and the need to protect. The so-called threat of black men renders white female sexuality hypervisualized. As Hall writes, "Rape and rumors of rape became the folk pornography of the Bible Belt" ("Mind" 335).

To take Hall's formulation one step further, it's important to realize that "victimized Womanhood" wasn't the only erotic component in this folk pornography. Although lynching worked in part to reinforce the political and social subjugation of women, it was a crime directed specifically at black male bodies. These bodies became a central part of the folk pornography Hall describes. More specifically, the focus on castration as a part of lynching rituals brought the black penis to the forefront of the cultural imaginary. As Kobena Mercer has written, in an essay on Robert Mapplethorpe's photographs of black male nudes, "In the fantasmatic space of the supremacist imaginary, the big black phallus is perceived as a threat not only to the white master . . . but to civilization itself, since the 'bad object' represents a danger to white womanhood and therefore the threat of miscegenation, eugenic pollution, and racial degeneration" ("Looking" 353). Scientific discourse on racial difference in the nineteenth century is filled with speculation concerning black male genitalia, with a particular focus on its alleged superiority in size to that of white males.[24] This widespread speculation bespeaks a fascination (Mercer calls it a "primal fantasy") that, if not itself erotic, is certainly based in erotic energies.

The act of castration itself, for all its obvious horror, does give us one of the few opportunities to witness culturally sanctioned physical interaction between white men and black male genitalia. This interaction is, of course, highly conflicted and, to borrow a phrase from Eric Lott, can be described as an act of "love and theft," in which the castrated penis is both revered and reviled. In her reading of lynching narratives, Trudier Harris reminds us that even as white men "castrated the black men, there was a suggestion of fondling, of envious caress" (22). Or as Robyn Wiegman writes, "The white male desires the image he must create in order to castrate" (98). In an epigraph to her essay, Hall quotes a member of a lynch mob in 1934: "After taking the nigger to the woods . . . they cut off his penis. He was made to eat it. Then they cut off his testicles and made him eat them and say he liked it" ("Mind" 329). This brutal moment tells the story all too well. The object of white male fascination is severed, only to be forcibly consumed by the black man himself, its threat and lure forever absorbed. The "Other's strange fruit" (to borrow Mercer's phrase) becomes less strange through the white men's control of it.[25]

Dixon accomplishes a similar negation by having Dick burned at the stake by a raging mob of white men, who finally succeed in diminishing his mythic power to "ashes and charred bones" (384). Although being burned at the stake is a different type of violence than castration, it's not without its own phallic overtones. Dick, whose name already casts him as the black penis itself, is forced to become the visual manifestation of black erection—tied to a stake, forced to stand up to endure the fire that consumes him. As in the ritual of castration, the perceived struggle between white men and black men over the bodies of white women culminates in white male fascination with and terror of the black penis.[26]

The larger result of this fascination is, as Wiegman points out, the simultaneous blurring and reification of those lines demarcating the difference between heterosexual and homosexual desire. In Wiegman's words, "we might understand the lynching scenario and its obsession with the sexual dismemberment of black men to mark the limit of the homosexual/heterosexual binary—that point at which the oppositional relation reveals its inherent and mutual dependence—and the heterosexuality of the black male 'rapist' is transformed into a violently homoerotic exchange" (99). The slippage between hetero and homo desire, as well as its role in the maintenance of white supremacy as a political and social structure, takes on additional importance in the novel's conclusion.

### Homosociality Unmediated

Having examined the homosocial underpinnings behind Dixon's rape narratives, I want to end by discussing the homosociality that enables not rape, but marriage. The novel's climax comes in Charlie Gaston's second major speech of the novel, this one directed to the Democratic Convention of North Carolina on the subject of how best to rule the Negro in the South. The speech is extremely important, since it decides an internecine struggle for control of the Democratic Party. Charlie is the leader of a faction of young men ready to wrest control of the party away from its more traditional, and elderly, base. They hope to do so by foregrounding the "Negro question" and taking a hard line on the absolute necessity for Negro disfranchisement and white supremacy. The contest takes on personal significance for Charlie, since Sallie's father, General Worth, is the de facto leader of the Democratic establishment, its current kingmaker. The general has refused Charlie's request for his daughter's hand, standing in the way of the "Ideal love" that so consumes him.

Charlie's speech is clearly a narrative device for Dixon himself, as it brings together into one document the racial ideology on which this novel is based. It begins, "Whereas, it is impossible to build a state inside a state of two antagonistic races, And whereas, the future North Carolinian must therefore be an Anglo-Saxon or a Mulatto, Resolved, that the hour has now come in our history to eliminate the Negro from our life and establish for all time the government of our fathers" (433–34). The speech continues in predictable fashion, touching on Anglo-Saxon "conquest of the globe" (435) and the "filth and degradation of a Negroid corruption" (436). Reiterating that this is a "white man's government," Charlie concludes with a call to Aryan manhood: "Citizen kings, I call you to the consciousness of your kingship!" (442).

As with the Memorial Day speech, Dixon eroticizes Charlie's oratorical powers, as his resolutions bring the crowd "to the highest pitch of excitement, and his words, clear, penetrating, and deliberate thrilled his hearers with electrical power" (434). Charlie "played with the heart-strings of his hearers . . . as a great master touches the strings of a harp. His voice was now low and quivering with the music of passion, and then soft and caressing" (439). In the midst of it all, of course, sits Sallie Worth, "her face . . . aflame with emotion, her eyes flashing with love and pride" (434).

Charlie's oratorical prowess finally overcomes the general's political opposition to his views on the race question as well as his opposition to Charlie as Sallie's suitor. As he tells Charlie after the speech, "My boy, I give it up. You have beaten me! I'm proud of you. I forgive everything for that speech. *You can have my girl*" (443, emphasis added). Whereas a speech celebrating the glories of the old South had served to introduce Charlie to Sallie, his emotional appeal for a new South built on the truths of white supremacy and Aryan domination secures him Sallie as a gift from her father. The exchange creates a kinship system that effectively unites the Old Democrats with the New, establishing a revitalized and expanded power base for a white-supremacist overthrow of republican/fusionist rule. Before the novel's last page, Charlie is elected governor, and he and Sallie are married on the morning of his inauguration.

What's intriguing about this marriage, however, is its redundancy;

Charlie and Sallie had actually been secretly married some thirty pages earlier. It is this move from a secret heterosexuality to a public heterosexuality that exposes the impossibility of Dixon's white nation. As long as a black threat to the state exists, Charlie and Sallie's marriage must remain a secret. Only with the victory of white supremacy—and the implied expulsion of the black threat—can that marriage become public, can the name of heterosexuality be spoken. Why is this the case? In Dixon's novel it's not whiteness that stands in for heterosexuality but blackness, which becomes, through the black troopers and black Dick, the transcendent sign of men who desire women. Blackness, as heterosexuality writ large, disrupts the homosocial kinship economy among white men. It stands as a too visible reminder of the reproductive possibilities that so threaten Dixon's white state. And so, the secret marriage between Charlie and Sallie can't withstand the public gaze until it is removed from the haunting presence of blackness, which is to say, from the haunting presence of heterosexual desire. With the expulsion of blackness and its attendants (reproduction, miscegenation, the body), whiteness can reign supreme as a homosocial economy of racial power.

That whiteness exists only in the realm of the homosocial is made clear by Sallie's role in the marriage that ends the novel. As she tells her husband in the novel's final pages, "I do not desire any part in public life except through you. You are my world. . . . I desire no career save that of a wife" (468–69). In other words, although Sallie is absolutely necessary to this consolidation of white-supremacist power, she must quickly disappear from it. Like Annie, Flora, and Dick, she is merely a transitional phrase within a heterosexual and white-supremacist grammar. Her vow of public silence at her most public moment speaks both to her necessity and to her ultimate irrelevance. Yet given that irrelevance, where is there for white male sexual desire to circulate at novel's end? With the creation of the white-supremacist state that Dixon and his white characters long for, desire between white men is really the only option left. The heterosexual union that reigns on the novel's final page is a dodge, its narrative insistence speaking to its fragility, as well as Dixon's anxiety. If the creation of the white-supremacist state depends on the forcible exclusion of black men, and the death or silence of white women—both exclusions signaling the desperate expulsion from the novel of heterosexual desire—then the inaugural ball must find a way to celebrate a new homosociality, one no longer dependent on mediating figures. But, of course, a homosociality absent mediating figures is nothing of the sort. Deprived of black Dick, and deprived of Sallie, General Worth and Charlie are left in a place of barren whiteness neither wanted to imagine, dancing with themselves.

## Heterosexual Failings

I concluded the previous chapter by suggesting that whiteness and heterosexuality come to occupy antithetical positions in Chesnutt's novel, that heterosexuality actually threatens whiteness because it breaks the closed circuit of white reproduction. This turns out to be true for Dixon's novel as well, though with a twist. As this chapter has shown, this twist most often takes the shape of overt homoeroticism, a homoeroticism that appears to be the necessary by-product of a gradually solidifying heterosexual imperative. As heterosexuality emerges as both a biological and a political requirement, it becomes, in many ways, more visible. And this visibility causes a certain anxiety, as it simultaneously produces the specter of heterosexuality's necessary corollary, homosexuality.[27] Charlie becomes the perfect emblem of this anxiety, as he doubts his ability to live up to the requirements of heterosexuality, yet recognizes the relation between those requirements and the political future of whiteness. Judith Butler gets to the heart of this in an oft-quoted and still resonant passage about drag, performance, and heterosexual anxiety:

> To claim that all gender is like drag, or is drag, is to suggest that "imitation" is at the heart of the *heterosexual* project and its gender binarisms, that drag is not a secondary imitation that presupposes a prior and original gender, but that hegemonic heterosexuality is itself a constant and repeated effort to imitate its own idealizations. That it must repeat this imitation, that it sets up pathologizing practices and normalizing sciences in order to produce and consecrate its own claim on originality and propriety, suggests that heterosexual performativity is beset by an anxiety that it can never fully overcome, that its effort to become its own idealizations can never be finally or fully achieved, and that it is consistently haunted by that domain of sexual possibility that must be excluded for heterosexualized gender to produce itself. (125)

This "domain of sexual possibility that must be excluded" is seemingly omnipresent in Dixon's novel—the clash of Dick and Hose that then leads, of necessity, to the burning of Dick at the stake. This excluded sexual domain is also, as Judith Roof argues, a constitutive part of narrative itself. Positing Freud's "Three Essays on the Theory of Sexuality" as something of a first text of modern heterosexuality, Roof writes: "The reproductive imperatives of the story produce heterosexuality as the magical, motiveless mechanism that turns everything right, while homosexuality and other perversions—also necessary elements—make all fail to cohere, exposing the story's parts in a meaningless, short-circuited, truncated, narrative gratification that heterosexuality seals up again" (xxii). Roof's gloss on Freud resonates with my own reading of Dixon, particularly the extent to which, in Dixon's story, that magical heterosexuality actually does a pretty miserable job of making everything okay at story's end, of making all cohere.

As it turns out, this is entirely appropriate. The whiteness that reigns in the final pages of Dixon's novel must necessarily be homoerotic at its core, a by-product of Dixon's antiamalgamationist fervor. As Young writes, "Same-sex sex, though clearly locked into an identical same-but-different dialectic of racialized sexuality, posed no threat because it produced no children; its advantage was that it remained silent, covert and unmarked. . . . In fact, in historical terms, concern about racial amalgamation tended if anything to encourage same-sex play (playing the imperial game was, after all, already an implicitly homo-erotic practice)" (25–26). In other words, the white nation is a homosocial nation. As long as it's really Charlie and General Worth who are married at novel's end—not Charlie and Sallie—then whiteness can remain pure, since only male-male relations can avoid racial contamination. Here then, as in Chesnutt's novel, heterosexuality threatens the very whiteness that it pretends to protect. Through its new pleasure-centered dispersal of sexual energy, heterosexual desire threatens the fall of the white state.

A question remains, however. Can Dixon's story be taken as a representative fable about the political structures of racial desire, or is it finally only an idiosyncratic example of one man's rather hysterical response to perceived racial threats? In other words, what does the novel tell us beyond itself? Can its bizarre lessons fuel a more general speculation about the cultural construction and propagation of white supremacy at the turn of the century? One way to answer these questions, if only briefly, is to think about Dixon's use of the elements of conventional romance as a framework for his less than conventional "romance of the white man's burden"—in other words, to trace the plight of convention when coupled with racial extremism. Dixon's conflation, for example, of a wedding scene with an attempted rape suggests that the one is necessary for the maintenance of the other, a relationship that Dixon would certainly contest. The troopers threaten white marriage at the same time that they bolster its reason for being—as an institution whose function was, at least partly, to preserve and claim white female chastity as well as to ensure the unsullied future of whiteness. The troopers' transgression against the newly constituted Norman heterosexual couple is the ultimate transgression, precisely because, in Dixon's hands, it reveals the homosocial underpinnings behind both white supremacy and heterosexual marriage.

Likewise, Dixon's suture of the Charlie/Sallie romance plot onto the "political plot" clearly indicates the politics of romance within a white-supremacist worldview. This narrative move suggests that heteromarriage is necessary for the creation of a white-supremacist state. That this marriage is more accurately a marriage between men than between a man and a woman dramatizes, as clearly as I think possible, the interdependence of white supremacy and masculinist control, and it does so in a way that queries the heterosexual constitution of that whiteness which it seeks to enthrone.

In short, Dixon's novel makes it difficult to think about white supremacy without simultaneously thinking about white male sexual desire. The overdetermined conflation of politicosocial hatred with conventional heterolove produces the novel's narrative desire, that "affective or social force," to return to Sedgwick's language, that tries so desperately to hold both the novel and its motivation together. But given the complexity of that desire, we're not surprised to discover that the new world Dixon creates already shows signs of wear and weakness. To construct that world through the slippery field of plot and language is to risk a contamination from within, as the heterosexual whiteness that reigns in the novel's final pages is revealed to depend on other—less hetero, less white—properties. Though Nelse, Mrs. Gaston, Dick, Hose, and Annie and Flora Camp are nowhere to be seen at Charlie's inauguration, or his wedding to Sallie, their presence is most acutely felt. Annie and Flora, martyred by Dixon for his cause; Dick, burned at the stake—these are the constitutive elements of whiteness, dead ravaged white women and burnt black flesh. Dixon, I think, would be the first to acknowledge the role of Dick's lynching in his grand scheme. The trail of dead and brutalized women, however, is another matter, and one he would most likely refuse to admit. Whether sacrificed to the pressures of narrative, or the dictates of whiteness, or more probably both, these white women cannot attend the novel's closing ceremony, a ceremony that Dixon couldn't imagine without them.

### Placing Blame

The second of this chapter's two epigraphs, taken from Samuel Butler's *Hudibras,* was borrowed by black mathematician, sociologist, and activist Kelly Miller for his rebuttal to Dixon's novel. In "As to the Leopard's Spots: An Open Letter to Thomas Dixon, Jr." (1905), Miller exercises his characteristic wit and sarcasm at Dixon's expense, time and time again exposing the surreal illogic of Dixon's arguments on behalf of innate white superiority. Although Miller chooses to confront Dixon's argument outside its fictional context (he makes no reference to the events of *The Leopard's Spots* or to its characters), his decision to include the quote from Butler's poem reveals his astute awareness of the energies driving Dixon's novel: "The self-same thing they will abhor / One way, and long another for." Although Miller deploys this quote in reference to white male feelings toward black women, the dynamic it suggests also references Dixon's complicated feelings about black male sexuality—feelings that oscillate wildly from loathing and repulsion to something like desire and need. Miller recognizes that behind Dixon's antiamalgamationist fervor lies an uneasy excitement, something like a sexual frenzy. He pokes fun at Dixon on this very point. As Miller writes in reference to amalgamation, "The Negro refuses to become excited or share in your frenzy on this subject" (62). Casting himself and other blacks as calm and reasonable observers, Miller effectively paints Dixon—the white man—as the oversexed and irrational subject, a position more commonly reserved for black men and women. Reversing the terms of Dixon's novel, Miller positions white masculinity as the site of various illicit desires and behaviors, not unlike what Chesnutt accomplished in *The Marrow of Tradition.* And he does so in a way that gets at the heart of the white man's frenzy: its foundation in the always conflicted circuit of desire and loathing marked by those lines from *Hudibras*.

And although it might go without saying, by this point, that such a conflicted circuit of white male desire has had disastrous real-world consequences, I want to say it again anyway—or, more accurately, to borrow Miller's saying of it. I can think of no more fitting ending to this chapter than the following passage from Miller's letter to Dixon, where he points the finger of blame with searing accuracy. Speaking to Dixon, he writes, "You preside at every crossroad lynching of a helpless victim; wherever the midnight murderer rides with rope and torch in quest of the blood of his black brother, you ride by his side; wherever the cries of the crucified victim go up to God from the crackling flame, behold, you are there; when women and children, drunk with ghoulish glee, dance around the funeral pyre and mock the death groans of their fellow-man and fight for ghastly souvenirs, you have your part in the inspiration of it all" (68–69). Although these words precede Steinbeck's *The Grapes of Wrath* by more than thirty years, they can't help but call to mind Tom Joad's famous good-bye to his mother, when he disseminates his newly acquired understanding of human struggle, sending himself out as the haunting force of social justice: "Wherever they's a fight so hungry people can eat, I'll be there. Wherever they's a cop beatin' up a guy, I'll be there" (572). Whereas Steinbeck uses this rhetoric of omnipresence to point the way to a better and more hopeful future, Miller keeps his eyes more firmly set on the present. And he was right to do so. By casting Dixon in such a spectral role—always everywhere, responsible for everything—Miller puts a face on whiteness, nailing it down, if only for a moment, to a specific man and a specific book. He does so, however, without discounting its omnipresent status as the air we breathe. Its role in the lynching Miller imagines is all-consuming, its presence felt in every breath of fire and victim.

# Chapter Six

# Becoming Visible: I'm White, Therefore I'm Anxious

This people must be saved . . . —Ethiop (William J. Wilson)

It would make sense to end with Dixon. Published exactly fifty years after *Uncle Tom's Cabin, The Leopard's Spots* stands as the omega to Stowe's differently conceived alpha. These two extremely popular novels look like fitting bookends to the sometimes surreal narrative I've traced in these pages. Invested in racist assumptions, both books encompass the multiplicity of ways in which race becomes text, in which racist ways of looking at the world can produce startlingly different representations of it. And also startlingly similar. That Stowe's radical piece of antislavery fiction shares a number of assumptions with Dixon's rabidly negrophobic work dramatizes how the text of racism is never neat and tidy, never linear and coherent. For my purposes, it is useful and instructive to locate Dixon's work at the other end of the narrative begun by Stowe, suggesting that the seeds of Stowe's antislavery sensibility sowed quite bitter fruit. I say this not to discount Stowe's remarkable achievement—rather, to suggest that the terms of that achievement, grounded as they were in white-supremacist assumptions, made Dixon's novel something like an inevitability.

Yet despite the pleasing symmetry of a Stowe/Dixon frame, there's a sense in which Dixon is actually too much of an endpoint, in which *The Leopard's Spots* closes the circle too neatly. Written at the beginning of the twentieth century, Dixon's novel remains firmly rooted in the century before, firmly grounded in a nineteenth-century genealogy of literary racism. Its gestures to the glorious prehistory of American Anglo-Saxonism are similar to Charles Peterson's in *The Cabin and*

*Parlor.* Its longing for a simpler time and a simpler whiteness casts its glance backward rather than forward, to the agrarian past rather than the industrial future. Its whiteness takes the shape of nostalgia, avoiding modernity with its dangerous taints and contaminations.[1]

And so I want to take one more step beyond Dixon and, in so doing, position him as the transitional figure I think he is. Fortunately, the step to take is an obvious one. When D. W. Griffith collaborated with Dixon to produce *The Birth of a Nation* (1915), taking Dixon's racism from the written page to the shiny new silver screen, he gave that racism a new birth in the modern world of technology and spectacle, of larger-than-life images and dreams. *Birth* allows us to witness the passing of the white-supremacist torch from one popular genre to another, from the literary romance to film. This new genre, which would become *the* popular American genre of the twentieth century, offered an invigorating array of new possibilities for the representation and projection of white fears, fantasies, and anxieties. With its emphasis on the visual, it makes sense that skin color would be its first topic. And, as I hope to show here, it also makes sense that the Klan would be its first star.

### Making the Seen

Before discussing Griffith's film, however, I should begin by admitting to a bit of situational irony in the title to this chapter. "Becoming Visible" was the name of a 1994 exhibit at the New York Public Library that traced the history of New York's lesbian and gay communities.[2] The metaphor of visibility was an appropriate one. Despite the accompanying textual material, the exhibit's primary weight was carried through photographs—pictures showing men and women in a variety of situations, some easier to read than others. Those men standing close together in a grainy black and white from 1928—just how close were they? The later photographs offered less resistance to the gaze, as emblems of collective identity—pink triangles, rainbow flags, ACT UP slogans—provided the viewer with the necessary interpretive clues. So in a literal sense this history had become visible because of the camera. But whereas it was finally visible to those of us at the New York Public Library, it was simultaneously not visible, since the strength of this remarkable exhibit lay in its ability to peel back the layers of what we see, showing the path toward visibility to be an incremental one, accomplished sometimes in small ways. Those early photos depended on lesbian and gay identity as something both seen and not seen. The process was—and still is, I think—one of "becoming."

Why visibility as privileged telos? It's become a critical commonplace (though no less true) that visibility is a necessary first step in the founding of communities based on shared identity. Such collective visibility can work in at least two contradictory ways: either as target of discrimination or as site of empowerment. In truth, though, it's rarely an either/or situation, as these antithetical possibilities exist simultaneously in a dialectic of strength and weakness, weapon and liability. As Foucault makes clear, visibility is a first step into the field of discipline: "Disciplinary power . . . is exercised through its invisibility; at the same time it imposes on those whom it subjects a principle of compulsory visibility. In discipline, it is the subjects who have to be seen. . . . It is the fact of being constantly seen, of being able always to be seen, that maintains the disciplined individual in his subjection" (*Discipline* 187). As Foucault's account of this double bind makes clear, visibility is the mechanism through which one achieves identity and through which that identity becomes subject to manipulation and control. Think of the distinction between a portrait and a mug shot. For lesbian and gay Americans to assume those basic rights promised in the Constitution, they must first be granted a rather simple yet grand admission: "Yes, you do indeed exist. We see you." Yet to be seen is to offer oneself as a target, opening up the potential for visibility as site of further abuse. In either case, visibility proves existence—it makes an abstraction real. Or to rewrite that age-old existential sound bite, and to provide the antecedent for my subtitle, "I'm visible, therefore I am."

The irony I announced at the outset becomes my transition, since I want to suggest that in *The Birth of a Nation* Griffith was engaged in a process not unlike that undertaken by the organizers of this exhibit on lesbian and gay history.[3] His project, which found its ideal vehicle in the visual spectacle of the Ku Klux Klan, was one of making whiteness seen. In his film, the Klan functions both as political antidote to the legions of black rioters and potential rapists, and as visual antidote to the fear created by the cinematic spectacle of black chaos. Having staged the fabulous and fearful scenes of black crowds run amok, Griffith needed an equally effective image capable of neutralizing the fear that both created the black mob and that radiates from it. With the Klan at its center, Griffith does indeed stage a "ride to the rescue," but it's not simply Lillian Gish as "Elsie" who needs rescuing—it's the audience, that crowd of white folks shut up in a dark room with what appear to be thousands of excited, jumpy, and dangerously absurd black folks.[4]

Whiteness has always contained within it the seeds for a serious identity crisis. Isn't it risky, after all, to found a collective identity not just on color but on a color most often perceived as the absence of color? Those virtues most frequently attached to it—purity, innocence, peacefulness—speak to its ethereal status as absence. As David Roediger writes, "Whiteness describes, from Little Big Horn to Simi Valley, not a culture but precisely the absence of culture. It is the empty and therefore terrifying attempt to build an identity based on what one isn't and on whom one can hold back" (*Towards* 13). Or in Edward Ball's formulation: "White people . . . don't exist. Until they come up against difference" (26). Or yet again, this time in Richard Dyer's words, as he confesses to the difficulty of writing about whiteness: "When whiteness *qua* whiteness does come into focus, it is often revealed as emptiness, absence, denial or even a kind of death" ("White" 45). Whiteness is because it isn't. There's the ever present fear, rendered clearly on the screen by Griffith, that whiteness, as noncolor, could disappear amid blackness, which everybody knows is very colored indeed.[5]

The Klan's subtitle, "the Invisible Empire," further encodes this anxiety over being seen and recognized. The phrase is ironic, given that the Klan's effectiveness—its claim to empire—depends absolutely on its visibility. Paradoxically, the Klan uniform works to provide the invisibility of empire at the same time that it creates its hypervisibility. Individual faces may be invisible, but the empire itself is nothing but visibility. White-sheeted men riding white-sheeted horses, traveling in large groups with flaming crosses—hardly the stuff of invisibility.[6]

As Griffith's biographer points out, film directors are often more interested in "imagistic possibilities" than the framework of plot and narrative (Schickel 213). This was certainly true at the inception of *Birth,* since Griffith's primary motivation was in getting the Klan up on the screen. Confronted with Thomas Dixon's *The Clansman,* which would serve as the partial basis for Griffith's film, he wrote, "I could just see these Klansmen in a movie with their white robes flying" (qtd.

in Schickel 212). One of the primary architects of the filmic "ride to the rescue," Griffith now saw the opportunity to film a "ride-to-the-rescue on a grand scale. Instead of saving one poor little Nell of the Plains, this ride would be to save a nation" (qtd. in Schickel 213).

Thus the film's genesis lay in Griffith's desire to visualize the Klan, to take what was already spectacular and make it a part of his own spectacle. A moment in the film provides a fictional analog for the director's moment of discovery. Ben Cameron, the film's hero, "in agony of soul over the degradation and ruin of his people," sits lost in thought on an overlook, pondering his next move in the fight to save whiteness from black overrun. Suddenly he sees two white children carrying a white sheet, which they use as a cover in their game of hide-and-seek. Next appear four black children, who see the white sheet fluttering in agitation from beneath. When the two white children stand up, still hidden by the white sheet, the black children become hysterical, with all the clichéd eye rolling that Griffith's camera had available to it. The black children flee while the white children laugh at their little joke. The next title card reads, simply, "The Inspiration." The following scene shows three Klansmen, in full regalia, preparing to frighten two superstitious black men.

Woodrow Wilson, writing about Thaddeus Stevens's policy toward the South in the days following the war, recounts a similar moment of birth for the Klan, one once again dependent on the power of the visual. White southerners discovered, he writes, "the thrill of awesome fear which their sheeted, hooded figures sent among their former slaves. . . . It threw the Negroes into a very ecstacy of panic to see these sheeted 'Ku-Klux' move near them in the shrouded night" (Wilson 60). This "ecstacy of panic," however, worked both ways. In Wilson's mind, the panic is purely the Negroes'; white sheets create black panic. However, this equation inverts the cause-and-effect relationship operable under Reconstruction. In fact, the panic Wilson is talking about isn't black panic but white panic, the very panic that makes the white sheets necessary. The white South's crisis of identity in the years following Reconstruction made necessary the sort of visual and collective identity the sheets provided. In a condition not unlike the commonplace usage of homosexual panic, white southerners feared the loss of something central to their identity: the power of whiteness as a normalizing and disciplinary trope. This fear called forth the necessity of display, the need for a projection of their white identity, an identity threatened by the very conditions that call it forth.[7]

## White Light/White Heat

In this context, Dana Polan's work on the ideology of spectacle offers a useful piece of connective tissue. He writes, "It is not accidental that two social practices of the modern age—cinema and psychoanalysis—both employ the concept of *projection* to describe the process(es) by which dreams and wishes come to be represented on a screen before the dreamer or spectator" (131). The image of the Klan that gave Griffith the reason for making his film can be seen as a wishful dream, an image of that comfortable homogeneity so rapidly slipping away. The Klan's visual presence restores an order and heroism increasingly lacking in the modern and mongrelized world. Griffith imagined the Klan's ride to the rescue before he had fully imagined the female character who would need rescuing. The damsel in distress was Griffith and, more importantly, the white South.

That Griffith's film signaled the birth of cinema as well as the new birth of a white nation offers us the opportunity to witness the interdependence of white identity and fear, of racial power and the power of the spectacle. As George Lipsitz notes, Hollywood films "have not merely reflected the racism that exists in social relations but have helped produce a unified white racial identity through the shared experience of spectatorship" (*Possessive* 99). Film, a popular genre by definition, achieved its first maturity amid a context of hysterical white projection, as white folks found a new way to shore up their stock in the rapidly declining value of whiteness as cultural capital. It's clear that in Griffith's film whiteness as visual symbol comes to the rescue of white folks anxious over the black mobs. Their anxiety in effect creates the need for the Klan as symbol of that power which they fear losing. But the relationship between white anxiety and white display isn't so much a cause-and-effect relationship as it is a relationship built on equivalence. Whiteness doesn't simply reassert itself in response to anxiety; rather, it *is* anxiety itself.

Lillian Gish's portrayal of Elsie Stoneman offers a demonstration of the equivalence between whiteness and hysteria that I'm suggesting. Gish, whose career spanned decades, achieved her first glimmerings of stardom in Griffith's films. Her portrayal of Elsie Stoneman is famous for the sexual vulnerability that lies at the heart of that portrayal, since her primary role in the story is to resist the lustful and scheming mulatto, Silas Lynch. The film's climax comes when the Klan rides to her rescue, preventing the forced marriage arranged by a drunken Lynch.

Writing on Gish as the epitome of the "white star," Richard Dyer argues that her presence in *Birth* makes "explicit the concatenation of gender, race and light that is a key part of her stardom" ("White Star" 24). Gish's figure on the screen demonstrates "the relationship between stardom and light, a relationship at once technical, aesthetic and ethical" (Dyer, "White Star" 23). Dyer unpacks this observation in relation to Gish's work in another Griffith film, *True Heart Susie:* "There is, in other words, a special relationship between light and Gish: she is more visible, she is aesthetically and morally superior, she looks on from a position of knowledge, of enlightenment—in short, if she is so much lit, she also appears to be the source of light" ("White Star" 23). Although Dyer's description of Gish's visibility certainly applies to her performance in *Birth,* qualities other than knowledge and enlightenment become attached to that visibility. In *Birth* what is most visible is her sexual vulnerability in relation to Lynch's advances. In a repeated shot, Griffith shows Gish in close-up with a white gag in her mouth. Just to her right looms a black fist, threatening immediate violence against her. A phrase Dyer uses to describe her in a different context—"a light shining in the darkness" ("White Star" 23)—takes on additional meaning here, as Dyer's metaphor is literalized at the expense of Elsie's safety and sexual integrity. The light that signifies calm superiority in *True Heart Susie* invokes nothing but vulnerability in the racialized context of *Birth.* The visibility that light produces is a double-edged sword. In this scene, Gish's white face stands in for whiteness, as the black fist metonymically signifies the rioting black mob outside. The sole purpose of the shot, quite effective in its composition, is to define Gish's whiteness against the blackness of fists, her sexual vulnerability against black-male violence. Her face, glowing from Griffith's lighting, is anxiety itself, as her features work overtime to signify her absolute helplessness.[8]

The close-up of Gish in peril exists not only in contrast to the blackness of fists but in contrast to the spectacle of crowds—both black and white. As Gregory Bush and others have argued, Griffith was the first fully to exploit the crowd scene in film, since most earlier work had been hampered by limited budgets and casts (Bush 216–17). In so doing, Griffith was simply taking his cue from precinema history, since crowds had been exploited for their visual appeal well before the birth of cinema, whether on the stage, in parades and pageants, at circuses and amusement parks, or in political rallies (Bush 214). According to Bush, Griffith's deployment of "mass man" breaks down into two categories: "fearful mobs and righteous crowds" (214). As this inherent dualism suggests, it's no surprise that Griffith's deployment of crowds lacks subtlety. A crowd, after all, isn't the most subtle of filmic instruments. As Bush argues, Griffith's crowds are either "righteous and imbued with the proper work ethic, or they [are] meanspirited, racially inferior, or snobbish" (217). In *Birth* this righteousness finds its vehicle in the Klan; out-of-control black mobs stand in for the danger of racial inferiority run amok.[9]

This running amok, this lack of order and control, becomes the primary color on Griffith's palette. It's a quality that was felt by early commentators on this new industry, particularly in relation to Griffith's work in *Birth*. In *The Art of the Moving Picture* (1916), Vachel Lindsay devotes an entire chapter, "The Picture of Crowd Splendor," to the crowd as an ideal dramatic image. Throughout the chapter, Lindsay resorts to oceanic metaphors to capture the effect of the crowd on screen. Just as "the shoddiest silent drama may contain noble views of the sea," the "sea of humanity" can serve an equally uplifting purpose (39). More specifically, in *Birth* "the Ku Klux Klan dashes down the road as powerfully as Niagara pours over the cliff" (47). Ben Cameron, the leader of the Klan, exists not as a mere individual but "as representing the whole Anglo-Saxon Niagara" (47). Lindsay also lauds Griffith's handling of the anti-image of this Niagara, "the rioting negroes in the streets of the Southern town, mobs splendidly handled, tossing wildly and rhythmically like the sea" (49).[10] Lindsay's consistent use of these metaphors of violent and moving water exposes a primary theme in Griffith's film: that these opposing mobs represent natural and inevitable forces, bound to encounter one another not in a battle of humanity but of nature, with its corresponding associations of good and evil. The contest between white and black is thus elevated far above and beyond the mere clash of multitudes of bodies. The struggle obtains mythic proportions.[11]

Lindsay is interestingly aware of how *Birth* is a "crowd picture" even beyond the confines of the screen, since it inevitably turns the audience in the theater "into a mob that is either for or against the Reverend Thomas Dixon's poisonous hatred of the negro" (47). Thus a film deriving its primary energy from the spectacle of crowds produces through that spectacle yet another crowd, one as racially identified as those white men on their horses. The audience, through the identification and transference available to them, comes to its own rescue. Simultaneously Elsie Stoneman as she avoids the lecherous sexual desire of Silas Lynch, and Ben Cameron as he and his Anglo-Saxon Niagara ride to her rescue, the audience has its primary fear created before its eyes only to experience the supreme joy of escape and racial victory.

But these myriad points of access get even more complicated if we consider the role of Silas Lynch. The white audience has the option of identifying there too, if only it looks hard enough, for the actor playing Lynch is, like most of the actors playing black or mulatto parts in the film, white. As Michael Rogin has argued, the film's use of white actors in blackface causes the ultimate collapse of the system of binary differences that Griffith longs to maintain. Shot in segments, the chase scenes offer rich irony. As Rogin puts it, "The obviousness of blackface, which fails to disguise, reveals that the Klansmen were chasing their own negative identities, their own shadow sides" (181). "The climax of *Birth*," Rogin writes, "does not pit whites against blacks, but some white actors against others" (181). The notion of whiteness chasing its own tail is one I will return to when I discuss Griffith's use of a moving camera to capture the Klan's climactic ride.

### Saving Lillian Gish

For now, I want to clarify these observations by looking at just a few moments near the end of the film and, in so doing, get a better sense of the specific quality in need of rescue by the Klan. In a scene introduced by a title card reading "The riot in the Master's Hall," Griffith takes South Carolina politics as a vehicle to literalize the postwar white South's fear and belief that blacks had actually taken over political power.[12] The scene shows scores of agitated and ridiculously dressed black men on the floor of the House. Casting actual blacks as the black legislators, Griffith's directorial emphasis is clearly on verisimilitude. Several of the men drink from whiskey bottles while others are busy eating peanuts and chicken. The controversy, however, and the subject of debate, isn't so much behavior as clothing. At the center of a repeated shot, we see a naked black foot propped up on one of the member's desks. The resolution on the floor is that "all members must wear shoes," and when it passes, the owner of the bare foot is made to cover it. The whole process is witnessed by the few white representatives, described as "the helpless white minority," and three white visitors in the gallery, two of whom are women. The women enter just in time for a discussion of a bill providing for legalized intermarriage. The white women and their escorts are so horrified by the spectacle of black chaos on the floor that they quickly exit.

Described as "the Master's Hall," the House functions metonymically to describe the alleged reorientation of southern power following slavery's collapse. Griffith's focus on the "helpless white minority," gendered female by the inclusion of the women on the balcony, attempts to suggest that the racial demographic seen here is actually the literal truth for the South itself. This numbers game—one that certainly doesn't hold up to actual scrutiny—dramatizes less the numerical truth of the South's population than the white South's perception of that "truth." The black mob is in control; black chaos sits where white government used to. Governed by the ungovernable, white women must leave the building and, implicitly, the state.

Griffith's emphasis on the black bare foot is equally interesting. The "black foot" has long been a fetish of those interested in the more physiological schools of white-supremacist thinking. Taken as a symbol of racial difference, writer after writer has described the alleged peculiarities of black feet, usually male: the lack of arch, the supposed backward protrusion of the heel. The black foot became an easy visual image for the racially grotesque.[13] Underlying this fascination was an association of the black foot with black male sexuality. With the focus on size and grotesque peculiarity, the discourse of the naked foot became the vehicle for a covert discourse about a different kind of nudity, one invisible but forever imagined. The black foot became the black penis.[14] Griffith's insistence on the bare foot as the center of his shot in the house of government (the owner of the foot actually flaunts it, repeatedly stretching and extending his toes), and the subsequent decision that government will function better if the foot is covered, placed black male sexual threat at the center of this riotous black chaos. The white visitors can't stand the vision.

With the triple emphasis on the black crowd, the white minority, and black male sexual threat, the scene in the State House works to justify and foreshadow the dual ride to the rescue that Griffith stages as his climax. The rescue is geared toward two sites: a cabin in which Dr. Cameron and his wife, their daughter Margaret, and Phil Stoneman are hiding from the black mob, and Silas Lynch's office, where Elsie has gone to plead for Dr. Cameron's life. Griffith's choice of these locales clearly indicates the larger ramifications of the rescue he effects.

It's significant, for example, that the cabin is actually owned and occupied by "two Union veterans." The title card reads, "The former enemies of North and South are united again in common defense of their Aryan birthright." The music accompanying the fugitive party's arrival at the cabin is "Auld Lang Syne." That these veterans agree to harbor Cameron and his party from the vengeful black mob posits black threat as the one thing capable of reuniting a wartorn country. This isn't, however, the only reunion accomplished in this "Union" space. Margaret and Phil, lovers separated by their fathers' antithetical loyalties, are thrown together in response to the black threat outside the cabin. In a moment of racial crisis they embrace, assuring the viewer that their union is fixed. The visual effect of this scene at the cabin is striking, as Griffith shows the doors of the small dwelling being pushed in while the black mob literally surrounds the cabin. At the center of this conflagration sits the newly constituted white family, symbol of the new Aryan nation that the film promises. (Griffith throws in a small white girl-child for good measure.)

The other of the Klan's two destinations is actually more important to Griffith, since it is in Lynch's cabin that his star, Lillian Gish, gets to enact the whirling-dervish ritual of white female sexual vulnerability.[15] With Gish as Elsie dressed all in white (with the exception of a black shawl, which she discards halfway during the scene) and lit like the star she is, the contrast with the rioting black troopers outside couldn't be greater.[16] As Lynch points out, these troopers provide visual proof of empire and power. He tells Elsie, "See! My people fill the streets. With them I will build a Black Empire and you as a Queen shall sit by my side." Black mobs metonymically signify a future black kingdom. As another title card informs us, these blacks in the streets were brought in by Lynch and his mentor Stoneman to "overawe the whites"; the sheer visual spectacle they create, both in the streets and on the screen, would have a significant effect not only on the white families looking out their windows at the chaos but also the white cinema patrons staring with a complicated mix of fear and joy at the silver screen.

For the next fifteen minutes, the screen is filled with Griffith's famous juxtapositions, as the camera cuts back and forth between Lynch and Elsie and the approaching Klan. The crisis inside Lynch's office begins when Lynch proposes marriage, later grabbing and kissing Elsie's white dress. As Lynch orders his henchmen to arrange a forced marriage, the two combatants run around the room, Elsie a frenzied spectacle of white anxiety and sexual vulnerability. The chase climaxes twice, first in Lynch's attempt to kiss Elsie after she has fainted in his arms and second in the shot of Elsie bound and gagged. Before it's "too late," however, the Klan finally arrives, led by Elsie's lover, Ben Cameron. Cameron takes Elsie into his arms and then lifts his Klan hood just enough for Elsie to recognize him beneath the layers of white. The hood lifting individuates Ben as a piece of the larger mass of whiteness, making visible just enough of the Invisible Empire to ensure the collapse of the romance plot with the "political plot."[17]

The dual rescue accomplished, Griffith stages the "Parade of the Clansman," with Margaret and Elsie as its leaders, since they are its reason for being. As the viewer watches this spectacle of whiteness's political and visual triumph (they've recovered the streets, which moments ago were a "sea" of black chaos), the viewer also watches individual white families watching the spectacle. These families, like the newly joined family in the Union cabin, are the real victors here, as Griffith posits the domestic as the guarantor of whiteness's future. Likewise, "the double honeymoon" near the film's conclusion highlights the intersection of heterosexual union and racial integrity in a manner similar to that at the close of *The Leopard's Spots*.[18]

### Crowding Whiteness

But as we discovered in Dixon's novel, the spectacular victory for whiteness in both personal and political terms isn't left entirely untroubled by film's end. In fact, it's through one of Griffith's most significant technical innovations that we come to realize the conflicted nature of this whiteness that appears to save us all. As many critics have noted, the visual success of Griffith's climactic Klan shots depends on his pioneering use of a moving camera, a huge technical and aesthetic step beyond the fixed perspective dominant before him.[19]

The effect of the moving camera is one of heightened participation for the audience, a sense of physical involvement in the action on the screen. Whereas the fixed camera functions as a sort of omniscient narrative voice, the moving camera necessarily obtains a subjectivity itself, becoming a character in the story.[20] The significance of this shift in *Birth* is tremendous, since Griffith pushed this new technology of motion to its highest effect in the shots of the Klan's ride to the rescue.

Yet the final effect of this audience involvement is interestingly ambiguous. Critics often speak of the camera's ride *with* the Klan. Gregory Bush, for example, writes that "a moving camera recorded the charging KKK as if the audience were riding with them, looking down upon both the disorderly mob of black soldiers and the well-dressed black sympathizers who had been pictured terrorizing innocent white victims" (219). Bush's observation is only partially true. The camera does indeed ride with the Klan, but the perspective is always one of looking *back* on the charging riders. The result isn't so much a participation in the Klan's glorious charge but the creation of a subjectivity not unlike those blacks being pursued. We're moving with the riders, but they're moving menacingly toward us. Not once does Griffith make the move we expect, never using his camera to capture the actual subjectivity of a rider looking forward at the fleeing blacks. Contrary to Bush's claim, the moving camera never views the blacks from "our" position on horseback.[21]

This is a crucial distinction, since the audience's absolute investment in the Klan's ride is Griffith's primary visual purpose. What does it mean that a white audience's sense of identification with the Klan is possibly troubled by this backward glance, this look over the shoulder? I want to suggest two possible answers, at least tentatively. On the one hand, our sense of being pursued by this frightening spectacle of horses and men simply works to reaffirm the power of the Klan. Getting a sense of what it means to be chased, we have a greater appreciation of the Klan's power to threaten the black rioters. Our brief antithetical relationship to the charging Klan further strengthens our subsequent identification, since we've gained a more visceral feel for "our" power as charging whiteness.

But I don't think this glimpse of an oppositional relationship between the white audience and the Klan can be fully recuperated within a larger pleasurable identification. Some of that fear created by the backward glance must remain. To the extent that it does, it becomes yet another piece of the fear and anxiety that require the Klan's presence in the first place. This force—created out of insecurity and panic—becomes yet another racial force that can't be reigned in or fully contained. Somewhere in that audiences's thrill of the spectacle lie traces of the anxiety and fear that caused the spectacle in the first place. Born in response to white panic in the face of black chaos, the Klan can't contain that panic without simultaneously proving its constitutive role in the DNA of whiteness.

The multiple and conflicted identifications I'm suggesting here are actually a fundamental part of the cinematic experience, creating an enormously complicated relationship between an audience and the images on the screen. As John Ellis suggests, there is rarely a simple and closed relationship between a viewer and his or her ideal image: "Identification involves both the recognition of self in the image on the screen, a narcissistic identification, and the identification of self with the various positions that are involved in the fictional narration: those of hero and heroine, villain, bit-part player, active and passive character. . . . Identification is therefore multiple and fractured, a sense of seeing the constituent parts of the spectator's own psyche paraded before her or him" (43).[22] This elasticity of identification, inherent to film as a visual genre, begins to explain the complicated dynamic at work in the white audience's relationship to the Klan. It doesn't, however, fully explain the terms of these various and malleable identifications.

To disentangle and clarify the implications of this circuitous dynamic—a dynamic that dramatizes the symbiotic relations between whiteness and anxiety—I want to borrow from those theorists of crowd psychology I mentioned earlier, Gustave LeBon and Freud, in order to get a clearer sense of what the various crowds in and around *Birth* mean. For both LeBon and Freud, crowds represent savagery and primitivism. Describing the transformation from individual to member of a crowd, LeBon writes, "By the mere fact that he forms part of an organized group, a man descends several rungs in the ladder of civilization. Isolated, he may be a cultivated individual; in a crowd, he is a barbarian" (52). Freud concurs: "When individuals come together in a group all their individual inhibitions fall away and all the cruel, brutal and destructive instincts, which lie dormant in individuals as relics of a primitive epoch, are stirred up to find free gratification" (*Group* 11). Such characterizations, although inevitably biased, are not surprising, given both men's investment in European notions of racial hierarchy and civilization. Likewise, their collective investment in masculinity as a state of order and control leads them to gender these savage crowds female. Describing the "impulsiveness, irritability, [and] incapacity to reason" of crowds, LeBon links these qualities to "beings belonging to inferior forms of evolution—in women, savages, and children, for instance" (55–56). Crowds, then, are both savage and female, primitive and hysterical.

I take LeBon and Freud's interpretation as typical of late-nineteenth- and early-twentieth-century attitudes toward mass behavior. Influenced as they are by racist, masculinist, and classist paranoia, they offer a window into cultural responses to the spectacle of the crowd. Turning our attention back to Griffith's film, LeBon and Freud can help us disentangle the various anxieties at work in the filmic spectacle of race and masses. To do so, I want to isolate three primary crowds in (and around) Griffith's film: the black mob in the street, the white Klan members on horseback, and the white audience sitting in the presumably comfortable confines of the theater.[23]

The spectacle of the black crowds running amok in the streets and on the screen provides a multivalenced scene for white viewers. The already assumed savagery and primitivism of blackness gets heightened by its visual density and collectivity. The black crowd is the apex of barbarism, simply by virtue of the transformation from black individuals to black mob. Its hysterical quality—referenced by LeBon's view of the mob as female—collapses gender demarcations. If mobs are generically female, the black mob combines out-of-control femininity with the always assumed phallic danger (remember Gus the rapist) of blackness, thus collapsing white cultural fears and assumptions. The black crowd is everything suggesting a loss of order and control, a diminution of civilization and a heightening of sexual frenzy.

The Klan—that white mob on horseback—owes its very existence to this spectacle of black masses. It is white anxiety writ large. Its white visibility is designed to counter the black incursion filling the screen. Yet at the moment whiteness assumes its salvational shape as a crowd, it gets saturated by suggestions of savagery and primitivism through the association of the crowd with barbarism. The white mob comes together to restore civilization, but if LeBon and Freud are right, that very coming together contributes to the further erosion of civilization. Charles Chesnutt wove this possibility into *The Marrow of Tradition* when he has Mr. Delamere connect white lynch mobs with "ethnic" barbarism: "I have lived to hear of white men, the most favored of races, the heirs of civilization, the conservators of liberty, howling like red Indians around a human being slowly roasted at the stake" (211). Civilization, Chesnutt tells us later, "is but a thin veneer, which cracks and scales off at the first impact of primal passions" (310). The African American activist and writer Ethiop (William J. Wilson) made a similar point in 1860 when he asked, "Whither are this people [whites] tending? If permitted in their course; if no restraining hand arrest them, who does not foresee that the goal at which they will ultimately arrive will be sure and certain barbarism" (64).

Griffith would also have found this connection between the white mob and savagery in his source material, *The Leopard's Spots*. After the mob has captured Dick and accused him of Flora's rape and murder, Charlie Gaston pleads with the men to let the courts take care of justice. The men, determined on a lynching, ignore Charlie's argument and burn Dick at the stake. As Dixon writes, "Under the glare of the light and the tears the crowd seemed to melt into a great crawling, swaying creature, half reptile, half beast, half dragon, half man, with a thousand legs, and thousand eyes, and ten thousand gleaming teeth, and with no ear to hear and no heart to pity!" (384). Dixon and Griffith, having created and unleashed the Klan as both narrative and visual spectacle, realize its potential for chaos and degeneration. The fear that creates it becomes a fear of its role in the further degradation of whiteness. Griffith's portrayal of black mass chaos renders salvation by white mobs both necessary and impossible. The inability to maintain itself as anything other than anxiety amid the spectacle of black mobs is whiteness's dilemma, caught, finally, by its own ontological contradictions.

Finally, there's the third crowd, the group of white people in the theater, enthralled and terrorized by the actions on the screen. Like the Klan, they come together in response to the black mobs. They too, like the men on horseback, are a collective white mass. But what happens as this crowd exits the theater? In *Crowds and Power*, Elias

Canetti spins a hypothetical scenario in which a crowd in a theater is forced to exit rapidly when someone yells "fire." With the cry of "fire," the audience, united in its common fear, "becomes something like a real crowd" (26). Yet in the rush to exit the theater, the crowd disintegrates rapidly, as the spatial confines of rows and exits reindividuate this collective and panicked mass. "Only one or two persons can get through each exit at a time," writes Canetti (26): "Each man sees the door through which he must pass; and he sees himself alone in it, sharply cut off from all the others. It is the frame of the picture which very soon dominates him. Thus the crowd, a moment ago at its apex, must disintegrate violently" (26). According to Canetti, the act of exiting the theater destroys the crowd formed during the panic experienced there. In the case of *Birth,* the white crowd is only fully itself within the theater, in the presence of the visual spectacle of black rioting and chaos. This isn't to say, however, as the Canetti example seems to suggest, that the crowd ceases to be a crowd once it exits the theater. Although whiteness achieves one of its particular forms in the white crowd, it also adheres to individuals in the absence of that crowd—or, more accurately, in the recollection of the now dispersed crowd. The memory of the white crowd—and the awareness that it can re-form—grants power to white individuals in a way that keeps the crowd intact as an idea, as a potential. Yet the crowd's exit from the theater does transform that crowd in a manner that resonates with the story Canetti tells. To get a sense of this transformation, I want to quote James Baldwin at some length. In "Going to Meet the Man," Baldwin describes the fearful reaction of a white community to the beginnings of the civil rights movement:

> They rarely mentioned anything not directly related to the war that they were fighting, but this had failed to establish between them the unspoken communication of soldiers during a war. Each man, in the thrilling silence which sped outward from their exchanges, their laughter, and their anecdotes, seemed wrestling, in various degrees of darkness, with a secret which he could not articulate to himself, and which, however directly it related to the war, related yet more surely to his privacy and his past. They could no longer be sure, after all, that they had done all the same things. They had never dreamed that their privacy could contain any element of terror, could threaten, that is, to reveal itself, to the

scrutiny of a judgment day, while remaining unreadable and inaccessible to themselves; nor had they dreamed that the past, while certainly refusing to be forgotten, could yet so stubbornly refuse to be remembered. They felt themselves mysteriously set at naught—while here they were, out-numbered, fighting to save the civilized world. They had thought that people would care—people didn't care; not enough, anyway, to help them. It would have been a help, really, or at least a relief, even to have been forced to surrender. Thus they had lost, probably forever, their old and easy connection with each other. (238)

The white crowd is, to again borrow Canetti's language, "sharply cut off from all the others" as they exit the theater. They are, as Baldwin understands, "mysteriously set at naught," having lost "their old and easy connection with each other." As they leave the theater—as they approach "the scrutiny of a judgment day"—they lose their status as parts of a greater whole, just as the Klan disappears once the last reel finishes. Created by white racial panic, the crowd doesn't cease to exist in its absence, but it does become aware, perhaps, of its fragility, of its impermanence. Whiteness begins to collapse as the projector beam fades.

### Escaping Whiteness

Before this collapse, however, Griffith tries one last time to make whiteness permanent and safe. Once the black crowds are vanquished by the Klan and thus removed from the camera's gaze, all that remain are two white crowds: the Klan parading gallantly toward the camera and the white audience staring in rapt attention at the screen. Whiteness gazing on whiteness. The pleasure and fear of narcissism. That Griffith refuses to end here is telling, as is the surreal directorial path he takes instead. Realizing the dilemma facing whiteness when the last reel is over, Griffith attempts, through the magic of this new technology, a relocation of whiteness to a world lacking the possibility of contamination. The postparade action of the film involves a three-stage move from the worldly to the mythic. A brief shot of "the next election" shows voting being overseen by a Klansman on a horse. Then comes the double honeymoon already mentioned, set at "the sea's edge," signifying a sort of jumping-off point to the otherworldly space Griffith creates next. Finally, we get a completely over-the-top staging of a world in which "War shall rule no more." This world is signified through another version of the Griffith crowd shot, this time centered on a man on a horse (presumably Mars, the war god) brandishing a huge sword. This figure of war finally gives way to a huge Jesus, standing in the middle of toga-clad white folks. As Jesus rather suddenly disappears (the result of shoddy editing rather than directorial intention), the scene dissolves into the film's final image: Ben and Elsie Cameron sitting on a hill, staring off into the distance at what must be the City of Peace, a medieval yet beautiful collection of castles and turrets.

The move from the worldly to the extraworldly—from the Klan to the City of Peace—is attributable to more than Griffith's desire for an epic ending to an epic film. It announces an escape, motivated by suspicion and fear, from the real to the ideal, from bodies to abstraction. Given the Klan's heroic and epic status throughout the film, one would think that the victory parade is Griffith's ideal, the film's final resting place. That he feels the need to transcend this vision suggests its worldliness and thus its capacity for degradation. Transported to the City of Peace, the audience experiences a release from the world and from the Klan. Whiteness, forced to take real shape in horses, men, sheets, and heterosexual union, finds itself returned to the land of abstraction. Less real, but also less dirty, and thus whiter, whiteness becomes once again a site of comfortable identification for the audience. Griffith's final images lull the audience into a security that the Klan couldn't entirely effect. This security is sweeter for its foundation in a disembodied, desireless abstraction. Returned to a vision of whiteness as ethereal goodness, the audience doesn't miss the more complicated version of whiteness that the Klan embodies. Griffith's move away from the Klan, like the Klan's filmic charge toward us, suggests an uneasiness, a fear, and the need for retreat.

Of course, Griffith's attempted projection of whiteness as pure abstraction was bound to fail. Like the sudden disappearance of Jesus I mentioned above—a disappearance inadvertently signaling the imperfections of this new technology of the imagination—the utopia Griffith constructs depends on celluloid and lights, wheels and electricity. It is most decidedly based in the material world and is thus subject to the ravages and degenerations of that world. And it can only exist in the noticeably artificial context of the theater, where scores of white people, sitting in rows in a dark room, face not each other, but the wall. This staged setting lends an unavoidable fragility to the vision of triumphant and carefree white folks fluttering on the screen. So does the awareness, in each of the audience members, that once the house lights come up, the show's over.

*Epilogue*

# The Queer Face of Whiteness

. . . if a few are determined to be white—amen, so be it; but don't let them argue as if there were no part to be played in life by black men and black women, and as if to become white were the sole specific and panacea for all the ills that flesh is heir to—the universal solvent for all America's irritations.—Anna Julia Cooper

But what on earth is whiteness that one should so desire it?—W. E. B. Du Bois

White folks who do not see black pain never really understand the complexity of black pleasure. And it is no wonder then that when they attempt to imitate the joy in living which they see as the "essence" of soul and blackness, their cultural productions may have an air of sham and falseness that may titillate and even move white audiences yet leave many black folks cold.—bell hooks

They thought he was a real sweet ofay cat, but a little frantic.—James Baldwin on black jazz musicians' response to Norman Mailer

Homosexuality is a sickness, just as are baby-rape or wanting to become the head of General Motors.—Eldridge Cleaver

Epilogues smell like freedom. It's not simply their proximity to the end that makes this so; rather, it's the distinction they bear in relation to that more burdensome first cousin, the conclusion. In a conclusion one has, of necessity, to conclude. The language of "In conclusion, I have argued that . . ." hovers over the whole enterprise. In an epilogue, however, there's a new sense of space, a withering away of constraint. Given that distinction, my goal here is epilogic rather than conclusive. What I have to say is, as the Greek root of "epilogue" reminds us, *in addition*. In short, I want to do two things here at the end: acknowledge a debt to the past and suggest a path toward the future.

## Studying Whiteness

As I indicated in my introduction, and as I have attempted to make clear throughout, my study of white-supremacist fictions should be understood as part of a larger project that's gaining tremendous momentum within the academy: whiteness studies. Though I began this project before the recent surge in whiteness scholarship, that surge has had a defining impact on the shape and texture of my own explorations. Since the recent increase in attention to whiteness feels like something of a "critical moment," it's worth pausing here to survey this "new" landscape and to ask ourselves what fruits it might bear.

The 1990s have witnessed an explosion of whiteness study, as evidenced in both popular and academic forums. Whiteness panels are becoming de rigueur at scholarly conferences; academic journals have devoted entire issues to whiteness scholarship (*the minnesota review, Transition, American Quarterly, Socialist Review*); trade papers and popular magazines have noted the increased attention to whiteness (*Chronicle of Higher Education, Black Issues in Higher Education, Lingua Franca, Newsweek, Time, New Republic*); *Race Traitor,* a journal whose motto is "Treason to whiteness is loyalty to humanity," has received increasingly wide exposure, from the *Utne Reader* to the hallowed halls of English departments; the *Village Voice* devoted a special issue ("The White Issue," edited by Edward Ball) to the topic, bringing together such diverse perspectives as Gary Indiana and Slavoj Žižek, Susie Bright and Michael Lerner. Work in whiteness crosses boundaries and disciplines. Film, communication, women's studies, education, sociology, queer studies, history, cultural studies, ethnic and American studies—all have devoted their particular methodologies and insights to the study of whiteness.

The extent to which "white" and "whiteness" find themselves increasingly in book titles provides yet another measure of growth in the whiteness industry. The following list stretches back only as far as 1993: *The Wages of Whiteness; Towards the Abolition of Whiteness;*

*Displacing Whiteness; Beyond the Whiteness of Whiteness; The Birth of Whiteness; Heart of Whiteness; Making Whiteness; Making Meaning of Whiteness; The Memory of Whiteness; White; Playing in the Dark: Whiteness and the Literary Imagination; The Possessive Investment in Whiteness; White Lies: Race and the Myths of Whiteness; White Lies: Race, Class, Gender, and Sexuality in White Supremacist Discourse; The Invention of the White Race; The Rise and Fall of the White Republic; White Women, Race Matters; White Reign; Whiteness: A Critical Reader; Whiteness: The Communication of Social Identity; Whiteness of a Different Color; Whiteness Visible; Dismantling White Privilege; The Word in Black and White; National Manhood: Capitalist Citizenship and the Imagined Fraternity of White Men; Racial Situations: Class Predicaments of Whiteness in Detroit; White Women Writing; Becoming and Unbecoming White; How the Irish Became White; Critical White Studies; Whiteness: Feminist Philosophical Reflections; How Jews Became White Folks and What That Says about Race in America; Looking White People in the Eye; Off White; Racechanges: White Skin, Black Face in American Culture; Was Blind, but Now I See: White Race Consciousness and the Law; White by Law; White Man Falling;* and *White Trash.* Chanted, this list becomes something of a mantra for our critical (white) moment.

Since I've described this new body of work as an "explosion," I should point out that explosions depend on fuses being previously lit. Depending on the length of those fuses, it's too often the case that we remember only the bang and not the person(s) with the match. Or, to shift the metaphor, as this new moment of whiteness studies gains institutional momentum, it's important that we resist an image of ourselves as new pioneers bravely charting untrammeled territory. We are not the first to set foot here. Attention to whiteness has a long and varied genealogy—one based in part in African American literary history and black and ethnic studies. As the title of Roediger's *The Wages of Whiteness* makes clear, much contemporary theorizing of whiteness can be traced back to W. E. B. Du Bois. Du Bois's vision of whiteness as a wage—both psychological and economic—has left a lasting imprint on scholars doing contemporary work on whiteness, myself included. Charles Chesnutt's "What Is a White Man?," published in 1889, makes it impossible for any of us to imagine that making whiteness visible is purely a twentieth-century preoccupation. Ralph Ellison's constant insistence on the ontological interdependence of whiteness and blackness has proven to be one of the foundational tenets of recent whiteness study. James Baldwin's essays provide a wealth of penetrating analysis, delivered in Baldwin's unique and biting voice. As he put it in the film *The Price of the Ticket*, "As long as you think you're white, there's no hope for you." Or at the end of "Dark Days," where he quotes Langston Hughes: "It's you who'll have the blues, not me. Just wait and see" (666). Toni Morrison and bell hooks have provided more recent contributions to whiteness scholarship, insisting that whiteness be interrogated, and that too much of the problem with contemporary race studies (particularly as practiced by white scholars) is that whiteness is allowed free and invisible reign, forever unmarked in contrast to the never-ending marking of blackness.[1]

As much as the contemporary work being done on whiteness owes to this long line of African American scholars, writers, and activists, there's another genealogy also worth tracing, one that leads to the heart of 1970s feminism and its early forays into the analysis of sexuality as an ideological structure. What might be called the central and transformative dilemma of seventies feminism—the gradual awareness that its general exclusion of women of color was no longer, and never had been, tenable—actually led to some of the earliest and most explicit theorizing of whiteness as a site of narcissistic and exclusionary privilege.[2] This theorizing often went hand in hand with a similar realization about heterosexuality. *Straight/White/Male*, a 1976 collection of feminist essays edited by Glenn Bucher, offers an interesting and instructive example of this early moment of white self-consciousness. Part 1 ("Attention! Honkies, Sexists, and Straights") quickly establishes its mode of address as well as its intended audience, and the essays collected here insist on marking whiteness and heterosexuality as interrelated categories. With such chapters as "The Meaning of Whiteness" and "Maleness and Heterosexuality," this volume provides a surprising early moment in which various normative categories—whiteness, maleness, heterosexuality, the middle class—were provocatively linked in an overarching analysis.

The feminist work of Marilyn Frye provides another example of how whiteness study has its roots in earlier modes of analysis. Her 1981 essay, "On Being White: Thinking toward a Feminist Understanding of Race and Race Supremacy," and subsequent essays on "whiteliness" and respectability locate some of the roots of whiteness study in the feminism of the 1970s and 1980s. Though Frye's essays, as well as those in the Bucher collection, too often betray the negative potential of guilty white liberalism, these earlier efforts to challenge whiteness's invisibility and its normative power deserve attention from critics doing whiteness study in the years to come.[3]

Queer studies in the 1980s and 1990s has become another site where whiteness has been poked and prodded. Cherrie Moraga and Gloria Anzaldúa's landmark collection *This Bridge Called My Back* (1981) has influenced and produced a significant body of work theorizing the varied intersections of race, class, ethnicity, and sexuality. The work of white lesbian writers Minnie Bruce Pratt and Mab Segrest offers evidence of Moraga and Anzaldua's continuing influence. Kobena Mercer has also made substantial contributions toward making whiteness visible, in part through his acute analysis of the raced homo-erotics of Robert Mapplethorpe's black male nudes. Like feminism, which has seen itself working against various normative and oppressive ideologies, queer scholars have begun to use their focus on heterosexuality as a productive place to think about whiteness as a part of the problem.[4]

### In Through the Out Door

Although this history of whiteness studies shows it to have a rich and varied past, it's also clear that white scholarly attention to whiteness too often reproduces what could be called the founding tenets of white critical practice: narcissism and an extreme narrowness of vision. To wrap up this brief genealogy and move toward a conclusion, I want to think through and problematize the often utopian cast to much contemporary whiteness study, asking what claims we should and shouldn't make about its potential payoffs. The title of Roediger's *Towards the Abolition of Whiteness* sets the stage. The title foregrounds provisionality (the "towards" is extremely important) at the same time that it suggests the possibility for something less provisional—abolition. Roediger sees whiteness as a second skin that must be shed, as a way of living in the world that can and must be radically reoriented. Yet he simultaneously suggests that such a shedding is ultimately impossible. Whiteness must be jettisoned, but "there is a sense in which whites cannot fully renounce whiteness even if they want to" (*Towards* 16). The tension between utopian desire and material reality is significant precisely because it isn't Roediger's alone. There's a sense in which it has become a defining quality of white self-awareness.

The journal *Race Traitor* faces a similar dilemma, but with less suspicion than Roediger voices. Here's how Noel Ignatiev, one of the journal's coeditors, defines "race traitor": "A traitor to the white race is someone who is nominally classified as white, but who defies the rules of whiteness so flagrantly as to jeopardize his or her ability to draw upon the privileges of the white skin" ("Treason" 82). *Race Traitor*'s reason for being is the abolition of whiteness through a collective renunciation of its privileges. As the title of one of its essays suggests, the journal is dedicated to mapping a way "out of whiteness." In this scenario, whiteness *is* ultimately something that can be shed, but only if enough people decide it's worth doing.[5]

But the essay to which I just referred—Christopher Day's "Out of Whiteness"—demonstrates the limits of this kind of rhetoric. Day identifies himself as a white, bisexual male. "I find it difficult," he writes, "to separate in my mind my queerness from my race treachery" (55). He believes that "it is possible for white people to break with whiteness and join the rest of humanity in the fight for a better world" (56). Although Day is absolutely right to argue that "heterosexuality and whiteness fulfill similar functions in the enforcement of authoritarian social relations" (55), I'm less persuaded by his suggestion that queerness opens up a path "out of whiteness." Such a claim depends on a dangerously reductive vision of this country's queer demographic, ignoring the scores of guppies who trade on whiteness daily, using it, in fact, as a relatively secure path to their own "outness." In short, rather than seeing queerness as a way out of whiteness, it's possible to see it as yet another constitutive part of what whiteness makes possible. This ironic relationship—queerness threatens whiteness, but whiteness makes queerness more palatable—demonstrates the risks in hastily granting the type of subversive potential to queer sexuality that Day does. It also demonstrates the danger in putting too much faith in the rhetorical stance of the new abolitionists. This rhetoric of "a way out of whiteness" is not merely naive; it insults those who understand through experience the effect of skin color on one's ability to survive American racism.

If whiteness can't be abolished, what is to be done instead? One answer to this question comes from what some are calling "whiteness pedagogy" or the "pedagogy of whiteness." Here the emphasis is on reinventing rather than abolishing whiteness, so that white students "gain a sense of hope that they can contribute to a better world by living their whiteness progressively" (Rodriguez 34). Joe Kincheloe and Shirley Steinberg describe a key goal of this reinvention: "the necessity of creating a positive, proud, attractive, antiracist white identity that is empowered to travel in and out of various racial/ethnic circles with confidence and empathy" (12). According to Kincheloe and Steinberg, "such pedagogical work is anything but easy; progressive Whites will require sophisticated help and support to pull them through the social, political, and psychological dilemmas they all will face. In such a context, those attempting to rethink their identity and to address the cultural and institutional racism they encounter always need strong support groups . . . if for nothing else to help them survive emotionally" (23). We are witnessing, according to Kincheloe and Steinberg, a "white identity crisis" (25), but there is hope, since, they argue, "a pedagogy of whiteness is one of the most compelling notions to emerge in decades in the struggle for racial justice" (26).[6]

Having arisen in opposition to the new abolitionist position, the notion that whiteness can be reinvented along a more progressive model shares the new abolitionist's naive utopianism and adds to it a rather insulting language of white victimization. I'm not sure now is the time for a "proud" and "empowered" whiteness, nor am I convinced that the reconfiguration of whiteness as something to be claimed and sought after should be our goal—at least not yet. Wouldn't such a reinvention merely reproduce the same under the sign of difference, even if that difference is cloaked in the language of social justice? One imagines newly empowered white folks, confident that they now hold the key to antiracism, making the same old blunders as they "travel in and out of various racial/ethnic circles."[7]

There's a sense, then, that this language of a "way out" of whiteness or a "reinvention" of whiteness simply reproduces the white liberal ruminations that achieved full force in the 1960s and that continue to this day. With guilt and complicity as the starting points, white liberals worked assiduously to assuage that guilt through a renunciation of the privileges that made them complicit in the first place. Did this offer them a way out of whiteness? Absolutely not. Rather, white liberal hand-wringing too often became a gestural response that further solidified, in a roundabout way, white privilege. Instead of providing a way out of whiteness, it offered a way back in. Guilt became a constitutive part of what we now mean when we think about whiteness. Although Kincheloe and Steinberg recognize the paralyzing effects of white guilt, their substitution of white empowerment strikes me as a poor one.

In thinking spatially about the ins and outs of whiteness, a pattern begins to emerge. Intended movements out of whiteness inevitably become retrenchments. One seems always to move in through the out door. I want to offer one more example to clarify this cyclical and recuperative movement, a movement that I take to be the clearest indicator of whiteness's hegemonic power. In *Towards the Abolition of Whiteness,* Roediger argues that white suburban youth who adopt hip-hop style are engaging in a subversive critique of whiteness without a consequent expropriation of blackness. He writes, "Hiphop offers white youth not only the spontaneity, experimentation, humor, danger, sexuality, physical movement and rebellion absent from what passes as white culture but it also offers an explicit, often harsh, critique of whiteness" (15–16). Well, yes and no. Since this race trading depends on the consumerist logic of hip-hop—since it is always already part of the commodification of "blackness"—then we ought to be very careful about the claims we make for its subversive potentials. Are white kids, in their baggy pants and borrowed sexuality, really critiquing whiteness, or has whiteness here found a way to reinvent itself, though always as whiteness? It may very well be that these white kids aren't critiquing whiteness so much as they are keeping it relevant, making it new, making it marketable. Even if there are elements of critique in this new white style, it's a critique that leaves whiteness firmly intact, simultaneously reinforcing the invisibility— the lack—that makes whiteness so effective. This racial cross-dressing pretends once again to make blackness the focus—the thing that we see—while reestablishing whiteness as the normative and colonizing subject. The ability of whiteness to recover itself has played a significant and unfortunate role in the history of white self-consciousness.[8]

We would do well to keep this history in mind at the current moment. Let's be honest: white people have never been very good at thinking about their own whiteness. Despite Marilyn Frye's contention that whites "in some ways know themselves best" ("White Woman" 152), I put more faith in bell hooks's point about the "special knowledge" blacks have gathered about whites through the ages, information obtained from the seldom-noticed space of black subjectivity. As hooks writes, "For years black domestic servants, working in white homes, acted as informants who brought knowledge back to segregated communities—details, facts, observations, psychoanalytic readings of the white "Other" (338). Given whites' only partial successes in seeing themselves as clearly as blacks have been forced to see them, I'm not convinced that the current critical moment is going to mark a turning point. We might instead find ourselves at yet another stage in the "changing same," as whiteness finds a way to incorporate a late-nineties self-awareness into its usual game.

It's worth noting, however, that the hesitation I just enacted in the previous two sentences has become something of a stock scene in whiteness studies (though it usually happens at the beginning of works such as this rather than at the end). To take just a few examples: in the introduction to *Whiteness: A Critical Reader,* Mike Hill wastes no more than a page before he begins to list the problems created by the study of whiteness, going so far as to suggest that "the desire for white critique may be nearly impossible" (3). Ruth Frankenberg, in the introduction to *Displacing Whiteness,* gets no farther than a paragraph before she points out the very real danger of "recentering rather than decentering" whiteness (2). In *White,* Richard Dyer only makes it through a single sentence before he mentions the "problems" inherent in his project. In his foreword to *White Reign: Deploying Whiteness in America,* Michael Apple takes two and a half pages before he points out that "there are dangers" in making whiteness the subject of analysis (xi). These "anticipatory flinches" (x), to borrow Fred Pfeil's language from another context, reach a remarkable apex near the end of the introduction to *Off White: Readings on Race, Power, and Society,* edited by Michelle Fine, Lois Weis, Linda C. Powell, and L. Mun Wong. In a section subtitled "Worries" ("As for our worries for the volume, yes, we have a few"), the editors write:

> We worry that in our desire to create spaces to speak, intellectually and empirically, about whiteness, we may have reified whiteness as a fixed category of experience and identity; that we have allowed it to be treated as a monolith, in the singular, as an "essential something." We despair that a terrifying academic flight toward something called white studies could eclipse the important work

being done across the range of race, postcolonialism, ethnicity, and "people of color"; that research funds could shift categories; that understanding whiteness could surface as the new intellectual fetish, leaving questions of power, privilege, and race/ethnic political minorities behind as an intellectual "fad" of the past. (xi–xii)

This justifiably anxious catalog not only emblematizes the stock scene of whiteness studies; it also takes that scene one step further. The editors continue, "We worry, therefore, that there will follow a spate of books on whiteness when, in part, we (arrogantly? narcissistically? greedily? responsibly?) believe that maybe this should be the last book on whiteness" (xii). Although I applaud the editors' parenthetical honesty about their possibly conflicted motivations, I worry that their anxiety will become what anxiety often becomes: paralysis. Though this paralysis may have different origins than the white guilt that preceded it, it nonetheless makes it impossible to move forward.

By pointing out this repetition of critical hesitation, I in no way mean to suggest that an unselfconscious approach to whiteness study would yield richer results. After all, an unselfconscious relation to whiteness is precisely the problem of whiteness, the thing that keeps it unmarked and uninterrogated. But what does it mean that the solution to this problem brings with it a reinscription of the problem itself—that our attempt to displace whiteness triggers a need to talk about the problems of such displacement, resulting in, at best, a narcissistic critical practice and, at worst, the critical paralysis called for and displayed by the editors of *Off White*? Is it really time to cease this talk of whiteness, to send whiteness back to the invisible center from which it came? Wouldn't that simply be the latest trick up whiteness's sleeve, a supremely ironic manifestation of its continuous ability to avoid the glare of the spotlight?

## Three Men and a Baby

Although it should be obvious by this point that I have decided against heeding such a cease-and-desist order, it should also be obvious that a change is necessary in the way we talk about whiteness, in the way we have made it the center of our analysis even as we have tried to deny it that center. As I have argued in the preceding chapters, one way to avoid this problem is to yoke whiteness to other normative structures. For my purposes, the most important of these other structures has been heterosexuality. As a way to conclude, I want to risk one final reading (and I use "risk" here deliberately), this time borrowing from a more recent eruption of America's racial unconscious. Although I suggested above that queerness doesn't necessarily open a path "out of whiteness," here I want to suggest that whiteness is itself queer, and that this queerness can be useful to those of us seeking insight into whiteness's vulnerabilities. I have called this reading a "risk" because it depends on insights generated in the homophobic imaginary. Starring Eldridge Cleaver, James Baldwin, and Norman Mailer, this is the story of three men and a baby.

In his "Notes on a Native Son" (1968), black nationalist Eldridge Cleaver describes James Baldwin as "a talent capable of penetrating so profoundly into one's own little world that one knows oneself to have been unalterably changed and liberated" (96). In this formulation Baldwin is the phallic writer, whose penetrating thrust transforms the reader (in Cleaver's case the male reader) utterly. Before we can unpack the implications of Baldwin's thrust into Cleaver's world, however, Cleaver almost immediately revises this drama of artistic procreation: "I . . . lusted for anything that Baldwin had written. It would have been a gas for me to sit on a pillow beneath the womb of Baldwin's typewriter and catch each newborn page as it entered this world of ours" (96). Baldwin has shifted from penetrator to penetrated, Cleaver from penetrated man to lusting midwife.

In the same essay, Cleaver calls Norman Mailer's "The White Negro" (1957) "prophetic and penetrating" (97)—there's that word again—and chastises Baldwin for his "schoolmarmish dismissal" (97) of Mailer's work. In "The Black Boy Looks at the White Boy" (1961) Baldwin had indeed criticized "The White Negro"—had called it, in fact, "impenetrable" (228). Cleaver admits that "The White Negro" "may contain an excess of esoteric verbal husk" (97), but, he continues, "one can forgive Mailer for that because of the solid kernel of truth he gave us. After all, it is the baby we want and not the blood of afterbirth" (97). Like Baldwin, in Cleaver's hands Mailer changes from penetrator to penetrated, from phallic writer to writer in the stirrups.

Cleaver's obsession with childbirth is the offspring of his even greater obsession with heterosexuality. For Cleaver, heterosexuality is the force at the very center of the universe. As he writes in "The Primeval Mitosis," "When the Primeval Sphere divided itself, it established a basic tension of attraction, a dynamic magnetism of oppo-sites—the Primeval Urge—which exerts an irresistible attraction be-tween the male and the female hemispheres, ever tending to fuse them back together into a unity in which the male and female realize their true nature—the lost unity of the Primeval Sphere. This is the eter-nal and unwavering motivation of the male and female hemispheres, of man and woman, to transcend the Primeval Mitosis and achieve supreme identity in the Apocalyptic Fusion" (164). Not only does this passage explain why Cleaver was willing to tolerate Mailer's "esoteric verbal husk," but it also explains the slippages in the passages I quoted earlier. In Cleaver's mind the artist must be both male and female.

But here's where Baldwin complicates things. Although the homo-phobic imagination normally figures the gay man as both man and woman, Cleaver can't allow Baldwin that doubleness. Only Mailer can successfully play both roles—he himself claims as much in "The White Negro," where he associates white Negroism with bisexuality (351). When Baldwin plays both male and female, he, according to Cleaver, involves himself in a "racial death wish" ("Notes" 100). He involves himself in whiteness. As Cleaver writes in "Notes on a Native Son," "It seems that many Negro homosexuals . . . are outraged and frustrated because in their sickness they are unable to have a baby by a white man. The cross they have to bear is that, already bend-ing over and touching their toes for the white man, the fruit of their miscegenation is not the little half-white offspring of their dreams but an increase in the unwinding of their nerves—though they re-double their efforts and intake of the white man's sperm" (100). In this formulation Baldwin is once again penetrated and pregnant, but Cleaver is no longer so excited about sitting "beneath the womb of Baldwin's typewriter" to catch the offspring, that unwinding of black nerves. Cleaver does, however, maintain an admiration for Baldwin the writer, though this admiration of course gets mixed up in the dis-tortive logics of race and sexuality: "Baldwin has a superb touch when he speaks of human beings, when he is inside of them—especially his homosexuals" (106). Cleaver applauds, once again, Baldwin the pene-trator, the skillful writer inside "his homosexuals." Cleaver's problem comes, apparently, when Baldwin's homosexuals are inside him.

Cleaver is intent in "Notes on a Native Son" on reifying an equiva-lent relation of blackness and heterosexuality. Since Baldwin's homo-sexuality disrupts this equivalence, Mailer must stand in for what is really heterosexual about blackness, an odd substitution, to say the least, though one Mailer had earned, presumably, through the racial cross-dressing of his white Negro. The result is that homosexuality and whiteness turn out to be the same thing for Cleaver, both representing "a dying culture and civilization alienated from its biology" ("Primeval" 164). Despite the homophobia that generates this "insight," there is a way in which it can be useful to us. Cleaver's claim that whiteness is "alienated from . . . biology" anticipates a central claim of our current moment: that there is, in fact, nothing biological about whiteness. Although Cleaver wants to hang onto the biological as the final arbiter of the good—the natural—he nevertheless positions whiteness as a dead form, as a way of living in the world that cannot endure. Although Cleaver's homophobia is repugnant (though it wasn't his alone in 1968, nor would it be now), its relation to his thinking about whiteness is neither accidental nor arbitrary. There is, in fact, a logic to it—more specifically, a reproductive logic. When Cleaver claims that "homosexuality is a sickness," just like "baby-rape," he economically describes what he takes to be the problem of homosexuality: its inability to reproduce itself. For Cleaver, homosexuality is like baby-rape because it is an assault on the very idea of babies, on the notion of continuance, on the possibility of reproduction. Black nationalist Larry Neal makes a similar point when he describes Edward Albee's *Who's Afraid of Virginia Woolf?* (a play concerned in part with the failure of white reproduction) as "very American: sick white lives in a homosexual hell hole" (68–69).

Although Cleaver and Neal see the problem of whiteness to be a problem of reproduction, others of us might rearticulate this problem as a goal. What I'm talking about here is finding our way to a place where whiteness no longer reproduces itself, where it is no longer self-generating. It should go without saying that I'm not talking about the end of a "biological whiteness" or the end of white people. Rather, I mean the end of whiteness as a locus of identity; as a site for the production of culture; as an organizing trope for community and for politics. Although some may say that this goal of a nonreproductive whiteness merely reproduces the naive utopianism of the new abolitionists, I would offer an important distinction. The process I envision is a slow and gradual one. It's not something that can be willed or chosen. It's more a historical fact in the making than an act of politics, or of good intentions. Unlike abolition, it will not happen with the stroke of a pen.

We saw in chapters 1 and 2 that whiteness and heterosexuality can be usefully seen as analogous structures—normative copartners in the coercions of racial and sexual power. In this formulation whiteness imagined that it could guarantee itself a future by allying itself with the great white hope of reproduction, heterosexuality. Yet with Chesnutt, and even more so with Dixon, we witnessed a strikingly different relation between these two structures, a relation that shows up once again in the Cleaver/Baldwin/Mailer triangle. Because Cleaver and Dixon become distracted in their attention to whiteness by their anxiety over heterosexuality, whiteness has the room in which to behave naturally, to assume all sorts of contradictory and complementary shapes and guises. In both Cleaver and Dixon's formulations whiteness isn't so much the normative structure of racial power as it is the abject, barren, and impotent mark of racial death. Its alliance with the reproductive powers of heterosexuality turned out to be abortive. Or to borrow a suggestive phrase from Richard Dyer, Cleaver and Dixon both silently understand, from their radically different points of view, the "dead end of whiteness" (*White* xv). The irony of this is obvious and instructive. The white supremacist and the black nationalist end up agreeing. In both accounts, whiteness lacks a future.

If there's a lesson in this for our critical practice, I think it goes something like this: looking at whiteness is like looking at the sun. The only way to see it is to refract our vision. This refraction throws whiteness off, makes it vulnerable. It reveals "within the very integuments of 'whiteness,'" to quote Homi Bhabha, "the agonistic elements that make it the unsettled, disturbed form of authority that it is" (21). This unsettled and disturbed whiteness should be the primary goal of our critical practice, at least for the near future. Not the abolition of whiteness, à la the *Race Traitor* camp, since this invokes a dangerously utopian model. And not the reinvented whiteness championed by the pedagogy camp, since this not only leaves whiteness intact, but even more comfortable with itself. Rather, an unsettled and disturbed whiteness—because this is when whiteness is most revealed, most instructive, most worth learning from. This is when whiteness exposes its anxieties about the white future, its repressed awareness (à la Dixon) that such a future may, in fact, be an impossibility. Whiteness studies has a role to play in this unsettling. Its articulation of white power and white vulnerability is a necessary step forward.

That said, we need to be very humble about the claims we make. Whiteness studies isn't going to end racism. This merely states the obvious, of course, but it's important to say it anyway. In fact, whiteness studies may not even make a dent in racism. Given the history of the best of white intentions, this shouldn't surprise us. Despite our desire to believe otherwise, we need to accept a realistic vision of what's to be gained from this renewed attention to whiteness. If we stop pretending that whiteness studies will lead us to the promised land of a new racial justice, we can pay attention to more prosaic claims, to more realistic payoffs. We can say, at the very least, that the study of whiteness adds to our knowledge about race and ethnicity in American culture. We can say that it gives us a new and richer way of thinking about class, gender, and sexuality. Humble claims? Perhaps not. To claim this much is actually to claim a great deal. And so we go forward, poking and prodding whiteness until it ends up where it never meant to go—until it divulges secrets it didn't even know it was keeping.

# Notes

## Introduction: White Fictions

1  For discussions of Jacobs's location within the literary confines of sentimental fiction see Valerie Smith's introduction to the Schomburg edition of *Incidents* and Jean Fagan Yellin's introduction to the Harvard edition.

2  Henry Louis Gates Jr. describes the dynamic I'm tracing here as "the curious dialectic between formal language use and the inscription of metaphorical racial differences" ("Writing 'Race' and the Difference It Makes" 6). For more on the ambivalent connections between race and writing see this essay and the volume it appears in, *Race, Writing, and Difference*.

3  In other contexts Helper did indeed propose many of these "solutions." His goal was the complete removal of blacks from the presence of whites, and he didn't limit his suggestions to the purely discursive realm. The irony of his racist activism lies in his staunch antislavery beliefs, which were based on an economic argument against slavery's continuance in the southern states. For more on Helper see Fredrickson's introduction to *The Impending Crisis*.

4  Fredrickson suggests that "*Nojoque* is the product of an unbalanced mind" ("Introduction" li) and describes Helper's racism as "pathological" (lvii). Although grounds for these assessments certainly exist, I worry that pathologizing Helper in this way can create a false distinction between "crazy racism" and "sane racism," when it would be more accurate to see racism itself, no matter what the flavor, as a pathology. Helper's title (Nojoque = no joke) warns against taking his efforts too lightly.

5  Although Darwin is often assumed to have breathed new life into mid-nineteenth-century scientific racism, this assumption actually depends on a misreading of *On the Origin of Species* (1859). Midcentury scientific racism was increasingly based in physical anthropology, and as Peter Bowler argues, "there is little evidence . . . that the Darwinian theory of evolution had any major influence on physical anthropology" (139). In fact, Bowler argues, Darwin's theory of evolution through natural selection actually made it harder to sustain the view of a hierarchy of races with the "white race" on the top. As Bowler writes, "Although many Darwinians adopted the conventional attitude toward race, it can hardly be said that Darwin's particular theory of evolution flourished because it could be used to support the racial hierarchy. In fact, [Darwin's] image of branching, haphazard evolution was difficult to reconcile with the belief that the white race is in some absolute sense the most developed form of the human species" (163).

This does not mean, however, that Darwin doesn't bear some responsibility for the "survival of the fittest" language of Social Darwinism. George Fredrickson quotes Darwin from 1881: "Looking at the world at no very distant date, what an endless number of lower races will be eliminated by the higher civilized races throughout the world" (qtd. in *Black Image* 230). And as Darwin wrote in *The Descent of Man* (1871), "At some future period, not very distant as measured by centuries, the civilized races of man will almost certainly exterminate and replace the savage races throughout the world" (qtd. in *Black Image* 230). These predictions arise naturally from *Origin*'s subtitle, *The Preservation of Favoured Races in the Struggle for Life*.

Nancy Leys Stepan and Sander L. Gilman attribute the uses and misuses of Darwin to his reliance on "charged and metaphoric language" (80). As they write, "Darwin could not keep control over the metaphors he introduced. . . . Nearly every term he used was multivalent and was appropriated in selective and varied ways by very different groups for different purposes" (80). See also Thomas F. Gossett, *Race: The History of an Idea in America* (esp. 67–69, 145). For a more detailed discussion of the racial implications of Darwinism see Nancy Stepan, *The Idea of Race in Science;* Gould, 416–20.

6   Jennifer DeVere Brody points out this danger in her review of Ruth Frankenberg's *White Women, Race Matters.* Concerning Frankenberg's general exclusion of nonwhite responses to the narratives of whiteness she offers, Brody writes, "This tendency to marginalize women of color or, rather, to reference them without really using their differing ideas as tools for thinking about the simultaneity of race, class, and gender is one of the risks of recentering whiteness in an effort to make it visible in all its multiplicity" (157).

7   Lincoln's alleged familiarity with Victor's novel may be apocryphal. Kathleen Maio writes that *Maum Guinea* "is said to have been praised by both President Lincoln and Henry Ward Beecher" (303), and Charles Harvey tells a similar story, but I've been unable to document the source of this hearsay.

8   In choosing this methodology, I'm loosely following Richard Dyer's suggestion in "White" that close study of "images of the white race in avowedly racist and fascist cinema" might yield a clearer picture of whiteness as a lived cultural and representational form (46).

9   My decision not to focus on canonical representations of whiteness is also rooted in the encouraging fact that good work is already being done there. See Mary Sisney, "The Power and Horror of Whiteness: Wright and Ellison Respond to Poe"; J. Lasley Dameron, "Melville and Scoresby on Whiteness"; Toni Morrison, "Romancing the Shadow" in *Playing in the Dark.*

10   In positioning Tompkins's work in this way, I do not mean to imply that it is without flaws, simply that it marked a shift in institutional thinking. For critiques of Tompkins see Lauren Berlant's review of *Sensational Designs* in *Modern Philology* and Ann Cvetkovich's argument in *Mixed Feelings* (125). For a useful overview of the debates that Tompkins's book both participated in and prompted (particularly its relation to Ann Douglass's *The Feminization of American Culture*) see Laura Wexler's "Tender Violence: Literary Eavesdropping, Domestic Fiction, and Educational Reform."

11   Agreeing with Cvetkovich, Rita Felski writes, "Rather than either reproducing or heroically resisting a univocal dominant ideology, popular fiction can more usefully be read as comprising a variety of ideological strands that cohere to or contradict each other in diverse ways" (142).

12   See, for example, Gates, "Writing 'Race' and the Difference It Makes."

13   Cornel West dramatizes this necessary slippage in an interview with Noel Ignatiev and William "Upski" Wimsatt. At one point he "want[s] to insist on a distinction between whiteness and white supremacy" (180), but later he collapses that distinction when he says, "And so when we talk about whiteness, we talk about white

supremacy. I think in the end, that's the bottom line" (198). See West, "I'm Ofay, You're Ofay."

14 The word had made its first appearance—along with *homosexual*—in the private correspondence of German sex-law reformer Karl Maria Kertbeny in 1868 (Katz 52).

15 See, for example, Susan Fraiman's "Geometries of Race and Gender: Eve Sedgwick, Spike Lee, Charlayne Hunter-Gault."

16 Katz is following Foucault's discussion of the "deployment of alliance: a system of marriage, of fixation and development of kinship ties, of transmission of names and possessions" (Foucault, *History* 106). For Foucault, marriage is a structure used to produce and regulate "sexuality," which he defines as "a great surface network in which the stimulation of bodies, the intensification of pleasures, the incitement to discourse, the formation of special knowledges, the strengthening of controls and resistances, are linked to one another, in accordance with a few major strategies of knowledge" (105–6).

17 I was alerted to this matrimonial trend in Krafft-Ebing's case histories by Katz. See *The Invention of Heterosexuality*, 21–32.

*1. "De White Man in Season"*

1 Reprinted from the *Pennsylvanian* in the *Liberator*, June 11, 1852.

2 Peterson actually published the novel under the pseudonym J. Thornton Randolph. I use his real name throughout, however, since that was the name he was most widely known by.

3 See chapter 12 of Gossett's *Uncle Tom's Cabin and American Culture* for a descriptive catalog of anti–Uncle Tom literature.

4 As Anna Julia Cooper points out, however, not all novels about slavery were equally worthwhile. As Cooper writes, "Not many have had Mrs. Stowe's power because not many have studied with Mrs. Stowe's humility and love. . . . Some have taken up the subject with a view to establishing evidences of ready formulated theories and preconceptions; and, blinded by their prejudices and antipathies, have altogether abjured all candid and careful study. Others with flippant indifference have performed a few psychological experiments on their cooks and coachmen, and with astounding egotism, and powers of generalization positively bewildering, forthwith aspire to enlighten the world with dissertations on racial traits of the Negro" (186).

5 The primacy of slavery as the new middle-class entertainment extended beyond the written page. According to an ad in the *New York Tribune* of November 5, 1852, readers could now enjoy "the NEW and INTERESTING GAME of UNCLE TOM and LITTLE EVA," priced at twenty-five cents. The ad continues: "The interest which one may take in this Game is considerable, and the more it is played the greater the desire for it. . . . The execution of the cuts, which are colored, representing the characters of UNCLE TOM'S CABIN, are beyond all censure. They are life-like and expressive. For the workmanship displayed in getting up this Game, for the pleasing and endless enjoyment one may derive in its study, and for the extraordinary low price at which it is offered, stamps it the Game of the season [*sic*]." The point of the game was apparently to rescue slaves from slavery and to reunite broken families. That the cuts

are "colored" provides an obvious irony, as does the fact that the game perpetuates itself through an increase in pleasure. This parlor abolition ensures the continuation of the game's "slavery," since the slaves must find themselves in slavery once again for the game to continue. The novel I take up in the next chapter, *Maum Guinea and Her Plantation "Children,"* offers a literary parallel to this cycle of pleasure and enslavement.

6   These numbers, taken from the publisher's advertisement itself, may be slightly suspect. They are, however, the closest we can get to gauging the sales of the novel at the time of its publication.

7   According to the *National Union Catalog,* another edition of *The Cabin and Parlor* was published sometime in the 1850s under the new title, *Courtenay Hall; Or, The Hospitality and Life in a Planter's Family; A True Tale of Virginia Life.* Although no exact date for this rerelease is available, the retitling does signal a passing of the Uncle Tom mania, since Peterson dropped all mention of cabins and focused instead on the pleasures of the southern aristocracy.

8   A notice for the novel in the *Southern Literary Messenger* makes a similar point. Calling *The Cabin and Parlor* "good in all respects," the notice continues, "we can only regret that by similarity of title and the time of its publication, it should be associated, in any way, with Mrs. Beecher Stowe's volumes, of the very name of which the public are getting heartily tired, for 'The Cabin and Parlor' is excellent enough to have won for itself a wide popularity, in the absence of that surfeit of 'nigger' literature, which now sickens the popular taste" (703). A telling reversal of abolitionist opinion, this review worries that an association with Stowe's book might taint Peterson's better and saner production, rather than vice versa.

9   Graham never uses Peterson's name in reference to *The Cabin and Parlor,* using instead the pseudonym under which the book was published. Peterson and Graham were friends, though they ran competing magazines. Graham was largely responsible for Peterson's start in the magazine business and even suggested that Peterson start his own magazine.

10   The antislavery response to Graham's article was so lively and widespread that Graham devoted space in the next issue of his magazine to a personal response. Graham responded specifically to Frederick Douglass's charge that he simply hates "niggerism" by revealing that he has "taught blacks in a Sunday-school for years, as a duty" (*Graham's,* Mar. 1853, 365). Focusing on what he calls abolitionist hypocrisy in reference to the treatment of free blacks in the North, Graham ends his editorial with the italicized line, "'FRIENDS OF THE BLACK MAN!'—Face the music" (366).

11   These seven refutations are worth quoting in full, if only by way of showing the extent to which Whipple took Peterson's novel, and its argument, seriously. Peterson's novel depends, Whipple writes, on the following "false and sophistical positions": "1st. That the negroes of Philadelphia fairly represent those of all the Northern States and Canada. 2d. That the most vulgar and brutal portion of the white people of Philadelphia fairly represent the entire white population of the North. 3d. That slaves are very rarely sold from the Northern slave regions to the Southern, and that families are very rarely separated in the selling. 4th. That both the happiness and welfare of the slaves generally are abundantly cared for by their

masters. 5th. That it is wrong, and that the more intelligent slaves think it is wrong, for slaves to take and keep their own liberty, and that of their wives and children; in other words, that religion approves the enslavement, and discourages the emancipation of the colored people. 6th. That the condition of the slave is always made worse by running away. And finally, 7th. That the injustice and contumely with which colored people are treated at the North, (instead of being, as it is, a direct and natural consequence of slavery, and incapable of even the commencement of a radical reform until slavery shall cease,) is an independent fact, leading fairly to the inference that slavery is better for the colored race than freedom." Whipple concludes that arguments like Peterson's actually further the cause of abolition, since they so economically demonstrate the sophistry of proslavery rhetoric.

12   Phyllis Palmer makes a similar point: "A wife's association with physical dirt contaminates her character in much the same way as her association with illicit sex. In the Western unconscious of the past two centuries, indeed, dirt and sex live in close association" (138). See Palmer, *Domesticity and Dirt.*

13   If we chart the flow of Thompson's language, we again notice the distinctions between women, ladies, and females. Women write; ladies read. When women write, they use female pens. The "mind of woman" is in danger. Men "think" of ladies reading with "shame and repugnance."

14   See chapter 11 of Gossett's *Uncle Tom's Cabin and American Culture* for a discussion of the southern response to Stowe's novel.

15   It's important to note that southern white men weren't the only ones offended by Stowe's novel. Blacks—both northern and southern—found a great deal in *Uncle Tom's Cabin* offensive and counterproductive to their fight against slavery and racism. Stowe's emphasis on black docility and her seemingly favorable views on forced black colonization met a loud and vocal black resistance. Speaking of Stowe's complicity with the country's procolonization forces, Martin Delany wrote that "I will never, knowingly, lend my aid to any such work while our brethren groan in vassalage and bondage" (qtd. in Banks 220). And as black Garrisonian Robert Purvis put it in a letter to the *Pennsylvania Freeman*, "Save us from our friends" (Ripley 124). For more on black responses to Stowe's novel see Marva Banks, "*Uncle Tom's Cabin* and Antebellum Black Response."

16   Mid–nineteenth century feelings about miscegenation tended toward two strains. On the one hand, as George Fredrickson has argued, the rise of a scientific racism in the 1840s and 1850s lent a certain legitimacy to taboos against miscegenation. As J. Aitken Meigs wrote in 1857, "As long as the blood of one citizen . . . differs from that of another, diverse and probably long forgotten forms would crop out . . . as indications of the past, and obstacles to the assumption of that perfectly homogenous character which belongs to true stocks alone" (qtd. in Fredrickson, *Black Image* 132).

On the other hand, this scientific approach simply played on more visceral responses to intermarriage. As William Drayton wrote in 1837, "But is such amalgamation possible? The fanatics, who pause not at the prospect of insurrection and slaughter, may, perhaps, regard without nausea, this process of harmonization. They may have sufficiently schooled and perverted their natural feelings, to endure a prospect at which ordinary human nature sickens. . . . But this subject can scarce be even referred to, without a breach of propriety, without feelings of nauseated disgust and excited indignation. The man who can insult the fair and accomplished ladies of this country, by conceiving, much less avowing, a belief of the possibility of such deep, unnatural and damning degradation—deserves the most emphatic expression of the abhorrence of society" (234–35).

17    See Lipsitz, "The Possessive Investment in Whiteness: Racialized Social Democracy and the 'White' Problem in American Studies." Lipsitz argues that whiteness perpetuates itself because its adherents have a great deal at stake in its continuance. The phrase "possessive investment" echoes Du Bois's notion, and more recently Richard Dyer's, of whiteness as both an economic and a psychological wage that makes an adherence to its values worthwhile. Eric Sundquist makes a related point in his reading of *Puddinhead Wilson* in the context of "Homer V. Plessy," where he emphasizes whiteness as a form of property. The problem for Tom Driscoll and Homer Plessy, however, was that this "property is not self-possession or identity but a sign of the rights of others" (Sundquist, *To Wake* 268).

18    The equation of slavery with Paradise provides an interesting counterpoint to the Paradise imagined in the texts I examine in chapter 3.

19    See Roediger, *Wages* 133–67.

20    St. Clare makes a version of this argument in *Uncle Tom's Cabin* when he tells Ophelia that the wage laborer "is as much at the will of his employer as if he were sold to him. The slave-owner can whip his refractory slave to death,—the capitalist can starve him to death. As to family security, it is hard to say which is the worst,— to have one's children sold, or see them starve to death at home" (Stowe 231).

21    Peterson probably wouldn't see it this way. His point in crafting this chicken scenario has more to do with proving how loyal slaves can be—how willing they are to help their masters in their time of greatest need. Contrary to Charles and Cora, Peter and Violet never thought of running away. Peterson's point here is meant to counter those abolitionists who argue that slaves naturally hate their slavery and their masters. If Peter and Violet are eager to stand by their masters, even when the yokes of slavery are broken, then they, and countless others like them, are meant for the kind of servitude that makes slavery viable and moral.

22    Baym concedes that such a move may have been necessary in the earlier part of the century, but laments its continued occurrence once women had come to dominate the field of fiction. See Baym 256–57.

23    See, for example, Roediger's "White Slaves, Wage Slaves, and Free White Labor" in *The Wages of Whiteness*. Abolitionists were able to invoke the notion of "wage slavery" because this phrase had become a key component of labor rhetoric during the 1830s. See chapter 4 of Eric Foner's *Politics and Ideology in the Age of the Civil War*.

*2. Sympathy and Symmetry: The Romance of Slavery in Metta V. Victor's*
Maum Guinea and Her Plantation "Children"

1    Born March 2, 1831, in Erie, Pennsylvania, Metta Victoria Fuller moved with her parents and older sister to Wooster Village, Ohio, when she was eight years old.

Her long and prolific literary career began with the publication of her first work in journals and newspapers when she was thirteen. She published her first novel, *The Last Days of Tul: A Romance of the Lost Cities of Yucatan,* when she was only fifteen years old, the same age she became a regular contributor to *New York Home Journal.* Though she cowrote a volume of poetry with her sister, the majority of her work took the form of novels or short stories. Her first best-seller, a temperance novel called *The Senator's Son* (1853), reflected her early interest in moralistic reform literature aimed at curing specific social ills. As her career progressed, however, the range of her material widened considerably. Her more than fifty published novels include almost every popular genre imaginable, from domestic romance to Wild West adventure. Her most important and long-lasting literary contribution may have been to the genre of the detective novel, a genre she helped invent with her publication under the name of Seeley Regester of *The Dead Letter* (1866), arguably this country's first detective novel. In 1856 she married Orville J. Victor, a journalist and later one of the principal editors of the hugely successful Beadle's dime novel series. Metta Victor soon became one of Beadle's most talented and prolific sources, editing a Beadle journal called *Home* and contributing over twenty novels to the Beadle roster. Of these novels, *Maum Guinea* was her most popular. Metta Victor died of cancer in 1885 at the age of fifty-four. For a slightly more expanded discussion of Victor's life see Kathleen L. Maio's article in *American Women Writers.*

2   Victor's play on the names of these young lovers is an early indicator of the drama she hopes to enact. "Virginia Bell" is the quintessential embodiment of southern white womanhood; Philip's surname links him both to that cradle of the southern aristocracy (Virginia, via Fairfax) and to his future bride.

3   Hazel Carby devotes a page to *Maum Guinea* in *Reconstructing Womanhood* but doesn't address this question of Victor's motivation. Rather, she positions *Maum Guinea* as an example of how white women writers "debated the parameters of the dominant sexual ideology and questioned its inherent value structure" without ever questioning the underlying notion "that woman meant white" (34). See *Reconstructing* 26, 33–34.

4   In the preface to *The Senator's Son,* Victor argues that only when literature contains "some effort at human improvement" should it be "tolerated" (vi). In this early preface she goes on to make the case for literature as a particularly apt vehicle for social reform. She writes: "so in this kind of fiction, while we cull its sweets, and linger entranced over its fascinating pages, the stern ideas of truth and right that meet us at every turn will gradually fasten upon our judgments, and linger in our memories, long after the sweet flowers that decked them have faded and been forgotten" (vi). Victor's later preface to *Maum Guinea* may best be understood as a more mature and strategic version of this earlier manifesto.

5   The distinctions between the novel's "black" characters and its "mulatto" characters are more complicated than my easy conflation suggests. For reasons of space and focus, however, I must let that conflation stand.

6   In Frank Luther Mott's *Golden Multitudes,* for example, *Maum Guinea* is listed as a "better seller," which Mott classifies as a book not quite reaching the necessary sales figures for "best seller" classification. For Mott's purposes, a book published

in 1861 would have needed sales of three hundred thousand to be considered a best-seller. In other sources *Maum Guinea* is usually noted as selling over one hundred thousand copies. See, for example, Charles Harvey's "The Dime Novel in American Life," James Kinney's *Amalgamation!,* and Helen Waite Papashvily's *All the Happy Endings.*

7   Dime novels rarely achieved the stamp of legitimacy that warranted literary notices in the review journals of the day, especially in the first years of the dime novel's popularity. As Michael Denning notes, however, only four years into the production of Beadle's dime novels, the *North American Review* reviewed the Beadle books, noting their unparalleled sales (Denning 11). In that review, William Everett devotes a paragraph to brief descriptions of several of Victor's novels, calling *Maum Guinea* "one of the thousand stories of negro life which owe their style, character, and very existence to 'Uncle Tom's Cabin' " (307). Other than this unenthusiastic blurb published four years after the novel's publication, *Maum Guinea* seems to have flown well under the radar of review journals. Its publication only a year or so into the Beadle series may partially explain this silence.

8   Albert Johannsen's two-volume *The House of Beadle and Adams and Its Dime and Nickel Novels: The Story of a Vanished Literature,* published in 1950 by the University of Oklahoma Press, remains the definitive scholarly study of the Beadle publishing house. A third volume, listing corrections to the first two, was published in 1962.

9   Beadle maintained a strict set of standards for the types of stories he would accept, as this set of "Instructions" for prospective writers indicates: "We prohibit all things offensive to good taste in expression and incident— We prohibit subjects of characters that carry an immoral taint— We prohibit the repetition of any occurrence which, though true, is yet better untold— We prohibit what cannot be read with satisfaction by every right-minded person—old and young alike— We require your best work— We require unquestioned originality— We require pronounced strength of plot and high dramatic interest of story— We require grace and precision of narrative, and correctness in composition. Authors must be familiar with characters and places which they introduce and not attempt to write in fields of which they have no intimate knowledge. Those who fail to reach the standard here indicated cannot write acceptably for our several Libraries, or for any of our publications" (Johannsen 1: 4–5).

10   E. D. E. N. Southworth's highly popular *The Hidden Hand, or, Capitola the Madcap,* published in serial form in 1859, is just one example of this common plot.

11   For example, Edward Magdol's demographic study *The Antislavery Rank and File* shows that 64.4 percent of the antislavery societies of Lynn and Worcester, Massachusetts, in the 1830s were made up of "skilled" laborers, compared to only 2.2 percent who were either "semi-professional" or "professional"; 18.4 percent of the respondents described themselves as "proprietor-manager-official (47).

12   The alliance is explicitly set forth in a letter from a partner in a northern mercantile house to a prominent abolitionist: "We cannot afford, sir to let you and your associates succeed in your endeavor to overthrow slavery. It is not a matter of principle with us. It is a matter of business necessity. We cannot afford to let you succeed.

And I have called you out to let you know, and to let your fellow laborers know, that we do not mean to let you succeed. We mean, sir, to put you Abolitionists down—by fair means, if we can, by foul means, if we must" (Wright and Wright 84).

13   The connective tissue between the labor reform movement and the antislavery forces was institutionalized in 1848 with the creation of the Free-Soil Party. As Eric Foner has argued, the party's birth dramatizes the awareness among the labor reformers that slavery's encroachment on the western territories would further diminish their own opportunities for financial advancement and social mobility ("Workers" 27).

14   David Roediger, although praising the work of Aptheker and Magdol, complicates somewhat their view of a vibrant and sustained working-class abolitionism, though not to the point of discrediting it. By focusing on the complicated ways in which whiteness functioned in the construction of "the working class," Roediger adds a necessary note of sober realism to our view of the relations between labor and antislavery. As Roediger puts it, "In a nation in which whiteness was so important and emancipation so hard to imagine, abolition was bound to be a minority movement within the working class as in the larger society. If the rhetorical framework of white slavery was limited because it asked white workers to liken themselves to Black slaves, working class abolitionism was limited because it asked white workers to organize energetically on the Black slaves's behalf" (Wages 86–87). Although Roediger is certainly right to note this sort of anticoalition dynamic, his doing so doesn't detract from my larger point that abolitionism did indeed find a receptive audience within the ranks of the white working class. For a full discussion of the give-and-take between whiteness, labor, and abolition see Wages chap. 4.

15   Victor's description of the African's "native character" bears an important kinship with Stowe's "romantic racialism" (the phrase is George Fredrickson's; see Black Image chap. 4). Although both authors assume such a thing as a "native character," Stowe's Christian framework changes the inflection of her portrait. According to Stowe, blacks are characterized by "their gentleness, their lowly docility of heart, their aptitude to repose on a superior mind and rest on a higher power, their childlike simplicity of affection, and facility of forgiveness" (181).

16   Thus Maum Guinea is itself a mirror, an object that when held up to an empirical reality is capable of capturing that reality, of creating its symmetrical double. People or novels with philanthropic motives, we are told, are denied this kind of direct and true access. Their mirrors are flawed, always distorted by what they think they already see. Their images, Victor imagines, are constructed before the fact. Literature then, free of the biases of interested criticism, is the perfect reflective product, showing us only what is already there. This is the fiction of Victor's central metaphor—the idea that a novel can become such an undistorted reflective space.

17   Stowe offers a similar reading of the relationship between "reality" and romance: "The note-book of a missionary . . . contains truth stranger than fiction. How can it be otherwise, when a system prevails which whirls families and scatters their members, as the wind whirls and scatters the leaves of autumn?" (433). However, while Stowe argues that slavery produces romance, Victor uses romance to "re-

produce the slave." These inverse formulations differ primarily on the question of agency; Victor grants primary agency to the novelist, who "makes" slavery; Stowe sees slavery as the creator of her novel.

18   A word on this notion of incoherence—a concept I find myself repeatedly drawn to in reference to *Maum Guinea*. In his work on the French artist Gustave Courbet, art historian T. J. Clarke uses a Freudian analogy to explain how incoherence speaks much more clearly and rationally than we might expect. He writes: "Like the analyst listening to his patient, what interests us, if we want to discover the meaning of this mass of criticism [the forty-five or so critics who have written on Courbet], are the points at which the rational monotone of the critic breaks, fails, falters; we are interested in the phenomena of obsessive repetition, repeated irrelevance, anger suddenly discharged—the points where the criticism is incomprehensible are the keys to its comprehension" (12). If we apply this psychoanalytic model to *Maum Guinea*, the strategy shows definite advantages. Not only does it render the novel's narrative hiccups useful to us, but it nicely conceptualizes the role of "the public" in the act of writing. As Clarke puts it, "The public, like the unconscious, is present only where it ceases; yet it determines the structure of private discourse; it is the key to what cannot be said" (12). Victor's mirrored narratives depend on the repetitions that Clarke mentions, since mirrors multiply single objects into apparent copies. The copies are only apparent, however, since "what cannot be said" necessarily complicates the reflective process. "What cannot be said" can be taken to mean anything that would threaten the commercial success of Victor's novel.

19   Although Maum fully approved of Judy's marriage to Slocum, the fact that the marriage was interracial made Maum's virtual banishment from Judy's life a necessity. Slocum makes this clear in a conversation with Maum: "Mrs. Ginny, though I've overcome my prejudices, I never could dose of my relatives; I'd never like to tell 'em dat my wife had African blood in her—I'd never like 'em to know dat you was her mudder. . . . If you're willing to keep it secret dat you're her mudder . . . it'll be all right" (176–77). The dialect in this passage is presumably Maum's in the retelling, not Slocum's in the initial conversation.

20   Victor's method here is not unlike Stowe's when Uncle Tom arrives at the St. Clair plantation and feels instantly at home in the exotic and oriental beauty of the place. See Hortense Spillers, "Changing the Letter: The Yokes, the Jokes of Discourse, or Mrs. Stowe, Mr. Reed."

21   This split is complicated by the homosocial quality of the scene's circulating desires. Presumably dreaming of Virginia (metonymically rendered "sweet and vague"), Philip's "every nerve" thrills to Hyperion's song—"the music of his own hopes." Hyperion's voice pores forth "deep" and "unrestrained." Victor's equation of black bodies with rich voices raises the question of where precisely Philip's hopes tend, as he unconsciously matches his step to the rhythm of his slave's melody. The interrelation of the men's desire is a necessary result both of Victor's racism and of her insistence on parallel romances.

22   It would be impossible for Victor (or Philip and Virginia) to imagine a social interaction with Rose and Hyperion not scripted by slavery. Outside the context of slavery, social interaction between whites and blacks would threaten the whites'

sense of their own superiority. Slavery makes such interaction superficially possible because the interaction is always a fiction underwritten by the power dynamics encoded within slavery.

23   A repetition of this epiphany occurs later when Hyperion, like Rose, finally understands his status as slave. After having overheard Judge Bell discuss his plans to sell Rose, Hyperion cries to Maum Guinea, "I can't be notting—I can't hab notting—I'm a slave, Maum Ginny, dough I nebber knew what it meant, till I hear massa Bell talk yesterday" (73).

24   His immediate attraction is not that surprising, as Victor has gone to great lengths to sketch in detail the "dangerously handsome" beauty of this "refined, gentle, [and] womanly" waiting maid (44). Rose is "touched with that pensive grace which makes the vivacity of her race so charming" (44) and "which no thoroughly Caucasian blood could ever emulate" (43). Victor expresses indignation at Talfierro's classification of Rose as a "superb creature": "Yes, a *creature*—a slave—that was what that beautiful woman was" (44). However, Talfierro's sexual desire and Victor's representation collude in their mutual objectification of the beautiful waiting maid, as Rose becomes nothing more than an exotic site of displaced and concentrated sexuality.

25   To be precise, Ellis used the term *narcissus-like,* later suggesting that Paul Näcke, who introduced the term *Narcismus* in 1899, deserved partial credit for the birth of "narcissism" as a diagnostic category.

26   That there are real problems in Freud's characterization should go without saying. As Michael Warner has suggested, "The theorization of homosexuality as narcissism is itself a form of narcissism peculiar to modern heterosexuality" (202). Warner's point about the structural relation between narcissism and heterosexuality resonates with my own argument about the relation of narcissism and whiteness. See Warner, "Homo-Narcissism; or, Heterosexuality."

27   In *Borderline Conditions and Pathological Narcissism* (1975), Otto Kernberg also defines narcissism in a way that can't help but resonate with the notion of whiteness—particularly vis-à-vis American slavery. The relationships that narcissists have with other people, Kernberg writes, "are clearly exploitive and sometimes parasitic" (227). He continues, "It is as if they feel they have the right to control and possess others and to exploit them without guilt feelings—and, behind a surface which very often is charming and engaging, one senses coldness and ruthfulness" (228).

28   John Irwin offers a helpful way to understand the possible uses of psychoanalytic criticism, and he does so in reference to the concept of repetition, which has a rather obvious relevance to Victor's text: "The analyst who listens while a patient repeats again and again the story or stories of his life is simply trying to understand the relationship between the narrator and the story or stories that he tells, trying to decipher a hidden story by analyzing the variations among the patent translations of that story, trying to discover the laws of condensation, distortion, substitution that govern the different oblique repetitions of that same hidden story" (3). Although Irwin's model has its attractions, especially in the case of a text like *Maum Guinea,* it carries the danger of pathologizing the author—of putting Victor on the couch. However, if we remember T. J. Clarke's reading of "the public" as a form of or figure

for the unconscious, the pathology associated with the analyst/analysand model adheres not to an individual author but to a cultural moment—or in this case, a cultural force like whiteness. For a good account of the debate that still rages over the application of psychoanalytical terms to authors and characters see Jeffrey Berman, *Narcissism and the Novel*.

29   Before we allow ourselves fully to condemn Virginia here, it should be pointed out that Victor transfers a great deal of agency in this transaction from Judge Bell, who actually has the power to buy and sell, to Virginia, who herself bears a relation of property to her father and his money. Virginia can neither buy nor sell, but Victor makes her responsible for the sale of Rose. Judge Bell is let off the hook, since it is Virginia's need for wedding finery that makes the sale necessary.

30   This passage also economically dramatizes the shape and pitfalls of compromise unionism, which repeatedly sought to defer the problem over slavery in order to maintain the fiction of a *united* states.

31   For a differently voiced rendition of this dilemma, think of Stowe's treatment of Shelby in the first chapter of *Uncle Tom's Cabin*. Like Judge Bell, Mr. Shelby is driven by financial necessity to sell beloved slaves to an unsavory purchaser. Stowe's biting irony in referring to Shelby as "A Man of Humanity" makes it clear that she does not condone his actions—even if driven by financial exigency. Shelby "had the appearance of a gentleman," Stowe writes, and we hear the emphasis on the word *appearance* (3). For Stowe, slavery is wrong precisely because well-intentioned men like Shelby lose their humanity in its proximity; for Victor, financial necessity justifies slavery in the absence of a moral keystone.

32   Slocum's hesitation before "purtiest babies" may actually signify a more significant hesitation in accepting the products of this amalgamationist marriage—on the part of both Slocum *and* Victor. How pretty—that is, how *light*—are these babies?

33   The text is silent concerning Virginia and Philip's apparent awareness and acceptance of Judy's marriage to a white man. As the novel hastens toward its happy ending, Victor apparently preferred not to confront the issues raised by Virginia and Philip's location as the houseguests of an interracial couple.

34   Harriet Jacobs's *Incidents in the Life of a Slave Girl* (1861) offers an interesting parallel here. Though passing isn't an issue, Linda Brent's heroic efforts to rescue her children from slavery ironically keep her from those children in the North, as her work and lack of a home necessitate separation. *Incidents* offers a provocative counterexample to Victor's text in other ways, and I return to it in my conclusion.

35   One way to fix the novel's present is to use Sophy's telling of the Nat Turner story. The Turner insurrection took place in 1831, and near the end of her story Sophy mentions that her children, who were babies at the time of the uprising, would be "growed big men now" (99). This detail allows us to assume that enough years have passed to make the present-day events part of a post–Fugitive Slave Law landscape.

36   Interestingly, Victor stages Rose and Hyperion's union at a time when many slaves would be experiencing the pain of separation. Slaves hired out to work for others usually began their new work at the first of the year. As Eugene Genovese writes in *Roll, Jordan, Roll*, "For many slaves, January 1 brought the holiday season

to a grim close, for those hired out had to bid friends and families farewell as they left to take up their duties for the coming year. The slaves often called New Year's Day 'heartbreak day'" (576).

37   I don't think my use of the word *compelled* is too strong here, since it signals both the force of genre and the changes suggested by Jacobs's editor, Lydia Maria Child. Jacobs had wanted to end her narrative with a recounting of John Brown's raid on Harper's Ferry. Child suggested that the chapter on Brown be omitted and that the narrative end with a return to Jacobs's grandmother. Although there are valid reasons for Child's preference, especially as it concerns the framelike use of the figure of the grandmother, it's also true that the omission of the Brown chapter returns the narrative to the generic confines of the sentimental romance—a genre more comfortable ending in the remembrance of a dead grandmother than in violence against slavery as an institution. For a fuller discussion of Child's role in the production of Jacobs's narrative see Bruce Mills, "Lydia Maria Child and the Endings to Harriet Jacobs's *Incidents in the Life of a Slave Girl.*"

*3. Someone's in the Garden with Eve: Race, Religion, and the American Fall*

1   Agreeing with Nancy Leys Stepan and Sander Gilman, I am resisting the urge to refer to these ethnologists as "pseudoscientists" rather than scientists. As Stepan and Gilman argue, "calling scientific racism a pseudoscience . . . allows scientists to refuse to confront the issue of the inherently political nature of much of the biological and human sciences, and to ignore the problem of the persistence of racial metaphors of inferiority in the sciences of today." "Pseudoscience" becomes a distancing rhetoric that covers over the political resonances and effects of so-called mainstream science. See Stepan and Gilman 76.

2   Written five years before Darwin's *On the Origin of the Species*, "Claims" reveals the ambivalence toward evolutionary thought that characterizes Douglass's later relationship to Darwin's work. As he put it as late as 1883, "I do not know that I am an evolutionist, but to this extent I am one. I certainly have more patience with those who trace mankind upward from a low condition, even from the lower animals, than with those that start him at a high point of perfection and conduct him to a level with the brutes. I have no sympathy with a theory that starts man in heaven and stops him in hell" (Blassingame 5: 129).

3   Antonio Gramsci offers another way to understand this struggle. My earlier reference to "commonsense racism" is meant to suggest Gramsci's notion of common sense as a "chaotic aggregate of disparate conceptions," where "one can find anything that one likes" (Forgacs 345). For Gramsci, common sense is itself a product of hegemony and becomes a means through which oppression and inequality are naturalized. Gramsci is interested in how intellectual systems can tap the productive possibilities of common sense so as to create a *new* common sense, one that would be less conducive to systemic inequalities. In the context of the argument I am tracing here, then, common sense becomes the site where religion (which Gramsci calls "an element of fragmented common sense") and philosophy (an "intellectual order" for which we can read "science") contest for dominance (Forgacs 327). The shape of common sense as "an ambiguous, contradictory and multiform concept" (Forgacs

346) makes it a rich space of cultural mediation where "truth" gets simultaneously created and distributed.

4   I want to stress the allegorical nature of this narrative, and in so doing borrow Toni Morrison's insistence that allegory works by emptying history of its content. According to Morrison, one of the "common linguistic strategies" (*Playing in the Dark* 67) that white writers have used to "engage the serious consequences of blacks" (67) is a "dehistoricizing allegory" (68), one that renders historical and cultural tension mute before a larger, mythical contest between Blackness and Whiteness. The theorists of the Garden erased the specific history of slavery, and their own cultural moment, in order to stage their contemporary fears and concerns at a far-distant site, and in a larger-than-life symbology.

5   Or as Elaine Scarry puts it, their awareness of their bodies signifies their new location within a corporeal economy, where "the body is made a permanently preoccupying category in the pain of childbirth, the pain of work," etc. (210). This sudden embodiment also signifies their radical distance from God, who is omnipotently disembodied, and the new power relation this disembodied/embodied binary brings with it.

6   For a more complete overview of how the story of the Fall functioned as a moral tale involving sexual desire and sin see Elaine Pagel's *Adam, Eve, and the Serpent.* Pagel offers a convincing argument for the Genesis story as a shaper of cultural values in the first four centuries C.E. She traces the arguments of those who saw sexuality itself as original sin (Augustine, for example) and those who tried to recoup sexuality from the apparently denigrated position where Genesis left it. Kate Millett offers another interesting gloss on the sexual politics of the Eden story in *Sexual Politics,* 52–54.

7   In *The Yemassee* (1835), William Gilmore Simms derives a perverse pleasure from emphasizing the connection between snakes and phallic power. Simms portrays Bess Matthews's encounter with a rattlesnake this way: "She sees him approach—now advancing, now receding—now swelling in every part with something of anger, while his neck is arched beautifully like that of a wild horse under the curb; until, at length, tired as it were of play, like the cat with its victim, she sees the neck growing larger and becoming completely bronzed as about to strike—the huge jaws unclosing almost directly above her, the long tubulated fang, charged with venom, protruding from the cavernous mouth" (172). The reader will remember Simms from his mistreatment of Stowe in chapter 1.

8   Ariel, of course, is the good spirit of Shakespeare's *The Tempest,* coinhabitant of the island with the savage Caliban.

9   As John David Smith points out, scholars have had difficulty confirming that Berry actually wrote this reply to Ariel. Maxwell Whiteman has suggested that an earlier volume attributed to Berry (*Slavery and Abolitionism, as Viewed by a Georgia Slave*) was possibly written by, or at least unduly influenced by, his master. And as Smith points out, Monroe Work's *A Bibliography of the Negro in Africa and America* does not identify Berry as a black author. See Whiteman's introduction to Berry's *Slavery and Abolition* and John David Smith's introduction to *Anti-Black Thought,* 6, xxviii–xxix.

10   Of course, it was possible to reach different conclusions about the relation between amalgamation and biblical truth. Frederick Douglass, for example, cleverly invoked America's amalgamationist history as evidence against racist interpretations of the biblical story of Ham. As he writes in his *Narrative,* "It is nevertheless plain that a very different-looking class of people are springing up at the south, and are now held in slavery, from those originally brought to this country from Africa; and if their increase will do no other good, it will do away the force of the argument, that God cursed Ham, and therefore American slavery is right. If the lineal descendants of Ham are alone to be scripturally enslaved, it is certain that slavery at the south must soon become unscriptural; for thousands are ushered into this world, annually, who, like myself, owe their existence to white fathers, and those fathers most frequently their own masters" (50).

11   Prospero is the duke in Shakespeare's play who comes to rule over the slavish and deformed Caliban. This choice of pseudonym in response to Ariel clearly reveals the colonial power dynamic at work here. If we remember Harrison Berry's charge that Ariel's argument was "founded on the interest of the great diabolical slave power," this joint work of Ariel/Prospero becomes an appropriate metaphor for the viability of slavery as a social structure. Though a servant himself in Shakespeare's play, Ariel aligns himself not with Caliban, who is also a servant (though classed as a "slave"), but with Prospero, his master. As Jerry Phillips has argued, the difference between Ariel's status as "servant" and Caliban's as "slave" is necessary to the "architecture of whiteness" (338). In Phillips's words, "In the logic of class conflict underpinning the play's dramatic action, Ariel must be seen as representing a counterrevolutionary position. Ariel is a servant, but instead of demonstrating solidarity with other servants and slaves, he looks on them with the eyes of the master. . . . In the ideological profile of Ariel, we can see the repressive capability historically located in the colonial soldier, the overseer, the lowly 'white' man, who defends the house of the master against the violence of rebellious slaves" (341). See Phillips, "Literature in the Country of 'Whiteness': From T. S. Eliot to *The Tempest.*"

12   Although I have highlighted the sexual nature of Eve's wandering, I should also mention its more overtly political aspect. Prospero, writing in the context of ever-expanding feminist activism, offers Eve's wandering as a cautionary tale against a more general feminine move away from the domestic space. When women are not happy in the home, they are liable to take that unhappiness to the streets, in the service of voting rights, for example. I return to this threat of feminist activism in my discussion of Charles Carroll.

13   My slippage from "Mongol" to "black" is not meant to erase ethnic distinctions but to signal how nonwhite sexual threats got lumped together in these accounts. For all their care in disentangling the various "races," these theorists still felt a threat to whiteness from any nonwhite source. "Mongol" and "black" created the same fear, though the representations of that fear may differ in regard to degree.

14   The full title of this work is *The Negro a Beast, or, "In the Image of God": The Reasoner of the Age, the Revelator of the Century! The Bible as It Is! The Negro and His Relation to the Human Family!* The title-page copy continues: "The Negro a Beast, but created with articulate speech, and hands, that he may be of service to his master—

the White man. *The Negro not the Son of Ham,* Neither can it be proven by the Bible, and the argument of the theologian who would claim such, melts to mist before the thunderous and convincing arguments of this masterful book. By Chas. Carroll, Who has spent fifteen years of his life, and $20,000.00 in its compilation."

15   This, despite the apparent failure of the Adamic Publishing Company. *Tempter* was the first in a series of books to be published in the Adamic Library, and it is safe to assume that this series never got off the ground. An advertisement included with *Tempter* mentions future publications on the Book of Revelation and the dangers of Spiritualism. If nothing more, this advertisement reveals Carroll's almost ludicrous ambition: "The fourth, fifth, sixth, seventh and eighth books of this series will each be devoted to a history of one of the five continents from the Deluge to the Twentieth century," all to be written by Carroll himself (504). These works apparently never materialized, and the Adamic press does not appear in turn-of-the-century St. Louis directories.

Carroll would be pleased to know, however, that *The Tempter of Eve* reappeared in the 1970s—not in a scholarly edition but in an enthusiastic reprint dedicated to Carroll's debunking of evolution. As its editor writes, "This work is a scientific and scriptural refutation of the atheistic theory of evolution, or descent. . . . Read it and be warned—take heed—and move quickly and decisively to save our country and our descendants from a destruction that has befallen so many countries and peoples down through the ages" (vi). See Charles Carroll, *The Tempter of Eve: A Book of Absorbing Interest and Profound Concern to Everyone* (Eufala, Ala., 197–?), a copy of which is located in the Auburn University Library.

16   Fredrickson argues that the accommodationists failed in influence largely because "they were, for the most part, intellectuals—clergymen and professors—attempting in vain to shape public policy in a profoundly antiintellectual society" (*Black Image* 297).

17   See F. Wood 241.

18   See Fredrickson 277. Whether Carroll's religious arguments were generally accepted remains somewhat of a mystery. Wood suggests that Carroll's ideas "were popular only among the most fanatical religious racists" (241). However, I am suspicious of arguments that cast Carroll—and other racial extremists—entirely beyond the pale. Firmly of his moment, Carroll helps us see the more commonplace realities that extremism is designed, in part, to cover up, and thus to facilitate. Whether Carroll's theory of the tempter gained wide currency is ultimately less important to me than the ways in which Carroll's version of the story shared common assumptions with—and made visible—a more "mainstream" culture of racism.

19   I have been unable to determine the artist responsible for this illustration.

20   It could be argued that the illustration does not defeminize the tempter so much as it dehumanizes her. In other words, the tempter's difference from the obviously feminine Eve is not a difference of gender but of species. Carroll, for example, might say that the female beast is not feminine in the same way as the female human. Although this could partially explain the tempter's appearance, the issue of gender should not be allowed to drop out of the equation, since gender does indeed play a role in the imagining of this supposed difference in "species." The tempter's lack of

femininity cannot be fully separated from her lack of humanity. Rather, these qualities function in something like a dialectical relationship, where the absence of one contributes to and is reinforced by the absence of the other.

21   This conflation is both obvious and complicated. The notion that blackness is always already gendered male has a lengthy history and is usually generated, in part, by racist fascination with black male sexuality. But since racist cultures often want things both ways, it is not surprising that blackness, in certain contexts, appears first and foremost as a female property. One respondent to the Ariel debate makes this point visually apparent when he provides a pictorial hierarchy of the races, in which the only examples gendered female are the Ethiopian and the Negro. Since the argument's emphasis is on the gradations of weakness and stagnation, it makes sense for this writer to see Ethiopians and Negroes as women, passive bodies reflecting the end of the family line.

22   James Fenimore Cooper's *The Last of the Mohicans* offers a resonant analog to this conflation of ethnic and reptilian threats. When Cora and Alice Munro are captured by the Indian Magua, who then threatens Cora with marriage, Natty Bumppo arrives to "save these tender blossoms from the fangs of the worst of sarpants" (105). For more on the sexual and racial politics in the territories see Leland S. Person Jr., "The American Eve: Miscegenation and a Feminist Frontier Fiction." The material Person examines provides somewhat of an antecedent to the material I read here, since novels of the frontier often placed white women (American Eves carving out new territory) in dangerous or romantic proximity to Indians.

23   For more on visual representations of the Hottentot Venus see Sander Gilman, "Black Bodies, White Bodies."

24   In fact, Sander Gilman links the corrupting sexuality of black women—specifically the Hottentot—to lesbianism. As Gilman points out, a standard gynecological handbook of the late-nineteenth-century suggested that the "Hottentot Apron" (the supposedly deformed labia of the Hottentot) was responsible for the "over-development of the clitoris," which the handbook associates with the "excesses" of "lesbian love" (237). Though this linkage of black femininity to lesbianism could have intriguing ramifications for my reading of Carroll's temptation scene, I am reluctant to pursue them. Although Carroll's tempter corresponds to certain images of the "mannish woman," that is, the lesbian, the linkage between black female sexuality and lesbianism that Gilman traces depends on the physically observable and pathological genitalia of the Hottentot. Since Carroll's tempter does not share the Hottentot's "excessive" physiology, the link from "black female" to "lesbian" in Carroll's illustration is not as obvious as it may first appear.

Esther Newton's influential discussion of the "mannish lesbian" offers another way to introduce lesbian sexuality into a discussion of Carroll's illustration, though here too I am not persuaded that lesbian temptation stands at the center of the picture. Describing women whose behavior or dress contained "masculine" elements, Newton writes that "from about 1900 on, this cross-gender figure became the public symbol of the new social/sexual category 'lesbian'" (283). As Newton points out, the assumed link between "mannish" behavior and lesbianism can also be found in late-nineteenth-century medical discourse, particularly the writings of influential sexologists Richard von Krafft-Ebing and Havelock Ellis. And yet neither Newton, Krafft-Ebing, nor Ellis consider how this linkage between mannishness and lesbianism gets complicated by race—or more specifically, by blackness. Although it is safe to assume that mannish representations of bourgeois white women carried associations of lesbian degeneracy (Radclyffe Hall's Stephen Gordon is the most obvious literary example), it does not follow that similarly masculine black women could be read in the same way. In other words, mannishness in bourgeois white women is seen as degenerate because it represents a fall from a so-called purely feminine state; under the cultural logic of white racism, however, black women had no such state from which to fall in the first place. See Newton, "The Mythic Mannish Lesbian: Radclyffe Hall and the New Woman."

Finally, Lynda Hart has argued that the category of lesbian has historically been marked as white, which she says is "an inheritance from nineteenth-century sexology and criminology that became further encoded in the discourse of psychoanalysis." See Hart 106.

25   Wiegman uses this phrase to signify the multiplicity of stories that govern and attach themselves to actual and narrative instances of rape and lynching in the nineteenth and twentieth centuries. Tracing a shift in the cultural framework through which rape and lynching were viewed, Wiegman highlights the "performative" and "specular" aspects of lynching at the end of the nineteenth century, insisting that we understand lynching as "a disciplinary activity that communalizes white power while territorializing the black body and its movement through social space" (13). For an earlier and indispensable treatment of lynching as a literary figure see Trudier Harris, *Exorcising Blackness: Historical and Literary Lynching and Burning Rituals.*

26   See also Frederick Douglass's brilliant analysis of lynch law in "Why Is the Negro Lynched?" (1894).

27   The reverse of this conspiratorial scenario would come some eighty years later, when black men would blame white feminists for turning "their women" against them. Reviewing Alice Walker's *The Color Purple,* Darryl Pinckney argued that the novel's appeal "does not lie in its text, but, through representing the black woman's experience in the popular feminist vocabulary, in its power as a symbol of the reconciliation between black women and white women in the feminist movement." The vitriol spilled on Walker by Pinckney and others suggests their real fear of such a "reconciliation," however much a paranoid fantasy it might be. The repetition (with a racial reversal) of this conspiratorial vision of feminist alliances may say more about the underlying logic of patriarchy than it does about race relations. See Pinckney 18. For other examples of this criticism see Mel Watkins, "Sexism, Racism, and Black Women Writers"; Phillip M. Royster, "In Search of Our Fathers' Arms: Alice Walker's Persona of the Alienated Darling"; and Stanley Crouch's review of Toni Morrison's *Beloved,* "Aunt Medusa."

28   In fact, white women did not become a significant part of antilynching activism until the formation of the Association of Southern Women for the Prevention of Lynching in 1930, under the leadership of Jessie Daniel Ames. For more on this organization and its leader see Jacquelyn Dowd Hall, *Revolt against Chivalry: Jessie Daniel Ames and the Women's Campaign against Lynching.*

29   According to *Tempter*'s title page, Carroll was apparently living in St. Louis at the time of its publication. A search of St. Louis directories from the late 1890s to the early 1900s reveals several Charles Carrolls, most of whom were laborers. This information and Carroll's known birth date (1849) point to a Charles C. Carroll, who was a salesman born in Missouri to Virginia-born parents. The 1900 census shows this Carroll and his wife living with his sister Maggie Carroll Ennis and her husband James Ennis. I am grateful to Jean E. Meeh Gosebrink at the St. Louis Public Library for this information.

30   See Sundquist, 395; Williamson 119; Wood, *The Arrogance of Faith;* Smith's introduction to *Anti-Black Thought;* Thompson, *The Negro, Not a Beast;* and Work 576, 578.

31   Harrison Berry, the black respondent to Ariel mentioned earlier, makes a similar point when he takes Ariel's argument on its own terms, unpacking the power dynamic it reveals. Referring to Adam and Eve's deception at the hand of the black tempter, Berry asks, "Does it not look like the one kinky headed Negro had more sense than the straight-haired, high foreheaded, sharp nosed, thin lipped, white skin, Adam and his wife had?" (9). Ariel's argument, according to Berry, proves not only that the Negro "must have been Adam's superior by far" but that "his race is superior to Adam's race to-day" (10).

32   Kobena Mercer makes a similar point in a more recent context. With Clarence Thomas as his text, Mercer writes, "The dangerous simplifications of identity politics consistently fail to recognize that the political problem of power represented by straight white males is a problem not about persons but about ideological subject-positions that reproduce relations of oppression" ("Fear" 81). "Only by making a tactical shift from 'identity' to 'identification,'" Mercer continues, "can we preempt the perpetuation of a public discourse in which white men remain at the center" ("Fear" 122).

*4. Charles Chesnutt and the Masturbating Boy:*
*Onanism, Whiteness, and* The Marrow of Tradition
My title respectfully references Eve Sedgwick's "Jane Austen and the Masturbating Girl," an article first conceived as part of a 1989 MLA special session, "The Muse of Masturbation." The panel—and specifically Sedgwick's title—caused one of those periodic uproars both inside and outside the academy that serve to raise certain existential (and consequently, political) questions about the nature of interpretive work done in contemporary English departments. Like Sedgwick, I am indebted to feminist scholars, particularly in the field of lesbian and gay studies, who have begun rethinking sexuality as a product of various social relations, fluid over time, and never without a political valence. In her article Sedgwick locates masturbation as a site from which to theorize hetero/homo binaries in the past and present: "Thinking about autoeroticism is beginning to seem a productive and necessary switchpoint in thinking about the relations—historical as well as intrapsychic—between homo- and heteroeroticism: a project that has not seemed engaging or necessary to scholars who do not register the anti-heterosexist pressure of gay and lesbian interrogation" (821).

1   This passage appears in German in Chesnutt's journal, as do several others.

The English title of the book Chesnutt received is *The Sexual System and Its Derangements*. Brodhead's translation of *Unordnungen* as "disorders" instead of "derangements" probably results from Chesnutt's original translation of the title.

2   Chesnutt's strategy of demonizing white masculinity can be seen as an early version of what would later occur during the Black Arts Movement of the 1960s. In an effort to reclaim a black masculinity denied under white racism, Eldridge Cleaver and others portrayed white men as the epitome of sexual frailty. As Cleaver famously put it in *Soul on Ice*, "The upper classes . . . are perennially associated with physical weakness, decay, underdeveloped bodies, effeminacy, sexual impotence, and frigidity" (167). Or in Amiri Baraka's words, "Most American white men are trained to be fags" (qtd. in Phillip Harper 50). (Tom Delamere, it seems, got off rather easy.) For a critique of this retrieval of black masculinity via the negative portrayal of white masculinity see chapter 2 of Phillip Brian Harper's *Are We Not Men?*

3   This claim, of course, must to some degree remain at the level of conjecture, since it is absurd to try to "prove" a fictional character's off-the-page activities. This does not, however, pose a problem for the argument I make in this chapter, since my emphasis is on Chesnutt's intention to cast suspicion on Tom as the type of person who would engage in such behavior. Whether or not Tom masturbates, he signifies masturbation as an activity that takes place outside, and which thwarts, the procreative economy of whiteness. Like Onan, he is unable to channel sexual desire into its procreative and normalizing middle-class function.

4   A relatively recent article in the *Washington Post* demonstrates the continuing currency of this scene of discovery. In late 1995 authorities investigating the murder of a black couple in North Carolina searched the room of a white man suspected in the crime, only to discover, as the *Post* hastens to point out, "a Nazi flag, white-supremacist literature, pamphlets on Adolf Hitler and Nazi Germany, and a videotape of the movie 'Natural Born Killers' " (Branigin A6).

5   Barker-Benfield's *The Horrors of the Half-Known Life* (1976) remains one of the most extensive and useful treatments of male sexual attitudes in nineteenth-century America, though it is not without its critics. Paula Bennett and Vernon A. Rosario have criticized Barker-Benfield for ignoring the adverse effects of anti-onanism on male masturbators and for failing to stress the fact that many of the physicians cited by Barker-Benfield were refuted by their colleagues. See Bennett and Rosario 6.

6   Barker-Benfield makes a similar argument in *The Horrors of the Half-Known Life*, though he emphasizes the bad book as a figurative penis, rather than semen. See Barker-Benfield 173–74.

7   Though these various tracts carry significant weight, I don't want to leave the impression that anti-onanism existed solely as a discursive practice. For example, an 1897 patent application described a device to be used by boys to prevent erection. It consisted of a belt that could be locked, a metal plate, and an adjustable tube through which the boy would insert "the male organ." Inside the tube were several sharp points. According to the patent application, when "expansion in this organ begins, it will come in contact with the pricking points and the necessary pain or warning sensation will result. If the person wearing the device be asleep he will be awakened or recalled to his senses in time to prevent further expansion. . . . If . . . his thoughts

should be running in lascivious channels (in waking hours), these will be diverted by the pain from the pricking points" (qtd. in Bullough and Bullough 76–77). Lest such devices fail to do their job, Indiana and Wyoming enacted laws that made it a crime to encourage masturbation (Bullough and Bullough 73).

8   This version of the Onan story also carries the homosocial subtext that we've already seen associated with self-pollution. Onan's chief worry, it seems, is that "he should give seed to his brother." Tamar functions as the middle term in a homoerotic triangle between Onan and his dead brother, Er. That eighteenth- and nineteenth-century sexual moralists used this passage as proof of biblical sanction against masturbation exposes their unspoken fears about the practice and its relation to same-sex eroticism.

9   *The Sexual System* functions both as clinical treatise and as advertisement for Dr. Abbey's services, further enforcing the self-referentiality of its obsession with exalted manhood. Dr. Abbey is not short on ego. Referring to the loss of erectile possibility, he writes, "none but particular treatment can restore this, and no doctor under heaven understands this but myself. I was the first to discover this, and now make the fact known for the first time to the world, and I alone know and possess the only specific remedy for this deplorable condition" (4).

10   For a related argument about how Chesnutt "evacuate[s] from the text the notion of victimized white womanhood" see Gunning chap. 2.

11   For a more detailed discussion of the racial metaphorics of blood see Susan Gillman, "Pauline Hopkins and the Occult: African-American Revisions of Nineteenth-Century Sciences."

12   Dr. Abbey is a significant exception to this medical wisdom. According to Abbey, "while a person is afflicted with Spermatorrhea [the condition resulting from too much masturbation], impotency, or private disease, he *should never marry*" (14), lest he "blast the lives of wife and children" (15). Although Tom urges marriage as a cure, Chesnutt's authorial refusal to allow the marriage aligns him with Abbey and can be seen as saving Clara from the type of misery Abbey describes. Most doctors, however, did indeed urge marriage as the best means to cure the chronic masturbator.

13   Both the rattle episode and the croup return us to Mammy Jane's suspicion about Dodie's mole. These medical emergencies—both of which dramatize the difficulty of breathing—metaphorically enact the lynching that Jane fears. In other words, Dodie *does* experience, if only figuratively, the fate of a black criminal, as the taint of color suggested by the mole becomes a narrative reality.

14   Stephen K. Knadler suggests that Chesnutt's intention, particularly in *Marrow*, "was less to effect the moral elevation of [his] white readers, or to coax their obliging philanthropy, than it was to deprive them of the privilege of whiteness" (429). As I suggest, however, Chesnutt's reliance on the moral codes of his white, middle-class readership actually reinforces the "privileges of whiteness."

15   Almost all writers on *Marrow* see Miller and Green as antithetical possibilities for black resistance. Andrews (197–201) and Sundquist (*To Wake* 440–47) offer just two examples. Others include Marjorie George and Richard Pressman, "Confronting the Shadow: Psycho-Political Repression in Chesnutt's *The Marrow of Tradition*"; Arlene Elder, "Charles W. Chesnutt: Art or Assimilation" in *The "Hin-*

*dered Hand": Cultural Implications of Early Afro-American Fiction;* Jay Delmar, "The
Moral Dilemma in Charles W. Chesnutt's *The Marrow of Tradition*"; John Reilly,
"The Dilemma in Chesnutt's *The Marrow of Tradition;* Michelle Wolkimir, "Moral
Elevation and Egalitarianism: Shades of Gray in Chesnutt's *The Marrow of Tradition.*
Stephen Knadler's "Untragic Mulatto" is somewhat of an exception to this critical
trend, in that Knadler positions Miller's wife Janet as the novel's chief hope for the
country's racial future.

16   The dialogue between Josh Green and Dr. Miller enacts, in significant respects, a fictional version of the turn-of-the-century dialogue between W. E. B. Du
Bois and Booker T. Washington. When Josh Green and his men encounter Dr. Miller
and the black lawyer, Mr. Watson, Green cries, "We're lookin' fer a leader" (281). This
search for leadership metaphorically stages the relationship between the black masses
and Du Bois's "talented tenth." By having Miller and Watson refuse this urgent plea,
Chesnutt subtly criticizes those who had faith that the black elite would act in solidarity with those "beneath" them. Chesnutt aligns Miller as a Du Boisian figure,
when, earlier in the novel, he writes both Du Bois and Washington into Miller's
family history. Speaking of Miller's father, Chesnutt writes, "He had brought up his
eldest son to the trade; the other he had given a professional education" (50). Playing Du Bois to his brother's Washington, Miller represents that talented elite who
offered themselves as models for black uplift. His refusal to "lead," then, takes on a
significantly negative valence, which is of course radically complicated by Chesnutt's
own identification with Miller.

17   As William Gleason has shown, there did exist a contemporary counterexample to Chesnutt's resolution of this question, since Chesnutt's was not the only
fictional treatment by a black author of the Wilmington violence. David Bryant
Fulton's *Hanover; or, the Persecution of the Lowly* (1900) offers what Gleason calls
a "more consistently militant, progressive voice" than Chesnutt was able to man-
age (23).

18   Sandra Gunning makes a different but related argument about Chesnutt's
dependence on the normative codes of race and gender. Gunning argues that Chesnutt ironically ends up replicating white-supremacist structures of gender by depending on the death of white women and the general silence of black women. As
Gunning writes, "In white supremacist thinking black women are invisible and their
experience of lynching and rape completely denied. Why, within Chesnutt's revised
representation of the new South, are black women still only barely visible as virtuous
figureheads?" (76). My own argument in this chapter partially replicates, in its focus
on the crisis of white masculinity, this silencing of black women and their stories.
Gunning's argument can be seen as a necessary companion, then, to the argument I
make here.

19   I make this claim in reference to Chesnutt's "racial novels." Chesnutt's first
collection of conjure stories, *The Conjure Woman* (1899), did afford him a measure of
commercial success. He was unable to duplicate this success, however, outside the
dialect story genre.

5. *White Sex: Thomas Dixon Jr. and the Erotics of White Supremacy*

1 See Nelson, *National Manhood,* 47.

2 *The Leopard's Spots* was published on March 22, 1902, and within a few months sold over one hundred thousand copies (Cook 112). It appeared at number five on *Bookman*'s list of best-selling novels for the month of June, and the sectional breakdown of the *Bookman* data reveals a strong southern response to the book. It was the number one best-seller for that month in Atlanta, Dallas, and New Orleans, and number two in Norfolk. According to Raymond Cook's account of the novel's spectacular sales, it eventually sold over one million copies and was translated into several foreign-language editions. Its success was largely responsible for establishing Doubleday, Page and Co. as a major publishing house and netted its author several hundred thousand dollars in royalties (Cook 112). A special holiday edition was published December 19, 1903. Dixon's next novel in his proposed racial trilogy, *The Clansman* (1905), surpassed the sales of *The Leopard's Spots.* This success, coupled with both novels' eventual adaptation into the film *The Birth of a Nation,* made Dixon a household name in America, if his first novel had not already succeeded in doing so. Ironically, *The Leopard's Spots* also had its share in the making of African American literary history, as it motivated African American novelist Sutton Elbert Griggs to write *The Hindered Hand; or, The Reign of the Repressionist* (1905) as a response to Dixon's racism. The popularity and influence of Dixon's novel is the subject of chapter 31 of *The Hindered Hand.*

3 According to Michael Rogin, the transfer of the sword became a central scene in D. W. Griffith's film *His Trust* (1910). Griffith's appropriation of Dixon's idea was fitting, since early memories of his father's sword, along with his reading of *The Clansman,* inspired Griffith to film *The Birth of a Nation* (Rogin 172). Upon the release of *Birth* Griffith told an interviewer that "the first thing I remember was my father's sword. . . . As I started the book [*The Clansman*], stronger and stronger came to my mind the traditions I had learned as a child, all that my father had told me. The sword I told you about became a flashing vision. Gradually came back to my memory the stories a cousin, one Thurston Griffith, had told me of the Ku Klux Klan" (Geduld 13–14).

4 The novel's fascination with various mother/son relationships is too extensive to explore in any detail. Witness, for example, the following exchanges between Charlie and his mother:

"Do you remember, Mamma, how many times when you were so sick I used to slip up close and kiss your mouth and eyes?"

"I often dreamed you were kissing me."

"I thought you would know. I'll soon be a man. I'm going to be rich and build a great house, and you are going to live in it with me, and I am going to take care of you as long as you live." (55)

"I expect you will marry some pretty girl and almost forget your old Mamma, who will be getting gray."

"But I'll never love anybody like I love you, Mamma dear!"

His little arms slipped around her neck, held her close for a moment, and then he tenderly kissed her. (56)

5 Fraiman is quick to point out that Sedgwick does examine triangles in which conflict and hatred between men figure prominently. "It is not that Sedgwick leaves conflict out of these relations," Fraiman writes, "but that in her account hostility and violence are essentially the signs of a highly charged but unrecognized intimacy" (68).

6 Like Fraiman, I find Sedgwick's model of the homosocial triangle enormously productive, and I don't intend my revision of that model to be a replacement for it. Sedgwick is properly self-conscious about the specificity of the argument she makes: "To assume that sex signifies power in a flat, unvarying relation of metaphor or synecdoche will always entail a blindness, not to the rhetorical and pyrotechnic, but to such historical categories as class and race" (*Between* 10–11). Her brief discussion of *Gone with the Wind* is meant to demonstrate the diverse ways in which sex and power can circulate within radically different social structures. I do want to emphasize, however, as does Fraiman, that Sedgwick's choice of material shapes her argument in ways that might be worth unsettling. By deploying her notion of the homosocial triangle in an overtly racialized American setting, I think we can get an even clearer sense of its possibility as a tool of both literary and cultural analysis.

7 Dixon was apparently so taken with the possibility of "the one woman" that he repeated the phrase as the title of his next novel, *The One Woman: A Story of Modern Utopia* (1903). In this novel, Dixon deploys antithetical female characters in order to make his case against socialism.

8 Dixon's relation to white women and feminist activism is vastly more complicated than space here allows. For example, when planning his "Church of the People," which opened in New York City in 1895, Dixon decided that "half the members of the Board of Deacons would be women" (Cook 91), a move suggesting a rather progressive view of women's role in religious institutions. Yet Dixon remained adamantly opposed to women's suffrage, and later novels like *The Foolish Virgin* paint a clear picture of the evils awaiting women if they dare to step outside their prescribed place in society. As a reductive summation, it's fair to say that Dixon loved women in a fashion bordering on worship. This worship, however, whether directed at mothers or potential wives, seemed largely driven by a love for so-called feminine ideals: purity, nurturance, innocence, and chastity.

9 That Charlie is at least partially modeled on Dixon himself is certain. Like Charlie, Dixon was in love with a woman whose father forbade marriage. Dixon proposed anyway, "at the falls of the Chattahoochee River" ("Southern" 272), in a scene re-created in the novel when Charlie proposes to Sallie on an island in the middle of a river. Also, Dixon and Harriet were forced to elope, an inspiration for the secret marriage that Charlie and Sallie will enter into near the novel's final pages. Raymond Cook, Dixon's biographer, doesn't speculate about the resemblances between Charlie and Dixon, and instead offers Charles B. Aycock as the model for Charlie (121). Aycock was the governor of North Carolina at the time of the novel's publication. For more on the connections between Dixon's biography and *The Leopard's Spots* see Williamson, 151–76.

10   Durham is ventriloquizing Dixon's own views here, since the Durham character represents the other half of Dixon's fictional alter ego. Thus this conversation between Dixon's two alter egos can be seen as further proof of his troubled ambivalences in the realms of sex and love.

11   This business with the wooden leg is almost too rich. As Gunning notes, Tom's status as amputee signals an obvious "dephallicization of the white male" (39). Yet his use of his prosthesis as a club can be read as an attempt to reclaim a phallic power taken from him by the war. Significantly, it's only in the presence of the black troopers that he can in fact accomplish such a reclamation.

12   This is less Dixon's intended message than an embarrassing and revealing byproduct of his (and Tom's) paternalism. Because of the terms on which "protection" is defined here, Annie never really had a chance.

13   According to Dixon's biographer, Dick was apparently based on a boyhood playmate of Dixon's. See Cook 18–19. In the context of this biographical detail, Sandra Gunning makes an interesting argument about the childhood friendship between Charlie Gaston and Dick, suggesting that it was impossibly homosexual at its core. See Gunning 36–37.

14   Dixon's complicity in Flora's rape is also too plain. In her reading of *Tess of the D'Urbervilles*, Bronfen notes the collusion between the novel's narrator and Alec D'Urberville in Tess's rape. By using Tess's violated body as a space on which to meditate on the metaphysical meanings of ravaged femininity, "the narrator repeats Alec's turning her body into a sign which must bear another's inscription" (236). Dixon similarly turns Annie and Flora into signs bearing the meanings of masculinist and racist ideologies.

15   While Dixon appropriates the Camps as a narrative staging ground for white racism, other writers on the South offered a more nuanced analysis of the relation between class and race after the war. Frances Harper, for example, viewed southern poor whites not with contempt but with pity. As she wrote after a visit to South Carolina in 1867, "To me one of the saddest features in the South is not even the old rebel class. . . . the most puzzling feature of Southern social life is, what shall become of the poorer white classes? Freedom comes to the colored man with new hopes, advantages and opportunities. He stands on the threshold of a new era, with the tides of a new dispensation coursing through his veins; but this poor 'cracken class,' what is there for them? They were the dregs of society before the war, and their status is unchanged" (124). Whereas Dixon imagined a white fraternity linking the Camps with the best of the southern aristocracy, Harper understood how that aristocracy actually depended on white poverty to maintain the structures of white privilege.

16   See Freud, "Beyond the Pleasure Principle" 147–50.

17   The *Random House Dictionary of American Slang* cites the following passage from a work called *Stag Party* as the first use of *dick* in the manner I'm tracing here: "Student (turning her fairly around and putting his dick where his finger was) — Nice, isn't it, ducky?" (Lighter 583).

18   As an example of how "manhood" functioned euphemistically for "penis," remember Dr. Abbey's obsession with the masturbated penis as an emblem of wasted American manhood.

19 A minor moment late in the novel shows this to be not solely a racial drama. When Reverend Durham learns that Allan McLeod has been spreading scandal about his wife, his automatic impulse is to respond with violence. Again, however, Dixon renders this move in terms of male sexual arousal. Taking a sword down from the wall, Durham notices "how snugly its rough hilt fitted his nervous hand-grip! He felt a curious throbbing in this hilt like a pulse. It was alive, and its spirit stirred deep waters in his soul that had never been ruffled before" (453). Though Durham is about to defend his wife's honor, his throbbing hilt and deeply stirred soul waters are caused by Allan, not by his wife.

20 My association of Hose's last name with Scandinavia has confused some readers, who rightly point out that "Norman" actually references Normandy in Northern France. The settlers of Normandy, however, were Vikings from Denmark, Norway, and Iceland.

21 There was, apparently, a real-life model for Hose Norman. According to Cook, Dixon had a childhood friend named Hosea Norman, whom Cook describes as "a powerful, strapping young animal of a man" (21). (Hosea had a dog named Napoléon Bonaparte that was nicknamed "Old Boney.") Though the existence of this real-life Hosea shows that Dixon didn't choose this name out of thin air, it's still significant that he chose a version of it for this particular context, perhaps realizing its appropriateness for this psychosexual drama. In addition to this real-life Hose, Dixon may have had another Hose in mind as well: Sam Hose, a black man accused of rape and murder in Georgia in 1899. Soon after his arrest, Sam Hose was castrated and burned alive in a well-attended and highly publicized lynching. Assuming that Dixon was aware of the story of Sam Hose (it received widespread media coverage throughout the South), his naming of Hose Norman takes on added significance, since it shows him appropriating black Hose for the purposes of white Hose. Stewart E. Tolnay and E. M. Beck claim that this Sam Hose was actually a Sam Holt, but he seems to have been reported as Sam Hose. For more on Sam Hose see Eric Sundquist's introduction to Chesnutt's *The Marrow of Tradition;* Tolnay and Beck 23; Sledd 71.

22 In this formulation, the South itself is figured as a white woman, not an uncommon metaphorical move for antiblack theorists. William Benjamin Smith, for example, foreshadows Dixon's language when he warns the South that miscegenation would "taint the well-spring of her life" (9). He continues: "It is this immediate jewel of her soul that the South watches with such a dragon eye, that she guards with more than vestal vigilance, with a circle of perpetual fire" (9). Substituting fire for sword, Smith's "jewel of her soul" and Dixon's "holy of holies" both speak of the same thing.

23 Only four pages later Dixon uses the phrase "holy of holies" in a different context. Charlie is once again worried about other men dancing with Sallie, "the woman whom he had enthroned in the holy of holies of his soul" (340). The phrase has undergone an interesting transformation. Whereas earlier it referred, at least in part, to female genitalia, in connection with Charlie it takes on a less bodily connotation, one associated purely with his soul. This shift further underscores the di-

chotomized nature of Charlie's desire, since true desire cannot be located in the (sexual) body.

24  In *White over Black* Winthrop Jordan traces this nineteenth-century fascination back to the discovery in the early part of the seventeenth century of the tailless ape, an animal "gifted" with a disproportionally large penis. The discovery of this animal coincided both temporally and geographically with the first European awareness of Africans, creating what Jordan calls a "tragic happenstance" whereby the overly endowed ape and black men were conflated in the white imaginary (29).

25  James Baldwin brilliantly dramatizes this dynamic in his short story "Going to Meet the Man," where he describes a lynching in brutal detail: "The man with the knife took the nigger's privates in his hand, one hand, still smiling, as though he were weighing them. In the cradle of the one white hand, the nigger's privates seemed as remote as meat being weighed in the scales; but seemed heavier too, much heavier, and Jesse felt his scrotum tighten; and huge, huge, much bigger than his father's, flaccid, hairless, the largest thing he had ever seen till then, and the blackest. The white hand stretched them, cradled them, caressed them" (247–48).

26  It's worth asking where black women appear (or don't appear) in this racial/ sexual dynamic. As others have noted, Dixon is more concerned with blackness in its male rather than its female form. As Sandra Gunning argues, this has everything to do with the history of miscegenationist union, a history most often manifested in the union (forced or otherwise) of white men and black women, not of black men and white women. As Gunning puts it: "Given that an acknowledgment of the presence of black women would automatically alter the racial construction of white masculinity, it is not surprising that black women are, in large measure, absent from Dixon's fiction. If they were referenced in too much detail, the reader would have to confront white male desire for the black within the plot of rescuing the domestic, and as such reveal the white male to be the foe of his own household" (33–34). Gunning continues: "Since the black woman had been associated with the slaveholder's sexuality in the antebellum South, her apparent absence in Dixon's representation of postwar America speaks to denial of the tradition of white-authored miscegenation in a postemancipation context" (44). As Gunning observes, the notable exception to this absence in Dixon's fiction is his 1912 work *The Sins of the Father*. See Gunning 43–47. Sutton Griggs economically captures this disappearance of black womanhood under the logic of white supremacy in *The Hindered Hand,* where he writes, "The world at large has heard that the problem of the South is the protection of the white woman. There is another woman in the South" (71).

27  Etymologically speaking, hetero- and homosexuality only exist in relation to each other. As binary terms, they can't exist singly. As Katz points out, the two terms debuted together in 1868 in the private correspondence of Karl Maria Kertbeny, an early sex-law reformer in Germany (52). In Kertbeny's writings heterosexuality stands as both normative standard and perversion, as it did for Kiernan and Krafft-Ebing. As Katz writes, "Kertbeny's coinage of *heterosexual* in the service of homosexual emancipation is one of sex history's grand ironies" (53).

1  In making this claim, I disagree slightly with Walter Benn Michaels's reading of Dixon's attitude toward the southern past. "Unlike, say, *Gone with the Wind*," Michaels writes, "*The Clansman* makes no appeal to nostalgia for the prewar South and for the more amicable race relations of slavery" ("Souls" 188). Michaels then generalizes from this claim to Dixon's larger attitude toward racial nostalgia. Although Michaels may be correct in relation to *The Clansman*, a reading of *The Leopard's Spots* complicates his argument in significant ways. *The Leopard's Spots,* particularly in book 1, is suffused with a longing for the Negro of the past, that prewar type whose loyalty sustained plantation life for whites. The figure of Nelse is the most obvious example. See Michaels, "The Souls of White Folk." For his slightly revised argument about Dixon's relationship to American imperialism see Michaels, "Anti-American Imperialism," n. 1.

2  That exhibit has since become a book. See Molly McGarry and Fred Wasserman, *Becoming Visible: An Illustrated History of Lesbian and Gay Life in Twentieth-Century America.*

3  In my discussion I'll be concentrating exclusively on part 2 of Griffith's film, since it's in this second reel that the Klan is born. Although countless critics have tried to dismiss the film's second half as antithetical to Griffith's intentions and success, I wish to place it at the thematic center of his project, recognizing the extent to which the film owes its very existence to the Klan as an image.

4  My assumption of a white audience here requires explanation. It signals my partial location within (as white viewer, though eighty-five years removed), as well as my imagining of, the audience Griffith had in mind in making the film. In so doing I erase, at some cost, the experience of the film's black viewers, both at the time of its release and subsequently. Yet my focus on the response of a white audience is consistent with the history of the film's debut. In its long battle with the film, the NAACP attempted to secure over a hundred tickets to an advance screening. The National Board of Censorship issued only two tickets, and those on the condition that they be used by white members of the NAACP. In response, the NAACP tried to infiltrate the screening with light-skinned black members (Shickel 272). Shown in a climate of strict segregation, where blacks had access to films primarily in segregated theaters in the South and ghetto theaters in the North, *Birth*'s audience was both imagined and realized as white. Black participation in the film's early days happened primarily *outside* the theaters, as several organizations worked assiduously to keep the film from being shown. Advertisements for the film also assumed a white audience, featuring heroic images of the Klan in full regalia.

5  A more recent example makes this point for me. The May 1996 issue of *Harper's Magazine* includes a partial listing of the various shades of white being offered in the new Ralph Lauren designer-paint line: "Aspen Summit; Avalanche; Breakwater White; Candelabra White; Country Stove White; Design Studio White; Dover Cliffs; Dune White; Edwardian Linen; Flour Sack White; Garden Rose White; Journal White; Killington Traverse; Montauk Driftwood; Petticoat White; Picket Fence White; Pocket Watch White; Polo Mallet White; Poncho White; Portico White; Resort White; River Rapids; Riviera Terrace; Roadster White; Sail

White; Sailor's White; Sneaker White; Snowdrift; Starched Apron; Tennis Court White; Tackroom White; Tuxedo Shirt" ("Ralph" 16). Whiteness only exists, and can only be differentiated, when it's attached to other, more concrete, properties: a starched apron, for example, or a polo mallet.

6    Walter Benn Michaels makes a similar point in reference to Dixon's *The Clansman:* "The purpose of the sheets, then, is not to conceal the identities of individual clansmen for, far from making their visible identities invisible, the sheets make their invisible identities visible. The Klan wear sheets because their bodies aren't as white as their souls, because *no* body can be as white as the soul embodied in the white sheet" ("Souls" 190).

7    The perceived loss of whiteness attaches to at least two of Griffith's primary characters. Lydia Brown and Silas Lynch, both mulattoes, represent perhaps the greatest threat to whiteness in the film, even more so than Gus does in his assault on a white woman. As mulattoes—products of the white South's greatest fear, miscegenation—Lydia and Silas complicate the binary system of relations that makes whiteness, as an abstraction, so powerful. For Dixon and Griffith, their very existence threatens the fall of Empire, whether their schemes for a racial power grab come to fruition or not.

8    For a more detailed discussion of light in *Birth* see Richard Dyer, "Into the Light: The Whiteness of the South in *The Birth of a Nation.*"

9    A more recent example—the announcement of the "not guilty" verdict in the O. J. Simpson criminal trial—helps clarify my point here. It's my suspicion that what angered and frightened white America most about the "not guilty" verdict in the Simpson trial is less the verdict itself than the televised spectacle of black response to that verdict. The television screen repeatedly showed jubilant, celebratory black crowds watching television at the moment the verdict was announced. From a large group of students at Howard University, to various "black restaurants" scattered around Los Angeles, to the predominantly African American crowd outside the courthouse, these shots of mass black celebration work in a number of ways. The most obvious, and I think least important, is the sense of some that a verdict in a double murder trial is nothing to celebrate, no matter what that verdict is. More significant is the visual representation of black segregation as celebratory power and exclusion. These are blacks "out of control" and thus out of white control. Their collective joy, visualized through shots of kinetic movement—jumping up and down, fists pumping in the air, hugging—signifies a coming together as physical power. These shots are usually juxtaposed against white reactions to the verdict that emphasize the opposite of this black collectivity. Whites are startled, and in their surprise wander off by themselves. They react to the screen, but not with one another. The difference in responses can be seen most clearly in those shots that show blacks and whites watching television together. In Times Square traffic stopped as multiracial crowds stared up at the Sony screen. When the verdict was announced, pockets of blacks shared their joy together, jumping up and down and hugging one another. On the periphery of these celebratory pockets stand white businessmen, clutching briefcases and watching the black celebrations in disbelief and apprehension.

10    In *Crowds and Power* (1960), Elias Canetti offers "the sea" and "rivers" as pri-

mary symbols of crowd behavior. Like crowds, "the sea is multiple, it moves, and it is dense and cohesive. Its multiplicity lies in its waves; they constitute it" (80). A river, Canetti writes, "is the crowd in its vanity, the crowd exhibiting itself" (83).

11    The study of crowd psychology, which began in the 1890s with the publication of Gustave LeBon's *The Crowd* (1895), was attaining critical mass around the time of Griffith's film. Based on the notion that the principles of individual depth psychology could be applied to this new "individual"—the crowd—behavioral scientists and psychoanalysts devoted their attention to the various modes of this collective psyche. Freud's *Group Psychology and the Analysis of the Ego* (1921) is perhaps the most famous example in this genre.

12    The remainder of the title card reads, "The negro party in control of the State House of Representatives, 101 blacks against 23 whites, session of 1871." Griffith's (and Dixon's) choice of South Carolina as a backdrop was far from accidental, since, as Eric Foner reminds us, South Carolina was the only state during Reconstruction in which blacks actually dominated the legislative process. Griffith's focus on the South Carolina House erases, through its visual emphasis, the actual legislative history of Reconstruction, in which blacks never achieved the striking political gains often attributed to them. See Foner, *Reconstruction* 151.

13    For example, this passage comes from an essay, "The Black Man," by Burmeister: "The negro foot impresses the beholder very disagreeably; its exceeding flatness, its low heel, projecting backwards, the prominent yet flat contour of the sides, the thick bolster of fat in the inner hollow of the foot, and the spread-out toes, serve to make it excessively ugly" (Helper 58). In a more visual example, the *Raleigh News and Observer* ran a cartoon on the front page of their October 5, 1898, edition. With the caption "Scene on the Atlantic and N.C. Railroad: What Occurred When Negro troops Were Travelling on that Railroad Under Republican Management," the cartoon shows a black man sitting with his bare feet propped up on the seat in front of him. A well-dressed woman looks in horror at the huge feet, which occupy the center of the frame.

14    Sandra Gunning makes a similar point about a scene in Thomas Dixon's *The Clansman*. In this scene, white men are able to identify a black man as the culprit in a rape through their discovery of abnormally large footprints. As Gunning writes, "One monstrous limb denotes another, so that Dixon can suggest the mark of black lust—the (apparently) abnormally large black genitalia—as the unmistakable symbol of the primitive black body at the scene of the crime" (34).

15    In no way do I wish to suggest that sexual vulnerability is itself a ritual—simply that for Griffith it became a stock scene in his repertoire, usually signified by the threatened woman twirling around with her arms up in the air and then fainting.

16    This black/white contrast proved instrumental to Gish getting the part in the first place. As she told *Stage* magazine in 1937, she never considered that she would get one of the main parts, having been one of the last to join the company. "But one day," she continues, "while we were rehearsing the scene where the colored man picks up the Northern girl gorilla-fashion, my hair, which was very blond, fell far below my waist and Griffith, seeing the contrast in the two figures, assigned me to play Elsie Stoneman" (qtd. in Bogle 14). Griffith's fondness for the visual appeal of this

black/white, male/female contrast influenced the films of another white star, Shirley Temple. According to Ann duCille, Temple's autobiography (*Child Star,* written under her married name, Shirley Temple Black) recounts how it was Griffith's suggestion that Temple work with Bill "Bojangles" Robinson. Black quotes Griffith as saying that "there is nothing, absolutely nothing, calculated to raise the gooseflesh on the back of an audience more than that of a white girl in relation to Negroes" (qtd. in duCille, "Shirley Temple" 17).

17　Though accomplished through a different method, Griffith effects a similar individuation earlier in the film, this time in reference to the black mob. The extended chase scene between Gus (the alleged rapist) and Flora Cameron serves to position Gus as a recognizable representative of the larger black mass. Whereas Ben's hood lifting gives the audience a knowable and attractive face to put on whiteness, Gus's pursuit of Flora allows a specific yet criminal face to be put on blackness.

18　Writing about the production and reception of *The Birth of a Nation* and the film version of *Gone with the Wind,* Gerald Wood theorizes their appeal by foregrounding "their common reliance on domestic melodrama that seeks to reaffirm social values about love, marriage, and the home and their integration of these domestic values with actual historical events so that our history becomes, in effect, the collective record of private American families" (123).

19　See Everett Carter, "Cultural History Written with Lightning: The Significance of *The Birth of a Nation* (1915)"; Scott Simmon, *The Films of D. W. Griffith;* Schickel, *D. W. Griffith;* William Everson, *American Silent Film.* Everson is a good example of those critics who have downplayed or dismissed *Birth*'s racism in defense of Griffith's technical achievements. "In terms of film history," Everson writes, "Griffith's opinion and treatment of blacks is not all that important" (87). This sort of form/content distinction ("film history" implies a history of purely technical moments divorced from substance) reigned in Griffith scholarship for much of this century and is fortunately being unsettled by more recent critics.

20　As Carter writes, "Before Griffith, the camera was treated as a fixed position, much like the spectator in the drama. The interpretation was by the actors, by their bodies, by their faces, by physical objects and by the settings before which these performed. Griffith made the ordering and interpretation—the art, in brief—one of the location, the angle, the movement of the camera and of the juxtaposition of the images the camera records by means of cutting and arranging these images to bring out their significance" (16).

21　In total, there are six shots of the Klan from the perspective of a moving camera. Five capture the Klan in its fast-paced charge; one shows the slow parade near the film's end. All five of the "ride shots" are of the over-the-shoulder type I'm discussing here. Further, the majority of Griffith's shots of the Klan riding are from a fixed perspective, most often in front of the Klan as it rides *toward* the audience. These fixed shots, however, are usually from a raised perspective, negating to some extent the sense of a Klan assault on the viewer.

22　Carol J. Clover depends on a similar formulation in her book on gender in modern horror films, *Men, Women, and Chain Saws.* Distinguishing between primary identification (the audience with the camera) and secondary identification (with the character of choice), Clover stresses the flexibility of these links between viewer and screen: "Both are fluid, character-identification on the psychoanalytic grounds that competing figures resonate with competing parts of the viewer's psyche (masochistic victim and sadistic monster, for example), and camera-identification on the cinematographic grounds that the camera can entertain different positions with ease" (8).

23  My inclusion of the Klan in this trio of crowds erases, to some extent, LeBon and Freud's assertion that the actions of crowds are never premeditated. Since the Klan's ride is premeditated, it could be argued that the Klan doesn't properly constitute a crowd in LeBon and Freud's sense. However, although there may be a premeditated goal at work in the Klan's ride (the rescue of Elsie Stoneman, for example), the route to this rescue, and the behavior of the rescuers, gets scripted moment to moment in response to the unregulated and unpremeditated movement of the black crowds in the streets. The Klan's ride is necessarily influenced by the unpremeditated movements of blackness and thus takes on the same quality.

### Epilogue: The Queer Face of Whiteness

1  See Du Bois, *Black Reconstruction in America;* Ellison, "The World and the Jug" and "The Shadow and the Act"; Baldwin, "On Being White and Other Lies" and "The Black Boy Looks at the White Boy"; Morrison, *Playing in the Dark;* hooks, "Representing Whiteness in the Black Imagination." In addition, see David Roediger's invaluable collection of African American writing on whiteness, *Black on White: Black Writers on What It Means to Be White.* For recent discussions of white scholarly work on racial identity and African American literature see Ann duCille, "The Occult of True Black Womanhood: Critical Demeanor and Black Feminist Studies"; Michael Awkward, "Negotiations of Power: White Critics, Black Texts, and the Self-Referential Impulse"; Elizabeth Abel, "Black Writing, White Reading: Race and the Politics of Feminist Interpretation"; Deborah McDowell, "Transferences: Black Feminist Thinking: The 'Practice' of 'Theory.'"

2  For a personal account of this awakening see Ruth Frankenberg's introduction to *White Women, Race Matters.* Mike Hill also addresses the link between contemporary whiteness studies and seventies and eighties feminism in his introduction to *Whiteness: A Critical Reader.*

3  See also Frye's "White Woman Feminist, 1983–1992" in her collection of essays, *Willful Virgin: Essays in Feminism, 1976–1992.* This essay marks the weaknesses as well as the strengths of Frye's work. Acknowledging her own middle-class identity, Frye refuses to recognize that this identity might substantially affect how she lives and understands her own whiteness. As a result, her delineation of "whiteliness" as an object of analysis isn't sufficiently differentiated from middle-class-ness, or something like respectability. Frye's unwillingness adequately to attend to the race/class dynamic is disappointing but also indicative of early mainstream feminism in the 1970s and 1980s. Although she's certainly aware that "the political significance of one's whiteliness interacts with the political significance of one's status as female or male in a male-supremacist culture" (160), she's unable to make this same connec-

tion in terms of class as a determining and often oppressive instrument of normative culture.

4   See Minnie Bruce Pratt, "Identity: Skin Blood Heart"; Mab Segrest, *Memoir of a Race Traitor;* Kobena Mercer, "Looking for Trouble" and "Skin Head Sex Thing."

5   *Race Traitor's* "new abolitionism" has become a dividing line for scholars working on whiteness, with many critics rejecting the notion that one can leave one's whiteness behind. See, for example, Kincheloe and Steinberg 21–22; Rodriguez 59–60; Homi Bhabha, "The White Stuff"; George Yúdice, "Neither Impugning nor Disavowing Whiteness Does a Viable Politics Make: The Limits of Identity Politics."

6   For other versions of this call to rearticulate whiteness see Yúdice, "Neither Impugning nor Disavowing Whiteness Does a Viable Politics Make"; Henry Giroux, "Racial Politics and the Pedagogy of Whiteness."

7   Noel Ignatiev offers a somewhat different critique of this call to reinvent whiteness, though he associates it with Matt Wray and Annalee Newitz's work on "white trash." See Ignatiev, "Abolitionism and the White Studies Racket."

8   Roediger readily admits to the limits of his hip-hop example. As he writes, "It would be ridiculous to claim that every white hip-hop fan is finding a way out of whiteness" (16). Roediger actually spends more time arguing the opposite point of view, that white investment in blackness is most often exploitative. Offering the examples of "guido" culture, Norman Mailer, and *Soul Man,* Roediger rightly foregrounds how white investment in blackness has historically worked not to critique whiteness but to reinforce it under the sign of black difference. Yet his faith in the subversive potential of such investment remains his final point: "If even MTV realizes that there is a mass audience for the critique of whiteness, we cannot fail to attempt to rally, and to learn from, a constituency committed to its abolition" (17). Roediger's claim for the subversive potential of white investment in hip-hop, first made in 1992, has acquired a new context here at the turn of the century, when miscegenated musical forms dominate the pop culture landscape. The huge popularity of white acts like Limp Bizkit and Kid Rock, both of whom craft a blend of hip-hop, eighties hardcore, and Skynyrd-era southern rock, raises anew this sense that white fans are somehow critiquing or resisting their whiteness. For an extremely useful account of this "new" white investment in blackness see Charles Aaron, "What the White Boy Means When He Says Yo."

# Works Cited

Aaron, Charles. "What the White Boy Means When He Says Yo." *Spin* Nov. 1998: 114–29.

Abbey, E. C. *The Sexual System and Its Derangements.* Buffalo, 1875.

Abel, Elizabeth. "Black Writing, White Reading: Race and the Politics of Feminist Interpretation." *Critical Inquiry* 19.3 (1993): 470–98.

American Psychiatric Association. *Diagnostic and Statistical Manual of Mental Disorders.* 3d ed. Washington, D.C.: American Psychiatric Association, 1980.

Andrews, William L. *The Literary Career of Charles W. Chesnutt.* Baton Rouge: Louisiana State UP, 1980.

Apple, Michael W. Foreword. *White Reign: Deploying Whiteness in America.* Ed. Joe L. Kincheloe, Shirley R. Steinberg, Nelson M. Rodriguez, and Ronald E. Chennault. New York: St. Martin's, 1998. ix–xiii.

Aptheker, Herbert. *Abolitionism: A Revolutionary Movement.* Boston: Twayne, 1989.

Atkinson, Edward. Rev. of "The Negro a Beast." *North American Review* 181 (1905): 202.

Awkward, Michael. "Negotiations of Power: White Critics, Black Texts, and the Self-Referential Impulse." *American Literary History* 2.4 (1990): 581–606.

Baldwin, James. "The Black Boy Looks at the White Boy." *Esquire* May 1961. Rpt. in *The Price of the Ticket: Collected Nonfiction, 1948–1985.* New York: St. Martin's, 1985. 289–303.

———. "Dark Days." *Esquire* Oct. 1980. Rpt. in *The Price of the Ticket: Collected Nonfiction, 1948–1985.* New York: St. Martin's, 1985. 657–66.

———. *Going to Meet the Man.* New York: Dial, 1965.

———. "On Being White and Other Lies." *Essence* Apr. 1984: 90–92.

Ball, Edward. "The White Issue." *Village Voice* 18 May 1993: 24–27.

Banks, Marva. "*Uncle Tom's Cabin* and Antebellum Black Response." *Readers in History: Nineteenth-Century American Literature and the Contexts of Response.* Ed. James L. Machor. Baltimore: Johns Hopkins UP, 1993. 209–27.

Barker-Benfield, G. J. *The Horrors of the Half-Known Life: Male Attitudes toward Women and Sexuality in Nineteenth-Century America.* New York: Harper and Row, 1976.

Baym, Nina. *Novels, Readers, and Reviewers: Responses to Fiction in Antebellum America.* Ithaca: Cornell UP, 1984.

Bennett, Paula, and Vernon A. Rosario II, eds. *Solitary Pleasures: The Historical, Literary, and Artistic Discourses of Autoeroticism.* New York: Routledge, 1995.

Berlant, Lauren. Rev. of *Sensational Designs,* by Jane Tompkins. *Modern Philology* Feb. 1988: 332–35.

Berman, Jeffrey. *Narcissism and the Novel.* New York: New York UP, 1990.

Berry, Harrison. *A Reply to Ariel.* Macon: American Union Book and Job Office Print, 1868. Rpt. in *Anti-Black Thought, 1863–1925: "The Negro Problem."* Ed. John David Smith. Vol. 5. New York: Garland, 1993. 223–56.

Bhabha, Homi K. "The White Stuff." *Artforum* May 1998: 21–24.

*The Birth of a Nation.* Dir. D. W. Griffith. Lumivision; International Museum of Photography at George Eastman House, 1991. Two videodiscs.

Blassingame, John W., ed. *The Frederick Douglass Papers*. Vols. 2, 5. New Haven: Yale UP, 1982. 5 vols. 1979–92.

Bogle, Donald. *Toms, Coons, Mulattoes, Mammies, and Bucks: An Interpretive History of Blacks in American Films*. New York: Continuum, 1989.

*Bookman*. July 1902: 472–74.

Bostwick, Homer. *Treatise on the Nature and Treatment of Seminal Diseases, Impotency, and Other Kindred Affections*. 2d ed. New York: Burgess and Stringer, 1848.

Bowler, Peter J. *The Non-Darwinian Revolution: Reinterpreting a Historical Myth*. Baltimore: Johns Hopkins UP, 1988.

Branigin, William, and Dana Priest. "3 White Soldiers Held in Slaying of Black Couple." *Washington Post* 9 Dec. 1995.

Brody, Jennifer DeVere. "Rereading Race and Gender: When White Women Matter." *American Quarterly* 48.1 (1996): 153–60.

Bronfen, Elisabeth. *Over Her Dead Body: Death, Femininity, and the Aesthetic*. Manchester: Manchester UP, 1992.

Brown, Sterling. *The Negro in American Fiction*. Washington, D.C.: Associates in Negro Folk Education, 1937.

Bucher, Glenn R., ed. *Straight/White/Male*. Philadelphia: Fortress, 1976.

Bullough, Bonnie, and Vern L. Bullough. *Sexual Attitudes: Myths and Realities*. Amherst: Prometheus, 1995.

Bush, Gregory W. "Like 'a Drop of Water in the Stream of Life': Moving Images of Mass Man from Griffith to Vidor." *Journal of American Studies* 25.2 (1991): 213–34.

Butler, Judith. *Bodies That Matter: On the Discursive Limits of "Sex."* New York: Routledge, 1993.

Canetti, Elias. *Crowds and Power*. 1960. Trans. Carol Stewart. New York: Continuum, 1981.

Carby, Hazel. " 'On the Threshold of Woman's Era': Lynching, Empire, and Sexuality in Black Feminist Theory." *Critical Inquiry* 12.1 (1985): 262–77.

———. *Reconstructing Womanhood: The Emergence of the Afro-American Woman Novelist*. New York: Oxford UP, 1987.

Carroll, Charles. *The Negro a Beast, or, "In the Image of God": The Reasoner of the Age, the Revelator of the Century! The Bible as It Is! The Negro and His Relation to the Human Family!* St. Louis: American Book and Bible House, 1900.

———. *The Tempter of Eve; or, The Criminality of Man's Social, Political, and Religious Equality with the Negro, and the Amalgamation to Which These Crimes Inevitably Lead. Discussed in the Light of the Scriptures, the Sciences, Profane History, Tradition, and the Testimony of the Monuments*. St. Louis: Adamic, 1902. Rpt. in *Anti-Black Thought, 1863–1925: "The Negro Problem."* Ed. John David Smith. Vol. 6. New York: Garland, 1993. 297–798.

Carter, Everett. "Cultural History Written with Lightning: The Significance of *The Birth of a Nation* (1915)." *Hollywood as Historian: American Film in a Cultural Context*. Ed. Peter C. Rollins. Lexington: UP of Kentucky, 1983. 9–19.

Chauncey, George, Jr. "From Sexual Inversion to Homosexuality: Medicine and the Changing Conceptualization of Female Deviance." *Salmagundi* 58–59 (fall 1982–winter 1983): 114–46.

Chesnutt, Charles W. *The Journals of Charles W. Chesnutt.* Ed. Richard H. Brodhead. Durham: Duke UP, 1993.

———. *The Marrow of Tradition.* 1901. Ed. Eric Sundquist. New York: Penguin, 1993.

———. *"To Be an Author": Letters of Charles W. Chesnutt, 1889–1905.* Ed. Joseph R. McElrath Jr. and Robert C. Leitz III. Princeton: Princeton UP, 1997.

———. "What Is a White Man?" *New York Independent.* 30 May 1889: 5–6.

Clarke, T. J. *Image of the People: Gustave Courbet and the 1848 Revolution.* London: Thames and Hudson, 1973.

Cleaver, Eldridge. *Soul on Ice.* New York: Dell, 1968.

Clover, Carol J. *Men, Women, and Chain Saws: Gender in the Modern Horror Film.* Princeton: Princeton UP, 1992.

Comstock, Anthony. *Traps for the Young.* 3d ed. New York: Funk and Wagnalls, 1883.

Cook, Raymond Allen. *Fire from the Flint: The Amazing Careers of Thomas Dixon.* Winston-Salem: John F. Blair, 1968.

Cooper, Anna Julia. *A Voice from the South: By a Black Woman of the South.* 1892. New York: Oxford UP, 1988.

Cooper, James Fenimore. 1826. *The Last of the Mohicans: A Narrative of 1757.* Ed. James Franklin. Albany: State U of New York P, 1982.

Crouch, Stanley. "Aunt Medea." *New Republic* 197 (1987): 38–43.

Cvetkovich, Ann. *Mixed Feelings: Feminism, Mass Culture, and Victorian Sensationalism.* New Brunswick: Rutgers UP, 1992.

Dameron, J. Lasley. "Melville and Scoresby on Whiteness." *English Studies* 74.1 (1993): 96–104.

Darwin, Charles. *On the Origin of the Species by Means of Natural Selection, or, the Preservation of Favoured Races in the Struggle for Life.* London: John Murray, 1859.

Day, Christopher. "Out of Whiteness." *Race Traitor* 3 (1994): 54–61.

Defoe, Daniel. *Conjugal Lewdness, or, Matrimonial Whoredom.* 1727. Gainesville: Scholars' Facsimiles and Reprints, 1967.

Delmar, Jay P. "The Moral Dilemma in Charles W. Chesnutt's *The Marrow of Tradition.*" *American Literary Realism* 14.2 (1981): 269–72.

D'Emilio, John, and Estelle B. Freedman. *Intimate Matters: A History of Sexuality in America.* 2d ed. Chicago: U of Chicago P, 1997.

Denning, Michael. *Mechanic Accents: Dime Novels and Working-Class Culture in America.* London: Verso, 1987.

Dixon, Thomas Jr. *The Clansman: An Historical Romance of the Ku Klux Klan.* New York: Gosset and Dunlap, 1905.

———. *The Foolish Virgin: A Romance of Today.* New York: D. Appleton, 1915.

———. *The Leopard's Spots: A Romance of the White Man's Burden — 1865–1900.* 1902. Ridgewood: Gregg, 1967.

———. *The One Woman: A Story of Modern Utopia.* New York: Doubleday, Page, 1903.

———. "Southern Horizons: An Autobiography." Unpublished (unfinished) manuscript.

Douglass, Frederick. "The Claims of the Negro Ethnologically Considered." 1854. *The Life and Writings of Frederick Douglass.* Ed. Philip S. Foner. Vol. 2. New York: International, 1955. 289–309.

———. *Narrative of the Life of Frederick Douglass, an American Slave.* 1845. Ed. Houston A. Baker Jr. New York: Penguin, 1986.

———. "Why Is the Negro Lynched?" 1894. *The Life and Writings of Frederick Douglass.* Ed. Philip S. Foner. Vol. 4. New York: International, 1955. 491–523.

Douglass, H. Paul. *Christian Reconstruction in the South.* New York: Pilgrim, 1909.

Drayton, William. *The South Vindicated from the Treason and Fanaticism of the Northern Abolitionists.* 1836. New York: Negro UP, 1969.

Du Bois, W. E. B. *Against Racism: Unpublished Essays, Papers, Addresses, 1887–1961.* Ed. Herbert Aptheker. Amherst: U of Massachusetts P, 1985.

———. *Black Reconstruction in America, 1860–1880.* 1935. New York: Atheneum, 1969.

———. *The Crisis Writings.* Ed. Daniel Walden. Greenwich: Fawcett, 1972.

———. *Darkwater: Voices from within the Veil.* New York: Harcourt, Brace, 1920.

duCille, Ann. "The Occult of True Black Womanhood: Critical Demeanor and Black Feminist Studies." *Signs* 19.3 (1994): 591–629.

———. "The Shirley Temple of My Familiar." *Transition* 7.1 (1998): 10–32.

Dyer, Richard. "Into the Light: The Whiteness of the South in *The Birth of a Nation.*" *Dixie Debates: Perspectives on Southern Cultures.* Ed. Richard H. King and Helen Taylor. New York: New York UP, 1996.

———. *White.* New York: Routledge, 1997.

———. "White." *Screen* 29.4 (1988): 44–64.

———. "A White Star." *Sight and Sound.* August 1993: 22–24.

Elder, Arlene A. *The "Hindered Hand": Cultural Implications of Early Afro-American Fiction.* Westport: Greenwood, 1978.

Ellis, Havelock. *Studies in the Psychology of Sex.* 3d ed. Vol. 2. Philadelphia: F. A. Davis, 1920.

Ellis, John. *Visible Fictions: Cinema, Television, Video.* London: Routledge and Kegan Paul, 1982.

Ellison, Ralph. "The Shadow and the Act." *The Reporter* 6 Dec. 1949. Rpt. in *Shadow and Act.* 1964. New York: Vintage, 1972. 273–81.

———. "The World and the Jug." *The New Leader* 9 Dec. 1963, 3 Feb. 1964. Rpt. in *The Collected Essays of Ralph Ellison.* Ed. John F. Callahan. New York: Modern Library, 1995. 155–88.

Ethiop [William J. Wilson]. "What Shall We Do with the White People?" 1860. *Black on White: Black Writers on What It Means to Be White.* Ed. David R. Roediger. New York: Schocken, 1998.

Everett, William. "Critical Notes: Beadle's Dime Books." *North American Review* 99.204 (1864): 303–9.

Everson, William K. *American Silent Film.* New York: Oxford UP, 1978.

Fanon, Frantz. *Black Skin, White Masks.* 1952. Trans. Charles Lam Markmann. New York: Grove, 1967.

Felski, Rita. *The Gender of Modernity.* Cambridge: Harvard UP, 1995.

Fine, Michelle, et al., eds. *Off White: Readings on Race, Power, and Society.* New York: Routledge, 1997.

Foner, Eric. *Politics and Ideology in the Age of the Civil War.* New York: Oxford UP, 1980.

———. *A Short History of Reconstruction, 1863–1877.* New York: Harper and Row, 1990.

———. "Workers and Slavery." *Working for Democracy: American Workers from the Revolution to the Present.* Ed. Paul Buhle and Alan Dawley. Urbana: U of Illinois P, 1985.

Forgacs, David, ed. *An Antonio Gramsci Reader: Selected Writings, 1916–1935.* New York: Schocken, 1988.

Foucault, Michel. *Discipline and Punish: The Birth of the Prison.* 1975. New York: Vintage, 1979.

———. *The History of Sexuality.* Vol. 1. Trans. Robert Hurley. New York: Pantheon, 1978.

Fraiman, Susan. "Geometries of Race and Gender: Eve Sedgwick, Spike Lee, Charlayne Hunter-Gault." *Feminist Studies* 20.1 (1994): 67–84.

Frankenberg, Ruth, ed. *Displacing Whiteness: Essays in Social and Cultural Criticism.* Durham: Duke UP, 1997.

———. *White Women, Race Matters: The Social Construction of Whiteness.* Minneapolis: U of Minnesota P, 1993.

Fredrickson, George M. *The Black Image in the White Mind: The Debate on American Character and Destiny, 1817–1914.* 1971. Hanover: Wesleyan UP, 1987.

———. Introduction. *The Impending Crisis of the South: How to Meet It.* By Hinton Rowan Helper. 1857. Cambridge: Harvard UP, 1968.

Freud, Sigmund. "Beyond the Pleasure Principle." 1920. Trans. C. J. M. Hubback. *A General Selection from the Works of Freud.* Ed. John Rickman. New York: Liveright, 1957. 141–68.

———. *Group Psychology and the Analysis of the Ego.* 1921. Trans. James Strachey. New York: Norton, 1959.

———. "On Narcissism: An Introduction." 1914. Trans. James Strachey. *The Standard Edition of the Complete Psychological Works of Sigmund Freud.* Ed. James Strachey. Vol. 14. London: Hogarth, 1957. 73–102.

———. "Three Essays on the Theory of Sexuality." 1905. Trans. James Strachey. *The Standard Edition of the Complete Psychological Works of Sigmund Freud.* Ed. James Strachey. Vol. 7. London: Hogarth, 1957. 135–243.

Frye, Marilyn. "On Being White: Toward a Feminist Understanding of Race and Race Supremacy." 1981. *The Politics of Reality: Essays in Feminist Theory.* Freedom: Crossing, 1983. 110–27.

———. "White Woman Feminist, 1883–1992." *Essays in Feminism, 1976–1992.* Freedom: Crossing, 1992. 147–69.

Gaines, Francis Pendleton. *The Southern Plantation: A Study in the Development and the Accuracy of a Tradition.* 1924. Gloucester: Peter Smith, 1962.

Gaines, Kevin. "Black Americans' Racial Uplift Ideology as 'Civilizing Mission': Pauline E. Hopkins on Race and Imperialism." *Cultures of United States Imperialism.* Ed. Amy Kaplan and Donald E. Pease. Durham: Duke UP, 1993. 433–55.

Gardner, Augustus K. *Conjugal Sins against the Laws of Life and Health and Their Effects upon the Father, Mother and Child.* New York: Hurst, 1874.

———. *Our Children.* Hartford: Belknap and Bliss, 1872.

Gates, Henry Louis, Jr. "Writing 'Race' and the Difference It Makes." *Critical Inquiry*

12.1 (1985): 1–20. Rpt. in *"Race," Writing, and Difference*. Chicago: U of Chicago P, 1986. 1–20.

Geduld, Harry M., ed. *Focus on D. W. Griffith*. Englewood Cliffs: Prentice-Hall, 1971.

Genovese, Eugene D. *Roll, Jordan, Roll: The World the Slaves Made*. New York: Random House, 1974.

George, Marjorie, and Richard S. Pressman. "Confronting the Shadow: Psycho-Political Repression in Chesnutt's *The Marrow of Tradition*." *Phylon* 48.4 (1987): 287–98.

Gillman, Susan. "Pauline Hopkins and the Occult: African-American Revisions of Nineteenth-Century Sciences." *American Literary History* 8.1 (1996): 57–82.

Gilman, Sander L. "Black Bodies, White Bodies: Toward an Iconography of Female Sexuality in Late Nineteenth-Century Art, Medicine, and Literature." *Race, Writing, and Difference*. Ed. Henry Louis Gates Jr. Chicago: U of Chicago P, 1985.

Giroux, Henry A. "Racial Politics and the Pedagogy of Whiteness." *Whiteness: A Critical Reader*. Ed. Mike Hill. New York: New York UP, 1997.

Gleason, William. "Voices at the Nadir: Charles Chesnutt and David Bryant Fulton." *American Literary Realism* 24.3 (1992): 22–41.

*Godey's*. 45 (1852): 579.

Gossett, Thomas F. *Race: The History of an Idea in America*. New York: Schocken, 1965.

———. *Uncle Tom's Cabin and American Culture*. Dallas: Southern Methodist UP, 1985.

Gould, Stephen Jay. *The Mismeasure of Man*. New York: Norton, 1996.

*Graham's Lady's and Gentleman's Magazine*. Feb., Mar. 1853.

Griggs, Sutton Elbert. *The Hindered Hand; or, The Reign of the Repressionist*. 1905. Miami: Mnemosyne, 1969.

Gunning, Sandra. *Race, Rape, and Lynching: The Red Record of American Literature, 1890–1912*. New York: Oxford UP, 1996.

Hall, Jacquelyn Dowd. " 'The Mind That Burns in Each Body': Women, Rape, and Racial Violence." *Powers of Desire: The Politics of Sexuality*. Ed. Ann Snitow, Christine Stanswell, and Sharon Thompson. New York: Monthly Review, 1983. 328–49.

———. *Revolt against Chivalry: Jessie Daniel Ames and the Women's Campaign against Lynching*. 1979. Rev. ed. New York: Columbia UP, 1993.

Harper, Frances Ellen Watkins. *A Brighter Coming Day: A Frances Ellen Watkins Harper Reader*. Ed. Frances Smith Foster. New York: Feminist P, 1990.

Harper, Phillip Brian. *Are We Not Men?* New York: Oxford UP, 1996.

Harris, Trudier. *Exorcising Blackness: Historical and Literary Lynching and Burning Rituals*. Bloomington: Indiana UP, 1984.

Hart, Lynda. *Fatal Women: Lesbian Sexuality and the Mark of Aggression*. Princeton: Princeton UP, 1994.

Harvey, Charles M. "The Dime Novel in American Life." *Atlantic Monthly* July 1907: 39, 43.

Hayne, Barrie. "Standing on Neutral Ground: Charles Jacobs Peterson of *Peterson's*." *Pennsylvania Magazine of History and Biography* 93 (1969): 510–26.

Helper, Hinton Rowan. *Nojoque; A Question for a Continent*. New York: George W. Carleton, 1867.

Higginson, Thomas Wentworth. *Cheerful Yesterdays*. Boston, 1898.

Hill, Mike, ed. *Whiteness: A Critical Reader.* New York: New York UP, 1997.

Holmes, George F. Rev. of *A Key to "Uncle Tom's Cabin,"* by Harriet Beecher Stowe. *Southern Literary Messenger* June 1853: 321–29.

hooks, bell. "Representing Whiteness in the Black Imagination." *Cultural Studies.* Ed. Lawrence Grossberg, Cary Nelson, and Paula Treichler. New York: Routledge, 1992. 338–46.

Hopkins, Pauline. *Of One Blood: Or, The Hidden Self. The Magazine Novels of Pauline Hopkins.* New York: Oxford UP, 1988. 440–621.

Ignatiev, Noel. "Abolitionism and the White Studies Racket." *Race Traitor* 10 (1999): 3–7.

———. Interview. "Treason to Whiteness Is Loyalty to Humanity." *Utne Reader* Nov.–Dec. 1994: 82–86.

Irwin, John T. *Doubling and Incest/Repetition and Revenge: A Speculative Reading of Faulkner.* Baltimore: Johns Hopkins UP, 1975.

Jacobs, Harriet. *Incidents in the Life of a Slave Girl.* 1861. New York: Oxford UP, 1988.

Jameson, Fredric. *The Political Unconscious: Narrative as a Socially Symbolic Act.* Ithaca: Cornell UP, 1981.

Jefferson, Thomas. *Notes on the State of Virginia.* 1784. Ed. William Peden. Chapel Hill: U of North Carolina P, 1955.

Johannsen, Albert. *The House of Beadle and Adams and Its Dime and Nickel Novels: A Story of a Vanished Literature.* 3 vols. Norman: U of Oklahoma P, 1950–62.

Jordan, Winthrop D. *White over Black: American Attitudes toward the Negro, 1550–1812.* 1968. New York: Norton, 1977.

Katz, Jonathan Ned. *The Invention of Heterosexuality.* New York: Penguin, 1995.

Kelly, Henry Ansgar. "The Metamorphosis of the Eden Serpent during the Middle Ages and Renaissance." *Viator: Medieval and Renaissance Studies.* 2 (1971): 301–28.

Kernberg, Otto. *Borderline Conditions and Pathological Narcissism.* New York: Jason Aronson, 1975.

Kincheloe, Joe L., and Shirley R. Steinberg. "Addressing the Crisis of Whiteness: Reconfiguring White Identity in a Pedagogy of Whiteness." *White Reign: Deploying Whiteness in America.* Ed. Joe L. Kincheloe, Shirley R. Steinberg, Nelson M. Rodriguez, and Ronald E. Chennault. New York: St. Martin's, 1998. 3–29.

Kinney, James. *Amalgamation! Race, Sex, and Rhetoric in the Nineteenth-Century American Novel.* Westport: Greenwood, 1985.

Knadler, Stephen K. "Untragic Mulatto: Charles Chesnutt and the Discourse of Whiteness." *American Literary History* 8.3 (1996): 426–48.

Krafft-Ebing, Richard von. *Psychopathia Sexualis, with Special Reference to Contrary Sexual Instinct.* Trans. Charles Gilbert Chaddock. 7th ed. Philadelphia: Davis, 1893.

Lallemand, Claude F. *A Practical Treatise on the Causes, Symptoms, and Treatment, of Spermatorrhoea.* Trans. Henry J. McDougall. London, 1847.

LeBon, Gustave. *The Crowd.* 1895. New Brunswick: Transaction, 1995.

Lester, A. Hoyle. *The Pre-Adamite, or Who Tempted Eve? Scripture and Science in Unison as Respects the Antiquity of Man.* Philadelphia: Lippincott, 1875. Rpt. in *Anti-Black Thought, 1863–1925: "The Negro Problem."* Ed. John David Smith. Vol. 6. New York: Garland, 1993. 129–94.

*Liberator.* 11 June, 5 Nov. 1852; 4 Mar. 1853.

Lighter, Jonathan E., ed. *Random House Dictionary of American Slang.* Vol. 1. New York: Random House, 1994–.

Lindsay, Vachel. *The Art of the Moving Picture.* New York: Macmillan, 1916.

Lipsitz, George. *The Possessive Investment in Whiteness: How White People Profit from Identity Politics.* Philadelphia: Temple UP, 1998.

———. "The Possessive Investment in Whiteness: Racialized Social Democracy and the 'White' Problem in American Studies." *American Quarterly* 47.3 (1995): 369–87.

Lott, Eric. *Love and Theft: Blackface Minstrelsy and the American Working Class.* New York: Oxford UP, 1993.

MacDonald, Robert H. "The Frightful Consequences of Onanism: Notes on the History of a Delusion." *Journal of the History of Ideas* 28.3 (1967): 423–31.

Magdol, Edward. *The Antislavery Rank and File: A Social Profile of the Abolitionists' Constituency.* New York: Greenwood, 1986.

Mailer, Norman. "The White Negro: Superficial Reflections on the Hipster." 1957. *Advertisements for Myself.* New York: Putnam's, 1959. 337–58.

Maio, Kathleen L. "Metta Victoria Fuller Victor." *American Women Writers: A Critical Reference Guide from Colonial Times to the Present.* Ed. Lisa Mainiero. Vol. 4. New York: Ungar, 1982. 302–4. 4 vols. 1979–94.

McDowell, Deborah E. "Transferences: Black Feminist Thinking: The 'Practice' of 'Theory.'" *"The Changing Same": Black Women's Literature, Criticism, and Theory.* Bloomington: Indiana UP, 1995. 156–75.

McGarry, Molly, and Fred Wasserman. *Becoming Visible: An Illustrated History of Lesbian and Gay Life in Twentieth-Century America.* New York: Penguin, 1998.

Mercer, Kobena. "Fear of a Black Penis." *Artforum* 32.8 (1994): 80–81, 122.

———. "Looking for Trouble." *The Lesbian and Gay Studies Reader.* Ed. Henry Abelove, Michele Aina Barale, and David M. Halperin. New York: Routledge, 1993. 350–59.

———. "Skin Head Sex Thing: Racial Difference and the Homoerotic Imaginary." *How Do I Look? Queer Film and Video.* Ed. Bad Object-Choices. Seattle: Bay, 1991. 169–222.

Michaels, Walter Benn. "Anti-Imperial Americanism." *Cultures of United States Imperialism.* Ed. Amy Kaplan and Donald E. Pease. Durham: Duke UP, 1993. 365–91.

———. "The Souls of White Folk." *Literature and the Body.* Ed. Elaine Scarry. Baltimore: Johns Hopkins UP, 1988. 185–209.

Miller, Kelly. "As to *The Leopard's Spots:* An Open Letter to Thomas Dixon, Jr." 1905. Rpt. in *Radicals and Conservatives, and Other Essays on the Negro in America.* 1908. New York: Schocken, 1968. 42–70.

Millet, Kate. *Sexual Politics.* Garden City: Doubleday, 1970.

Mills, Bruce. "Lydia Maria Child and the Endings to Harriet Jacobs' *Incidents in the Life of a Slave Girl.*" *American Quarterly* 64.2 (1992): 255–72.

Moraga, Cherrie, and Gloria Anzaldúa, eds. *This Bridge Called My Back: Writings by Radical Women of Color.* Watertown: Persephone, 1981.

Morrison, Toni. *Beloved.* New York: Knopf, 1987.

——. *Playing in the Dark: Whiteness and the Literary Imagination.* New York: Vintage, 1992.

Mott, Frank Luther. *Golden Multitudes: The Story of Best Sellers in the United States.* New York: Macmillan, 1947.

Neal, Larry. "The Black Arts Movement." *Visions of a Liberated Future: Black Arts Movement Writings.* Ed. Michael Schwartz. New York: Thunder's Mouth, 1989. 62–78.

Nelson, Dana D. *National Manhood: Capitalist Citizenship and the Imagined Fraternity of White Men.* Durham: Duke UP, 1998.

——. *The Word in Black and White: Reading "Race" in American Literature 1638-1867.* New York: Oxford UP, 1993.

Nelson, John Herbert. *The Negro Character in American Literature.* College Park: McGrath, 1926.

Newton, Esther. "The Mythic Mannish Lesbian: Radclyffe Hall and the New Woman." *Hidden from History: Reclaiming the Gay and Lesbian Past.* Ed. Martin Bauml Duberman, Martha Vicinus, and George Chauncey Jr. New York: New American Library, 1989.

*New York Tribune.* 2, 29 Oct., 5, 6, 18 Nov. 1852; 6, 11, 12, 13, 16 Dec. 1861.

Nipps, Karen. "Charles Jacobs Peterson." *Dictionary of Literary Biography.* Ed. Matthew J. Bruccoli. Vol. 79. Detroit: Gale, 1978–. 236–41.

*Onania: or, The Heinous Sin of Self-Pollution, and All Its Frightful Consequences, in Both Sexes Consider'd, & c.* 16th ed. London, 1737.

Ovid. *Metamorphoses.* Trans. Frank Justus Miller. Ed. G. P. Goold. Cambridge: Harvard UP, 1977.

Pagels, Elaine. *Adam, Eve, and the Serpent.* New York: Random House, 1988.

Palmer, Phyllis. *Domesticity and Dirt: Housewives and Domestic Servants in the United States, 1920-1945.* Philadelphia: Temple UP, 1989.

Papashvily, Helen Waite. *All the Happy Endings: A Study of the Domestic Novel in America, the Women Who Wrote It, the Women Who Read It, in the Nineteenth Century.* New York: Harper and Brothers, 1956.

Payne, Buckner H. [Ariel]. *The Negro: What Is His Ethnological Status? Is He the Progeny of Ham? Is He a Descendant of Adam and Eve? Has He a Soul? Or Is He a Beast in God's Nomenclature? What Is His Status as Fixed by God in Creation? What Is His Relation to the White Race?* 2d ed. Cincinnati, 1867. Rpt. in *Anti-Black Thought, 1863-1925: "The Negro Problem."* Ed. John David Smith. Vol. 5. New York: Garland, 1993. 1–48.

Person, Leland S., Jr. "The American Eve: Miscegenation and a Feminist Frontier Fiction." *American Quarterly* 37.5 (1985): 668–85.

Peterson, Charles Jacobs [J. Thornton Randolph]. *The Cabin and Parlor; or, Slaves and Masters.* Philadelphia: Peterson, 1852.

*Peterson's Magazine* 22.6 (Dec. 1852): 297.

Pfeil, Fred. *White Guys: Studies in Postmodern Domination and Difference.* New York: Verso, 1995.

Phillips, Jerry. "Literature in the Country of 'Whiteness': From T. S. Eliot to *The Tempest.*" *Whiteness: A Critical Reader.* Ed. Mike Hill. New York: New York UP, 1997.

Pinckney, Darryl. "Black Victims, Black Villains." *New York Review of Books* 29 Jan. 1987: 17–20.

Polan, Dana B. "'Above all else to make you see': Cinema and the Ideology of Spectacle." *Boundary 2: A Journal of Postmodern Literature and Culture.* 11.1–2 (1982–83): 129–44.

Pratt, Minnie Bruce. "Identity: Skin Blood Heart." *Yours in Struggle: Three Feminist Perspectives on Anti-Semitism and Racism.* By Elly Bulkin, Minnie Bruce Pratt, and Barbara Smith. Brooklyn: Long Haul, 1984. 9–63.

Prospero. *Caliban. A Sequel to "Ariel."* New York, 1868. Rpt. in *Anti-Black Thought, 1863–1925: "The Negro Problem."* Ed. John David Smith. Vol. 5. New York: Garland, 1993. 191–222.

*Raleigh News and Observer.* 5 Oct. 1898.

"Ralph Lauren's Shades of Pale." *Harper's Magazine* May 1996: 16.

Reilly, John M. "The Dilemma in Chesnutt's *The Marrow of Tradition.*" *Phylon* 32 (1971): 31–38.

Richards, Leonard L. *"Gentlemen of Property and Standing": Anti-Abolition Mobs in Jacksonian America.* New York: Oxford UP, 1970.

Ripley, C. Peter, ed. *The Black Abolitionist Papers.* Vol. 4. Chapel Hill: U of North Carolina P, 1991. 4 vols.

Rodriguez, Nelson M. "Emptying the Content of Whiteness: Toward an Understanding of the Relation between Whiteness and Pedagogy." *White Reign: Deploying Whiteness in America.* Ed. Joe L. Kincheloe, Shirley R. Steinberg, Nelson M. Rodriguez, and Ronald E. Chennault. New York: St. Martin's, 1998. 31–62.

Roediger, David R., ed. *Black on White: Black Writers on What It Means to Be White.* New York: Schocken, 1998.

———. *Towards the Abolition of Whiteness: Essays on Race, Politics, and Working Class History.* London: Verso, 1994.

———. *The Wages of Whiteness: Race and the Making of the American Working Class.* London: Verso, 1991.

Rogin, Michael Paul. "'The Sword Became a Flashing Vision': D. W. Griffith's *The Birth of a Nation.*" *Representations* 9 (1985): 150–95.

Roof, Judith. *Come As You Are: Sexuality and Narrative.* New York: Columbia UP, 1996.

Royster, Philip M. "In Search of Our Fathers' Arms: Alice Walker's Persona of the Alienated Darling." *Black American Literature Forum.* 20.4 (1986): 347–70.

Rubin, Gayle. "The Traffic in Women: Notes on the 'Political Economy' of Sex." *Toward an Anthropology of Women.* Ed. R. Reiter. New York: Monthly Review, 1975. 157–210.

Scarry, Elaine. *The Body in Pain: The Making and Unmaking of the World.* New York: Oxford UP, 1985.

Schickel, Richard. *D. W. Griffith: An American Life.* New York: Simon and Schuster, 1984.

Schuyler, George S. "Our White Folks." *Black on White: Black Writers on What It Means to Be White.* Ed. David R. Roediger. New York: Schocken, 1998. 71–84.

Sedgwick, Eve Kosofsky. *Between Men: English Literature and Male Homosocial Desire.* New York: Columbia UP, 1985.

———. "Jane Austen and the Masturbating Girl." *Critical Inquiry* 17.4 (1991): 818–37.

Segrest, Mab. *Memoir of a Race Traitor*. Boston: South End, 1994.

Simmon, Scott. *The Films of D. W. Griffith*. Cambridge: Cambridge UP, 1993.

Simms, William Gilmore Rev. of *A Key to "Uncle Tom's Cabin,"* by Harriet Beecher Stowe. *Southern Quarterly Review* July 1853: 214–54.

———. *The Yemassee: A Romance of Carolina*. 1835. New Haven: College and UP, 1964.

Sisney, Mary F. "The Power and Horror of Whiteness: Wright and Ellison Respond to Poe." *CLA Journal* 29.1 (1985): 82–90.

Sledd, Andrew. "The Negro: Another View." *Atlantic Monthly* July 1902: 65–73.

Smith, John David. Introduction. *Anti-Black Thought, 1863–1925: "The Negro Problem."* Ed. John David Smith. Vol. 6. New York: Garland, 1993. xxv–xxix.

Smith, Valerie. Introduction. *Incidents in the Life of a Slave Girl*. By Harriet Jacobs. New York: Oxford UP, 1988. xxvii–xl.

Smith, William Benjamin. *The Color Line: A Brief in Behalf of the Unborn*. New York: McClure, Phillips, 1906.

*Southern Literary Messenger* 18 (1852): 703.

Spence, H. D. M., and Joseph S. Exell, eds. *The Pulpit Commentary*. London: C. Kegan Paul, 1880–.

Spillers, Hortense. "Changing the Letter: The Yokes, the Jokes of Discourse, or Mrs. Stowe, Mr. Reed." *Slavery and the Literary Imagination*. Ed. Arnold Rampersad and Deborah E. McDowell. Baltimore: Johns Hopkins UP, 1989. 25–61.

Squier, Ephraim G. "American Ethnology." *American Review* 9 (1849): 385–98.

Stanton, William. *The Leopard's Spots: Scientific Attitudes toward Race in America, 1815–59*. Chicago: U of Chicago P, 1960.

Stearns, Bertha Monica. "Philadelphia Magazines for Ladies: 1830–1860." *Pennsylvania Magazine of History and Biography* 69 (1945): 207–19.

Steinbeck, John. *The Grapes of Wrath*. 1939. New York: Viking, 1989.

Stepan, Nancy. *The Idea of Race in Science: Great Britain, 1800–1960*. London: Macmillan, 1982.

Stepan, Nancy Leys, and Sander L. Gilman. "Appropriating the Idioms of Science: The Rejection of Scientific Racism." *The Bounds of Race: Perspectives on Hegemony and Resistance*. Ed. Dominick LaCapra. Ithaca: Cornell UP, 1991. 72–103.

Stephens, Ann S. "Literary Ladies." *Lady's World* 6 (1843): 97–103.

Stowe, Harriet Beecher. *Uncle Tom's Cabin: or, Life among the Lowly*. 1852. New York: Harper and Row, 1958.

Sundquist, Eric. Introduction. *The Marrow of Tradition*. 1901. Ed. Eric Sundquist. New York: Penguin, 1993.

———. *To Wake the Nations: Race in the Making of American Literature*. Cambridge: Belknap P of Harvard UP, 1993.

Tabick, Jacqueline. "The Snake in the Grass: The Problems of Interpreting a Symbol in the Hebrew Bible and Rabbinic Writings." *Religion* 16.2 (1986): 155–67.

Taylor, G. Rattray. *Sex in History*. New York: Vanguard, 1954.

Thompson, John. Rev. of *Uncle Tom's Cabin: or, Life among the Lowly*, by Harriet Beecher Stowe. *Southern Literary Messenger* Oct. 1852: 630–38.

Thompson, M. B. *The Negro, Not a Beast, But a Descendant of Adam. A Reply to Prof.*

*Chas. Carroll's Work, "The Negro a Beast" or "In the Image of God."* Mount Juliet: Freeman, 1906.

Tissot, Samuel. *Onanism: A Dissertation on the Maladies Brought on by Masturbation.* Paris, 1760.

Todd, John. *The Student's Manual; Designed, by Specific Directions, to Aid in Forming and Strengthening the Intellectual and Moral Character and Habits of the Student.* 22d ed. Northampton: Hopkins, Bridgman, 1857.

Tolney, Stewart E., and E. M. Beck. *A Festival of Violence: An Analysis of Southern Lynchings, 1882–1930.* Urbana: U of Illinois P, 1995.

Tompkins, Jane. *Sensational Designs: The Cultural Work of American Fiction, 1790–1860.* New York: Oxford UP, 1985.

Tucker, David M. "Miss Ida B. Wells and Memphis Lynching." *Phylon* 32 (1971): 112–22.

Victor, Metta V. *Maum Guinea and Her Plantation "Children," or, Holiday-Week on a Louisiana Estate: A Slave Romance.* 1861. Freeport: Books for Libraries, 1972.

———. *The Senator's Son, or, The Maine Law; a Last Refuge; a Story Dedicated to the Lawmakers.* Cleveland: Tooker and Gatchel, 1853.

Walker, David. *One Continual Cry: David Walker's Appeal to the Colored Citizens of the World, 1829–1830.* Ed. Herbert Aptheker. New York: Humanities, 1965.

Warner, Michael. "Homo-Narcissism; or, Heterosexuality." *Engendering Men: The Question of Male Feminist Criticism.* Ed. Joseph A. Boone and Michael Cadden. New York: Routledge, 1990.

Watkins, Mel. "Sexism, Racism, and Black Women Writers." *New York Times Book Review* 15 June 1986: 1, 35–37.

Wells, Ida B. *Crusade for Justice: The Autobiography of Ida B. Wells.* Ed. Alfreda M. Duster. Chicago: U of Chicago P, 1970.

———. *Selected Works of Ida B. Wells-Barnett.* Ed. Trudier Harris. New York: Oxford UP, 1991.

West, Cornel. "I'm Ofay, You're Ofay: A Conversation with Noel Ignatiev and William 'Upski' Wimsatt." *Transition* 7.1 (1998): 178–98.

Wexler, Laura. "Tender Violence: Literary Eavesdropping, Domestic Fiction, and Educational Reform." *The Culture of Sentiment: Race, Gender, and Sentimentality in Nineteenth-Century America.* Ed. Shirley Samuels. New York: Oxford UP, 1992.

Wheeler, Marjorie Spruill. *New Women of the New South: The Leaders of the Woman Suffrage Movement in the Southern States.* New York: Oxford UP, 1993.

Whiteman, Maxwell. "Harrison Berry: A Georgia Slave Defends Slavery, a Bibliographical Note." Introduction. *Slavery and Abolition, as Viewed by a Georgia Slave.* By Harrison Berry. 1861. Wilmington: Scholarly Resources, 1977.

Wiegman, Robyn. *American Anatomies: Theorizing Race and Gender.* Durham: Duke UP, 1995.

Williamson, Joel. *The Crucible of Race: Black-White Relations in the American South since Emancipation.* New York: Oxford UP, 1984.

Wilson, Woodrow. *A History of the American People.* Vol. 5. New York: Harper and Brothers, 1902.

Wittig, Monique. *The Straight Mind and Other Essays.* Boston: Beacon, 1992.

Wolkomir, Michelle J. "Moral Elevation and Egalitarianism: Shades of Gray in Chesnutt's *The Marrow of Tradition*." *CLA Journal* 36.3 (1993): 245–59.

Womack, B. R. "A Kind Word for the Negro." *Baptist Standard* 14 (1902): 3.

Wood, Forrest G. *The Arrogance of Faith: Christianity and Race in America from the Colonial Era to the Twentieth Century.* New York: Knopf, 1990.

Wood, Gerald. "From *The Clansman* and *Birth of a Nation* to *Gone with the Wind*: The Loss of American Innocence." *Recasting: "Gone with the Wind" in American Culture.* Ed. Darden Pyron. Miami: UP of Florida, 1983. 123–36.

Work, Monroe N. *A Bibliography of the Negro in Africa and America.* New York: Wilson, 1928.

Wray, Matt, and Annalee Newitz, eds. *White Trash: Race and Class in America.* New York: Routledge, 1997.

Wright, P. G., and E. Q. Wright. *Elizur Wright.* Chicago: U of Chicago P, 1937.

Yellin, Jean Fagan. Introduction. *Incidents in the Life of a Slave Girl: Written by Herself.* By Harriet A. Jacobs. Cambridge: Harvard UP, 1987. xiii–xxxiv.

Young, Robert J. C. *Colonial Desire: Hybridity in Theory, Culture, and Race.* London: Routledge, 1995.

Yúdice, George. "Neither Impugning nor Disavowing Whiteness Does a Viable Politics Make: The Limits of Identity Politics." *After Political Correctness: The Humanities and Society in the 1990s.* Ed. Christopher Newfield and Ronald Strickland. Boulder: Westview, 1995.

# Index

Abbey, E. C., 213n. 9; on manhood
and the penis, 116–17, 217n. 18; on
masturbation and marriage, 213n.
12; on masturbation and uplift,
129, 130; on semen as lifeblood,
120. See also *The Sexual System and
its Derangements*
Abolitionism: class dynamics of, 60–
62; and labor: 61, 62, 200n. 11,
200–201nn. 12–14
Adamic Publishing Company, 95,
208n. 15
*Adventures of Huckleberry Finn, The*
(Twain), 55
African American literature: dilemma
of, 2, 6, 12, 127–28, 130–31; history
of, 11–12; as intervention in white
supremacy, 5–6, 109–10; as path to
freedom, 1–2. See also *The Marrow
of Tradition*
Aggasiz, Louis, 86
Albee, Edward, 190
Alger, Horatio, 39
Amalgamation. *See* Miscegenation
Ambivalence. *See* Desire; Hetero-
sexuality; Whiteness
American Book and Bible House, 95
American literature: history of, 5,
10–11
Ames, Jessie Daniel, 210n. 28
*Ancrene Riwle,* 90
Andrews, William, 127, 128
Anthropology, 1, 3, 193n. 5
Anti-Uncle Tom novels, 5, 7, 26, 28.
See also *The Cabin and Parlor*
Anzaldúa, Gloria, 182
Apocalypse of Moses, 89–90
Apple, Michael, 186
Aptheker, Herbert, 60–61
Ariel. *See* Payne, Buckner
Atkinson, Edward, 96
*Atlantic Monthly,* 54

Austen, Jane: and women writers, 32
Aycock, Charles B., 216n. 9

Baldwin, James: and Eldridge
Cleaver, 188–91; "Going to Meet
the Man," 174–75, 219n. 25; and
Norman Mailer, 178, 188–91; on
whiteness, 181
Ball, Edward, 161, 179
Baraka, Amiri, 106, 212n. 2
Barker-Benfield, G. J., 112, 212nn. 5–6
Baym, Nina, 31–32, 48–49, 198n. 22
Beadle and Company, 57, 59
Beadle's dime novels, 59–60, 200n.
9. See also *Maum Guinea and Her
Plantation "Children"*
"Benito Cereno" (Melville), 55
Bennett, Paula, 212n. 5
Berry, Harrison: on black superi-
ority, 211n. 31; identity of, 206n. 9;
response to Buckner Payne, 91–92,
207n. 11
Bhabha, Homi, 191
Bible, the: and miscegenation, 207n.
10; and racial purity, 86–87; and
racism, 4, 12, 85, 91; and slavery,
83, 86. *See also* Eve; Garden of
Eden; Genesis; Religion; Serpent;
Tempter
*Birth of a Nation, The* (Griffith), 159,
160–77; and black male sexu-
ality, 167–68; and crowds, 164–66,
171–75, 224n. 23; as domestic
melodrama, 223n. 18; and moving camera, 169–71, 223n. 21;
NAACP's response to, 220n. 4; and
ride to the rescue, 162, 168, 170;
and southern politics, 166–67,
222n. 12; and spectacle, 163; and
visibility, 159–62, 164; and white
audience, 170–71, 173–77, 220n.
4; and whiteness, 160–64, 168–69,

to, 25–26; and *The Leopard's Spots*, 135; and *Maum Guinea and Her Plantation "Children,"* 54, 57, 59

"Claims of the Negro Ethnologically Considered, The" (Douglass), 83, 84, 205n. 2. *See also* Douglass, Frederick

*Clansman, The* (Dixon), 10, 161, 215nn. 2–3, 220n. 1, 221n. 6, 222n. 14. *See also* Dixon, Thomas Jr.

Clarke, T. J., 202n. 18, 203–4n. 28

Class. *See* Abolitionism; *The Cabin and Parlor; The Leopard's Spots;* Whiteness

Cleaver, Eldridge, 178, 188–91, 212n. 2

Clover, Carol J., 223–24n. 22

Compromise of 1850, 78, 81

Comstock, Anthony, 112, 113

Cook, Raymond, 215n. 2, 216n. 9

Cooper, Anna Julia: and antilynching activism, 102; on novels of slavery, 195n. 4; on whiteness, 23, 84, 178; on William Dean Howells, 6

Cooper, James Fenimore, 209n. 22

Courtship, 51

Crowds: in *The Birth of a Nation*, 164–66, 171–75, 224n. 23; and O. J. Simpson verdict, 221n. 9; psychology of, 222n. 11; and water imagery, 221–22n. 10

Cvetkovich, Ann, 10, 194n. 11

Darwin, Charles, 4, 85, 96, 193–94n. 5

Davis, Jefferson, 117

Day, Christopher, 183

Defoe, Daniel, 114

DeGobineau, Joseph, 86

Delany, Martin, 197n. 15

D'Emilio, John, 51

Denning, Michael, 60, 200n. 7

Desire: ambivalence of, 13, 17, 155, 156–57; defined, 137; and the Garden of Eden, 88, 89; and heterosexuality, 13, 21, 132, 154; and

homosociality, 18, 134, 142; and nationalism, 138; racial, 136, 137, 138

Digourney, Lydia, 48

Dime novels, 7, 200n. 7; audience for, 7, 60, 62; and happy endings, 56. *See also* Beadle's dime novels; *Maum Guinea and Her Plantation "Children"*

Dixon, Thomas Jr., 127, 134, 161, 166, 191; and black male sexuality, 156; and Charles Chesnutt, 109, 117; *The Foolish Virgin*, 216n. 8; *The One Woman*, 216n. 7; as problem for black writers, 12; and sexual anxiety, 139, 141, 217n. 10; *The Sins of the Father*, 219n. 26; on Stowe, 5; as transitional figure, 159; and white women, 110, 216n. 8. *See also The Leopard's Spots*

Doubleday, Page, and Company, 7, 215n. 2

Douglass, Frederick, 1–2, 86; on abolitionism, 61–62; on ethnology, 83, 85; on evolution, 205n. 2; on miscegenation and the Bible, 207n. 10; *Narrative of the Life*, 1–2, 207n. 10; on religion and science, 84, 85; on religious slaveholders, 82

Douglass, H. Paul, 96

Drayton, William, 197–98n. 16

Du Bois, W. E. B., 5, 86, 178; and Booker T. Washington, 214n. 16; on Christianity and racism, 83; on miscegenation, 106; on scientific racism, 83; on whiteness as wage, 180, 198n. 17

duCille, Ann, 223n. 16

Dyer, Richard: on blood and white supremacy, 119; on heterosexuality and race, 16; on heterosexuality and whiteness, 21, 132; on Lillian Gish, 164; on the problems of whiteness studies, 186; on whiteness as absence, 161; on whiteness

Jameson, Fredric, 56–57
Jefferson, Thomas, 1
Jim Crowism, 91
Johannsen, Albert, 59–60
Jordan, Winthrop, 219n. 24

Katz, Jonathan Ned: on heterosexuality, history of, 14–15, 131, 219n. 27; on heterosexuality, tensions within, 141; on heterosexuality and women, 93–94; on marriage, 195n. 16; on masturbation, 117
Kelly, Henry, 89, 90
Kennedy, John Pendleton, 51
Kernberg, Otto, 203n. 27
Kertbeny, Karl Maria, 195n. 14, 219n. 27
Kid Rock, 225n. 8
Kiernan, James G., 14, 131, 219n. 27
Kincheloe, Joe, 184, 185
Knadler, Stephen K., 213–14nn. 14–15
Krafft-Ebing, Richard von, 14–15, 19–20, 94, 131, 210n. 24
Ku Klux Klan: in *The Birth of a Nation*, 159–66, 168–73, 175–76; in *The Clansman*, 221n. 6; in *The Leopard's Spots*, 144, 146

Lacan, Jacques, 135, 136, 137
Lallemand, Claude F., 115
LeBon, Gustave, 171–72, 173, 222n. 11, 224n. 23
*Leopard's Spots, The* (Dixon), 5, 125, 134–57, 158, 169, 173; autobiographical elements of, 216n. 9, 217n. 13, 218n. 21; and the black penis, 146–47, 149–50; and black women, 219n. 26; and Chesnutt, 109; and class, 141, 145–46, 217n. 15; and heterosexuality, 141–42, 144, 145, 150, 152–55; and marriage, 143–44, 150–53, 155; and miscegenation, 144, 147, 152,

154, 156; and mother/son bonds, 135–36, 215–16n. 4; and nostalgia, 220n. 1; and politics/sex, 139, 142–43; racial ideology of, 151; and sadomasochism, 140; sales of, 7, 215n. 2; and sexual anxiety, 139, 141, 146, 153; and slavery, 135; and southern womanhood, 145; and *Uncle Tom's Cabin*, 158; and white manhood, 136, 145, 146–47; and whiteness, 145–46, 147, 148, 152–57; and worship of the dead, 138–39
Lester, A. Hoyle, 93–95
Lévi-Strauss, Claude, 18
*Liberator*, 27, 33
Limp Bizkit, 225n. 8
Lincoln, Abraham, 54, 194n. 7
Lindsay, Vachel, 165–66
Lipsitz, George, 37, 163, 198n. 17
Lott, Eric, 149
Lowell, James Russell, 25
Lynching: and antilynching activism, 101–4, 210n. 28; Baldwin on, 219n. 25; in *The Leopard's Spots*, 149–50, 156, 157; as performance, 210n. 25; and sexual fascination, 133–34, 148–50.
Lynch law, 91

MacDonald, Robert H., 115, 120
Magdol, Edward, 200n. 11, 201n. 14
Mailer, Norman, 178, 188–91
Manhood. *See* Masculinity
Mapplethorpe, Robert, 149, 182
Marriage, 19–20, 195n. 16; as cure for masturbation, 120, 121, 213n. 12; and freedom, 80; and homosociality, 134, 150–53, 154, 155; and racial struggle, 125; and rape, 155; and slavery, 46, 80; and whiteness, 19–20, 45–46, 155; and white supremacy, 19–20, 155
*Marrow of Tradition, The* (Chesnutt), 6, 108–14, 117–32; and marriage,

120–21, 213n. 12; and masculinity, 109, 110, 113–14, 117, 121–23, 125–27, 212n. 2; and masturbation, 108–9, 111, 112–13, 120, 121, 123, 129–31, 212n. 3; and minstrelsy, 110, 123; and procreative economy, 109, 115, 117, 121, 122–23, 126, 127, 130, 131–32; and racial slippage, 122–24, 213n. 13; relation to white-supremacist fiction of, 6; sales of, 130, 214n. 19; and *Uncle Tom's Cabin,* 127; and white dependence on blackness, 122; and whiteness, 109, 110, 114, 117, 119, 120, 122, 123, 126–32, 213n. 14; and white savagery, 173

Masculinity, 110, 116–17; black, 99–101, 103–4, 113, 126, 127; and heterosexuality, 142; and marriage, 20; as order, 172; and rape, 31; and the serpent, 89–91; and Stowe, 31, 33; white, 109, 110, 113–14, 116–17, 121, 122, 123, 127, 140–41, 156, 212n. 2; and whiteness, 46–48. *See also* Castration

Masturbation: and black uplift, 129–30; and degeneracy, 114–15, 117–18; discourses against, 108, 112; evils of, 112, 115, 118 (illus.); and hetero/homo binary, 211 unnumbered note; and homosexuality, 113, 213n. 8; and homosociality, 113, 213n. 8; marriage as cure for, 120, 213n. 12; and Onan, 114–15, 121, 212n. 3, 213n. 8; and race, 115, 124, 126, 129–30; and reading, 112–13; treatment for, 212–13n. 7; and whiteness, 109, 120, 212n. 3

*Maum Guinea and Her Plantation "Children"* (Victor), 7, 12, 51–81; advertisements for, 57–59, 62; as antislavery, 55, 56; and economics of slavery, 70–71, 75, 76, 204n. 31; ending of, 52, 56, 76–80; and homosociality, 202n. 21; and inco-

herence, 53, 57, 64, 202n. 18; mirror as metaphor in, 52–54, 64–70, 81, 201n. 16; and miscegenation, 204n. 32; and narcissism, 53, 64, 71–72; plot of, 51–52; and political context, 81; and political impact, 54; popularity of, 57, 59, 194n. 7; and repetition, 65, 79, 202n. 18, 203–4n. 28; and representation and subjectivity, 62–63; review of, 200n. 7; sales of, 59, 199–200n. 6; scholarly reception of, 54, 56; and slavery, 50–81; temporal setting of, 204n. 35; and transracial identification, 52–54, 55, 64, 68–69, 70, 71–72, 73, 74, 75–76; and *Uncle Tom's Cabin,* 54, 55, 58; and Victor's political motivation, 55; and whiteness, 72–73; and white supremacy, 62

Meigs, J. Aitken, 197n. 16

Melville, Herman, 7, 55

*Memphis Commercial,* 101

Mercer, Kobena, 149, 182, 211n. 32

*Metamorphoses* (Ovid), 72

Michaels, Walter Benn, 220n. 1, 221n. 6

Miller, Kelly, 133, 156–57

Miscegenation: attitudes toward, 197–98n. 16; and blackness, 152; and black phallus, 149; and black/white binary, 221n. 7; and black women, 219n. 26; Buckner Payne on, 92; Charles Carroll on, 98; Du Bois on, 106; and heterosexuality, 17; and homoeroticism, 154; and Ida B. Wells, 101–2; and incest, 144; Kelly Miller on, 156; and spatial metaphors, 33; and temptation of Eve, 84, 87, 103–4; as threat to the South, 218n. 22; and white men, 147; and whiteness, 34–35, 41; and white women, 34–35. *See also* Racial purity

Moraga, Cherrie, 182

Morrison, Toni: on allegory, 206n. 4; *Beloved,* 2–3; on black surrogacy, 107; *Playing in the Dark,* 107; and whiteness studies, 181
Morton, Samuel, 85, 86
Mott, Frank Luther, 199–200n. 6

Näcke, Paul, 203n. 25
Narcissism: and heterosexuality, 203n. 26; in *Maum Guinea and Her Plantation "Children,"* 53, 64, 71–72; as term, 72–73, 203n. 25; and whiteness, 53, 72–73, 109, 175, 181, 182, 187, 203n. 27
*Narrative of the Life of Frederick Douglass* (Douglass), 1–2, 207n. 10. *See also* Douglass, Frederick
Neal, Larry, 190
*Negro a Beast, The* (Carroll), 95; circulation and reception of, 96; full title of, 207–8n. 14. *See also* Carroll, Charles
Nelson, Dana, 134
Nelson, John Herbert, 54
*New Orleans Picayune,* 33
Newton, Esther, 209–10n. 24
New woman, 94
*New York Tribune,* 26, 57–58, 62, 195n. 5
*North American Review,* 96, 200n. 7
Nott, Josiah, 86

Oedipal Complex, 135–36
Onan: story of, 114–15, 121, 212n. 3, 213n. 8
Onanism. *See* Masturbation
Ovid, 51, 72

Page, Thomas Nelson, 117
Pagels, Elaine, 88, 206n. 6
Palmer, Phyllis, 197n. 12
Payne, Buckner, 91–93, 98
*Pennsylvanian,* 23
Person, Leland S. Jr., 209n. 22
Peterson, Charles Jacobs, 7, 24, 84,

158; career of, 25; and moderation, 25–26; pseudonym of, 195n. 2; and women, 48. *See also The Cabin and Parlor*
*Peterson's Magazine,* 25, 48
Pfeil, Fred, 186
Phallus, the, 135
*Philadelphia Evening Bulletin,* 26
Phillips, Jerry, 207n. 11
Philo of Alexandria, 90–91
Pinckney, Darryl, 210n. 27
Poe, Edgar Allan, 7, 25
Polan, Dana, 163
Polygenesis, 83, 86, 87, 91. *See also* Preadamites
Popular fiction, 8–11
Powell, Linda C., 186–87
Pratt, Minnie Bruce, 182
Preadamites, 93, 95, 96, 97. *See also* Polygenesis
Procreative economy, 109, 121, 123, 130, 131, 212n. 3. *See also The Marrow of Tradition;* Reproduction; Whiteness: and reproduction
Prospero [pseud.], 93, 98, 99
Psychoanalysis: and literary criticism, 202n. 18, 203–4n. 28
Purvis, Robert, 197n. 15

Queerness: and whiteness, 183, 188
Queer studies, 182

*Race Traitor,* 179, 183, 191, 225n. 5
Racial purity: and the Bible, 86–87; and black men, 84, 134; and heterosexuality, 13, 21; and whiteness, 13, 21, 35; and white women, 35, 134, 144. *See also* Miscegenation
Racism: and American literary history, 10–11; and antimasturbatory discourse, 115; and antiracism, 184, 192; and the Bible, 4, 12, 85, 91; and black masculinity, 113, 212n. 2; black responses to, 5–6, 109–10; and blood, 119; and cinema, 159,

Victor, Orville J., 199n. 1
Visibility, 159–62; and gay and lesbian identity, 159–60; and whiteness, 25, 33, 160, 161–64, 169, 221n. 6

Walker, David, 82
Warner, Michael, 203n. 26
Washington, Booker T., 214n. 16
Weis, Lois, 186–87
Wells, Ida B.: and antilynching activism, 101–4; on Christianity, 82; *Crusade for Justice*, 5; *A Red Record*, 102
West, Cornel, 194–95n. 13
Wheeler, Marjorie Spruill, 102, 103
Whipple, Charles K., 27, 196–97n. 11
Whiteman, Maxwell, 206n. 9
White men: and black men, 17–18, 134, 146–47, 149–50; bodies of, 114, 117, 118, 133; and death, 138–39; as economic providers, 47; and lynching, 101; and prerogatives of manhood, 115–16; and racial desire, 136, 137; and racial purity, 35, 117, 119; and rape, 31; and savagery, 173; as sexually degenerate, 109, 117, 156, 212n. 2; and white supremacy as homosocial network, 134, 152–53. *See also* Castration
Whiteness: abolition of, 182–84, 190, 191, 225nn. 5, 8; as absence, 73, 161, 185; as abstraction, 19, 24, 29, 33, 44, 176, 221n. 7; and ambivalence, 17, 169–71; and anxiety, 6, 12, 13, 24, 29, 84, 146, 162–64, 169, 171, 173; as anxiety and norm, 13, 24, 162–63; and black male sexuality, 109; and blackness, 40, 122, 128, 162, 164, 180–81; and black sexuality, 130; and black/white binary, 106; and blood, 117, 119, 120; and class, 24, 145–46, 201n. 14, 224n. 3; and crowds, 173–75; as cultural commodity, 110, 163;

cyclical movement of, 35, 185; degradation of, 39–40, 42–43, 173; as distinct from white supremacy, 13, 194–95n. 13; and the domestic, 169; as failure of vision, 73; and fear, 163, 170–71; future of, 190–92; and gender, 24, 29, 41; and guilt, 182, 184–85, 187; as heterosexual economy, 131; and heterosexuality, 13–14, 16–21, 131, 132, 153, 154, 155, 181, 182, 188, 191; and homoeroticism, 18, 132, 154; and homosexuality, 189–90; and homosociality, 17–18, 152, 154; as identity, 106; as ideology, 7, 106; and impotence, 109, 110, 114, 122, 191; and Irishness, 39; as literary economy, 109; as live cultural form, 8; and marriage, 19–20, 45–46, 155; and masturbation, 109, 120, 212n. 3; and miscegenation, 34–35, 41; and narcissism, 53, 72–73, 109, 175, 181, 182, 187, 203n. 27; as norm, 13, 14, 24, 33, 44, 126, 128, 162, 185; as nostalgia, 159; and panic, 162–63; as pathology, 72–73, 131; and patriarchy, 17, 46–47, 48; possessive investment in, 37, 42, 198n. 17; and procreation, 123, 127, 130; as procreative economy, 123, 131–32; as projection, 163; and queerness, 183, 188; and racial purity, 21; and rape, 148; reinvention of, 184–85, 191; relation to, 110; and reproduction, 16, 17, 18, 98, 132, 152, 153, 190–91; and savagery, 172–73; and semen, 117, 119, 120; and slavery, 24, 29, 50; as text, 3–4, 158; as threat to heterosexuality, 20–21; as threat to itself, 109; as vacuum, 5; and visibility, 25, 33, 160, 161–64, 169, 221n. 6; vulnerability of, 35, 49, 50, 175, 188, 191–92; as wage, 180, 198n. 17; white masculinity as threat to,

Whiteness (*continued*)
109; and white women, 17, 35, 117,
119, 145, 148, 156; and work, 24,
28–29, 33, 35, 41, 48. *See also* White
supremacy

Whiteness studies, 12, 13, 179–87,
191–92; and African American
literary history, 180–81; and feminism, 181–82; problems of, 182–87,
191–92, 194n. 6; and queer studies,
182

White supremacy: African American response to, 5–6, 109–10;
and black women, 214n. 18, 219n.
26; and the body, 133; as distinct
from whiteness, 13, 194–95n. 13;
and heterosexuality, 13, 150, 152;
as homosocial network, 18, 134,
137–38, 143, 155; and marriage,
19–20, 155; and patriarchy, 102,
104, 134, 155; as popular discourse,
8; and textuality, 1, 4, 6. *See also*
Whiteness

White women: and agency, 101, 102;
and antilynching, 102–3, 210n.
28; as corpse, 144–45, 217n. 14;
and cult of southern womanhood,

31; in positions of exchange, 17,
18, 133, 134, 135–37, 151–53; as
the South, 218n. 22; as threat to
whiteness, 148; as victim, 109,
134, 143–49, 164, 168, 169; and
whiteness, 17, 35, 117, 119, 145, 148,
156

Wiegman, Robyn, 101, 103, 149, 150,
210n. 25

Williamson, Joel, 104

Wilson, William J. (Ethiop), 51, 84,
108, 159, 173

Wilson, Woodrow, 162

Winchell, Alexander, 96–97

Wittig, Monique, 14

Womack, B. R., 96

Women's Christian Temperance
Union, 16

Wong, L. Mun, 186–87

Wood, Forrest, 96, 104

Wood, Gerald, 223n. 18

Work, Monroe, 104, 206n. 9

Wright, Fanny, 30

Writing: and race, 1, 2, 4, 158, 193n. 2

Young, Robert J. C., 17, 98, 134, 154

*Mason Stokes* is Assistant Professor
of English at Skidmore College.

Library of Congress Cataloging-in-Publication Data
Stokes, Mason Boyd.
The color of sex : whiteness, heterosexuality, and the
fictions of white supremacy / Mason Stokes.
p. cm. — (New Americanists)
Includes bibliographical references and index.
ISBN 0-8223-2626-4 (cloth : alk. paper)
ISBN 0-8223-2620-5 (pbk. : alk. paper)
1. American fiction—History and criticism.   2. Whites in literature.
3. White supremacy movements—United States—History.
4. Heterosexuality in literature.   5. African Americans in literature.
6. Racism in literature.   7. Race in literature.   8. Sex in literature.
I. Title.   II. Series.
PS173.W46 S76 2001
813′.40935203034—dc21                    00-057815